Freedom's First Generation

University of Pennsylvania Press / 1979

FREEDOM'S FIRST GENERATION

Black Hampton, Virginia, 1861-1890

Robert Francis Engs

Library of Congress Cataloging in Publication Data

Engs, Robert Francis.
  Freedom's first generation.

  Bibliography: p. 225
  Includes index.
  1. Afro-Americans—Virginia—Hampton—History.
2. Hampton, Va.—History. I. Title.
F234.H23E54   975.5'412'00496073   79–5046
ISBN 0–8122–7768–6

Photo on title page courtesy
of the Hampton Institute Archives

For Jean and Robby

Contents

Illustrations

Acknowledgments

When a scholar completes a manuscript to which he has devoted many years of time and effort, there is the temptation to exult, "Well, *I* finally did it!" Upon reflection, he realizes that there may be faults still in his work, but that they are not there because he lacked help. Supporters, colleagues, good friends have all done their best. The question becomes has he done the best he could? The answer is something an author and his readers must decide. Before that decision is made, it is appropriate to thank those who, whatever the outcome, tried to aid the scholar as much as they could.

Modern scholarship does not occur without the generous support of public and private organizations. I am grateful to Yale University, the New Jersey Education Consortium, the University of Pennsylvania, the William Penn Foundation, and the Moton Center for Independent Studies for financial support while I did the research for and the writing of this book. I am especially grateful to the Moton Center whose excellent facilities provide the perfect setting for the writing, rewriting, and critique of a work in progress.

Although the topic of my research represented a new direction for many of the library staffs with whom I was associated, I found that I was welcomed and greatly aided at each institution visited. The staffs of the National Archives in Washington, at the University of Virginia, the University of North Carolina, Chapel Hill, and at Yale University were experts in knowledge of their collections and of great assistance to me. The staff of Fisk University's Library gave up part of their Christmas break so that I might study the American Missionary Association Papers, then located at Fisk. The collection's curator, Clifton Johnson, took special time to guide me to the most salient material. The staffs of the Hampton Association of Arts and Humanities, Hampton, Virginia, and of the Syms-Eaton Library provided me with free access to all of the valuable collection of materials on Hampton history that added so much to this study.

This study could not have been undertaken without the invaluable resources and generous assistance of the Hampton Institute Library. The excellent men and women of that institution determined that, to do a proper job, I should know all that I could. They were thorough in their guidance and tolerant of my "outsider's" ignorance. The staff at Hampton represents a scholar's dream of happy cooperation between researcher and library associates. Among those at the Institute, I am especially grateful to Professor E. K. Graham and to the late Miss Eleanor Gilman who guided me through the then uncatalogued archives of the school.

A project researched must still be made into a work readable to a scholar's audience. I owe a debt of thanks to Donald and Jane Mathews and to James McPherson for insisting that my study was worth doing and for offering valued criticism as the study progressed. More particularly, I owe a profound debt to C. Vann Woodward for insisting that the study would be completed and that it would be the best I could do. (Typically, he has always been gracious enough never to say whether it was, in fact, "good enough.")

It is standard to acknowledge colleagues who have assisted an author in writing his book. It is nonetheless true that many of my colleagues and friends devoted extraordinary time to helping me prepare and polish this manuscript. The fact that I did not always listen to their advice in no way diminishes their contribution. Among such associates at the University of Pennsylvania, I think especially of Houston Baker, Richard Beeman, Richard Dunn, Theodore Hershberg, Nell Painter, Charles Rosenberg, and Michael Zuckerman. Each brought their own perspective to my efforts, and the final result is better because of their help.

Many others, I am sure more because of kindness toward me than conviction about the worth of my prose, also read and reacted to this work. I wish to thank especially, Renee Fox, Morgan Kousser, James Green, Donald Mathews, Charles McCracken, Frederick Quinn, Alfred Rieber, and John B. Williams. Each provided valuable insight about the meaning of my work. The strongest qualities of this book are, at least in part, a product of their careful advice. One colleague, in particular, refused to allow me to lose faith as I struggled to revise and improve this study. To him, Leon Higginbotham, I also owe a special debt and many thanks.

Along with supportive colleagues, I was privileged to have a number of excellent graduate students who read pieces of this manuscript and offered their evaluations. Especially helpful were Lorenzo Griffin, Willie Griffin, Steven Lipman, and Walter L. Turner. Another graduate student, Henry Williams deserves special acknowledgment for assisting me in the preparation of the quantified sections of this study and for doing yeoman's service by helping to proofread the final manuscript.

The book which follows is, I think, a somewhat different view of a Southern post-bellum community. My deepest gratitude goes to those people who made that different view possible. They are the descendants of "Freedom's First Generation" and their friends in Hampton, Virginia.Without them I would have known and understood far less about that community. Most particularly among my guides in Virginia, I wish to thank Mr. and Mrs. Solomon Phillips. They took time and invested much trust in me so that I might meet many informants who theretofore had been unwilling to talk with me. I am also grateful to Mrs. Hattie Anderson whose knowledge of the black community guided me to many whom I needed to meet. Also of extraordinary assistance was Mrs. Hamilton Evans whose knowledge of Hampton both before and after the Civil War is unsurpassed. Very special thanks are due to Mrs. Louise Davis Stone, descendant of the extraordinary Davis family of Hampton. Her insights about the inner workings of the town's black community, her knowledge of the prominent families, and her expertise as an editor greatly aided the preparation of this work.

There are, in addition, each of the men and women I met in the process of reconstructing Hampton's post-bellum history. They were: Mrs. Dottie Peake Anderson, Mrs. Lillian Weaden Kemp, Mrs. Hattie McGrew, Mr. Alfonso Lively, Mr. John Mallory Phillips, Mr. and Mrs. Robert Nottingham, Mr. James W. H. Scott, and Mrs. Phoencie Armstead Tull.

Each scholar can think of contributions made by his family in the process of doing a book. Those I received were very tangible. My parents, Robert and Myrtle Engs, provided a place to stay, free lending of cars, and moral support during the course of this research. On occasion they even pitched in as research assistants. To them, my heartfelt thanks.

Finally, one is expected to thank one's spouse. My wife did not type but did proofread what follows. She gave moral support and helped to do the research as this study progressed. She insisted that this book be finished and the debt I owe her is fully acknowledged elsewhere.

Capahosic, VA
August, 1979

Introduction

When I began this study of Hampton, Virginia, I had two primary goals in mind. First, to contribute to the ongoing debate on slave personality by investigating the goals, values, and behavior of ex-slaves immediately after emancipation. Second, and more important, to analyze the process through which blacks and Northern whites in Hampton, Virginia, developed the most influential educational establishment for Negroes in the late nineteenth century, i.e., Hampton Institute.

My research, and that of others, reshaped both my focus and my goals. Others have now demonstrated that it is unnecessary to study blacks *after* slavery in order to discern what they were like *during* slavery. Recent works on slavery—especially John Blassingame's *The Slave Community* (New York, 1972), George Rawick's *Sundown to Sunup* (Westport, Conn., 1972), and, most important, Eugene Genovese's *Roll, Jordan, Roll* (New York, 1972)—have liberated the slave (and the historian) from Stanley Elkins and his theories about Sambo. Herbert Gutman, in *The Black Family in Slavery and Freedom, 1750-1925* (New York, 1976), has argued convincingly that black family instability is not a heritage of slavery and an earlier matriarchal society in Africa.

These books have given us a much more thorough picture of the slave than we have had heretofore. We now understand that the slave was a complete human being with many of the same desires and concerns as other Americans. But these studies have also underscored the need for a similar treatment of the ex-slave during and after the Civil War. Most of our works on blacks in the post-bellum era portray them primarily as victims either of Northern insensitivity and hostility—as in William McFeely's *Yankee Stepfather* (New York, 1968)—or of resurgent Southern racism—as in state studies like Joel Williamson's *After Slavery* (Chapel Hill, 1965). Those descriptions of the black man's plight in the postwar era are all too accurate. Nevertheless, we need to understand more about the black man's response to the problems he encountered in the War, Reconstruction, and New South. The people we now know to have been remarkably resourceful as slaves logically should not have been less so once they were emancipated.

Some recent historians have already demonstrated this point and have given considerable attention to black responses in the war and its aftermath. Willie Lee Rose, in *Rehearsal for Reconstruction* (New York, 1964), gives an excellent description of both the freedmen of the Sea Islands in South Carolina and of Northern missionaries who sought to aid them. Joel Williamson, in *After Slavery*, presents a sensitive and insightful analysis of South Carolina blacks from emancipation to disfranchisement in the 1890s. Finally, John Blassingame, in *Black New Orleans, 1860-1880* (Chicago, 1973), gives us a thorough study of the black response to the War and Reconstruction in that unusual city.

Each of these very important studies has certain drawbacks. Rose does not carry her study past the end of Reconstruction, so we have too little sense of how blacks coped with life after the reestablishment of native white control in the Sea Islands. Williamson's statewide study of South Carolina avoids this difficulty, but its very scope prevents attention to individual blacks and how they maneuvered among the various forces impinging on their lives. Blassingame offers us excellent insights about post-bellum black life in a large city, but most blacks did not live in large cities and, in any case, New Orleans was unlike any other Southern city.

The history of blacks in Hampton, Virginia, between 1861 and 1890, represents an opportunity to avoid some of the drawbacks of these earlier studies and to contribute to our understanding of blacks in the post-bellum era. Hampton, with never more than 20,000 total population during this period, is more typical in size of post-bellum black communities than a major Southern city. Because of continuity of records and population, it is possible to make an intimate study of interactions between blacks and whites and among the blacks themselves for the periods of War, Reconstruction, and Restoration.

Hampton's unique qualities make it important to do an in-depth study of the town and its people. In Hampton, Northern whites evolved and elaborated many of their most important responses to black freedom. In addition, freedmen evolved a most remarkable and resourceful black community which managed to acquire most of the benefits of freedom despite often halfhearted support from Northern whites and hostility from Southern ones.

Hampton was a major focal point in the restructuring of American race relations during the war and its aftermath. Between 1861 and 1865 the town was the site of three major developments: in Hampton, Southern slaves carried out their first mass escape of the Civil War; the Union military first developed the labor and race control policies that it would apply to ex-slaves throughout the South; and finally, the first Northern missionaries, members of the American Missionary Association, initiated their efforts to aid ex-slaves.

After the Civil War, Hampton continued to play a major role in influencing black and white attitudes toward one another. The town was an important regional headquarters for the Freedmen's Bureau. More important, however, Hampton became the home for Hampton Institute, a black teacher training college founded by Northern missionaries. During the last thirty years of the nineteenth century, the Institute was a major factor in shaping white attitudes toward black education and participation in society. The philosophy of black accommodation, espoused by the Institute's white founder, Samuel Chapman Armstrong, and by the Institute's most renowned graduate, Booker T. Washington, became the norm for white expectations of black behavior.

The role that Northern whites in Hampton played in shaping the life of that black community and of blacks throughout the South is only one part of the Hampton story. The blacks of the town were uniquely prepared to take advantage of the Northern white interest in their community and to turn these white initiatives to their own purposes. Ante-bellum blacks in Hampton experienced a slave system considerably more relaxed than elsewhere in the South. Fewer slaves in Hampton were simple fieldhands on plantations; many more slaves were permitted to "hire their own time." Other slaves were oystermen, fishermen, skilled craftsmen; a few were even foremen of their master's farms. A number could read and write; most had stable families. They were closely allied with the small but resourceful free black population of the town. Together they were well prepared to take advantage of freedom when it came.

The blacks' unusual opportunities continued once the war began. Hampton was behind Union lines through the war, and the town was abandoned by the native white population. Blacks used this situation to their advantage, attending schools established by the missionaries and renting abandoned farms from the Union army. They also undertook to learn more about freedom and to define their goals as a free people.

When blacks commenced this process of exploration and self-definition midway through the war, a tension began to develop between them and their Northern missionary allies. Blacks and missionaries were never very far apart on goals for the freed slaves—at least until Samuel Armstrong arrived in 1866; both wanted blacks to enjoy religious freedom, property ownership, education, and political rights. Differences over the means to achieve those goals, however, created a strain between the two groups that would last to the end of the century. The missionaries, and other Northern whites during Reconstruction and Restoration, sought to regulate the freedmen's behavior as well as their goals. This well-intended paternalism offended the freedmen's basic understanding of what freedom was about, i.e., the right to control their own lives as they had not been able to do as slaves.

The strains between missionaries and Hampton blacks did not lead to a break, but they did lead to divergent paths toward goals that were no longer entirely similar. The missionary path led to Hampton Institute and its principal's advocacy of black hard work combined with abstention from politics, acceptance of inferior education, and passivity in pursuit of equal rights. Ultimately it led to white America's acceptance of a blend of white paternalism and black accommodation as the proper course for American race relations.

The path chosen by blacks did not reject hard work nor Hampton Institute, but both were only means to an end: full civil and political equality. Blacks wanted property, voting rights, political office, education for their children, autonomy in their religious and social lives. By 1890 they had made tremendous strides toward achievement of their goals. One-fifth of all blacks in the town owned property; half of the businesses on Hampton's main street were black-owned. Hampton blacks participated fully in the political process throughout the 1880s, electing black local officials and delegates to the state legislature. Blacks held jobs across the entire spectrum from common laborer to professional; nearly half were in the category of skilled craftsman or above. Hampton blacks also saw to the education of their children, supporting the public elementary school and a private secondary school. Many sent their children to the Institute thereafter, but few of them proved susceptible to Armstrong's notions about the blacks' place in post-bellum society. Many went on to colleges and graduate schools in the North, and returned to become involved in local and state politics. Finally, blacks established a whole set of community institutions to serve the people: five churches, various fraternal organizations, women's associations, young people's groups, and temperance societies. The Hampton black community by 1890 was an elaborate one which shared the styles, values, and problems of many other American communities, whatever the geographical location or racial composition.

In that year, blacks began to suffer major setbacks after more than twenty years of progress. Native whites, in alliance with Northern white immigrants, launched an onslaught against black office-holding which removed blacks from local office and marked the beginning of black Hampton's decline as a unique and successful entity. The end of this remarkable experiment in black equality was ignored by most Americans; their attention was held by the other product of the Hampton experience: accommodation and its chief spokesman, Booker T. Washington.

Between 1861 and 1890, in a single town—Hampton, Virginia—two disparate visions of post-bellum black life developed side by side and were often interwoven with each other. One looked to full equality in the present; the other postponed that equality to some distant future. The two visions were inexorably linked together. The blacks acquired much of their definition of full equality from association with Northern missionaries. The missionaries retreated somewhat from that goal because they were not sure blacks were ready for full equality or would be granted it in any case. Hampton Institute was created to serve blacks, and was established at Hampton because of the high educational level and resourcefulness of its black inhabitants. Yet, the Institute advocated a philosophy that most of the black residents rejected. The Institute was, nevertheless, a valuable resource to the black community and played an important role in the community's achievement of goals that the school officially rejected. Analyzing the interaction between blacks and whites as they evolved these contrasting views and appraising the consequences for the black community are the central themes of this study.

It is true that black Hampton was hardly a typical post-bellum black community; it staved off defeat longer and accomplished more than most, in part because of the assistance of Northern whites. There is, nevertheless, much in Hampton's history that speaks to the national state of race relations in the late nineteenth century. The disingenuousness of Americans arguing that blacks were unfit for full freedom is plainly revealed by a special irony in the Hampton experience. There, where the postponement of equality was being most loudly advocated, was one of the few places in America that blacks had most nearly achieved it!

The Hampton experience also provides us with a new perspective on the defeat of most Southern blacks early in Reconstruction, as well as informing us about black Hampton's own, lesser known, tragedy two decades later. The story of the first generation of freedmen in Hampton is a tale of "what might have been" for the black post-bellum South. It is a model of what freedmen might have accomplished if they had shared Hampton's opportunities, if they had had the same resources within their own communities at the time of emancipation; if the Northern missionaries had been more stalwart allies and had stayed longer in the South; if the federal government had kept even a few of the promises it made to blacks after the war; if white Southerners had been less devastatingly effective in thwarting black advancement almost immediately after the war.

The forces of repression ultimately engulfed black Hampton just as they had the rest of the black South, but the twenty years of respite enjoyed by Hamptonians made a crucial difference. During that period a whole new generation of blacks had reached maturity in a community in which their parents owned property, voted, held elective office, and knew more about the outside world than many white Hamptonians. Even in political and economic defeat, black Hampton's first free generation could look with pride at its major achievement: its children. They were well educated, ambitious, sophisticated in business, in education, and in the ways of the world, white as well as black, Northern as well as Southern. They and their descendants would continue to play a major role in American black life long after accommodation had been repudiated.

Freedom's First Generation

In Search of Freedom: Hampton During the War

During the Civil War, the groups which would shape the post-bellum life of black Hampton came together for the first time. Over that same period, the issues that would inform black and white approaches to freedom, in Hampton and in the South as a whole, crystallized.

It was neither a time nor place for carefully considered and executed planning. Throughout the war, conditions in Hampton were chaotic. The town and its military base, Fortress Monroe, were the principal bastions in the Union's control of the Virginia coast and Chesapeake Bay. Hampton was the staging area for the two huge Union assaults against Richmond from the South: McClellan's unsuccessful campaign of 1862 and Grant's triumphant one of 1864-65. In addition, the *Monitor* and *Merrimac* battled each other to a standstill within sight of Hampton in March of 1862; and, in February, 1865, President Lincoln and Secretary of State Seward met Confederate representatives on board a warship anchored off Hampton in an abortive peace effort. Hundreds of thousands of Union troops and their generals passed in and out of Hampton during the war, often bringing additional chaos through jealousies and rivalries with each other. Most important for the black man's post-bellum future, thousands of refugee slaves were settled in Hampton to remove them from the battlefront. They suffered from constant shortages of food and housing, and they were prey to all the diseases caused by poor sanitation and overcrowding.

In these unstable circumstances, Northern whites and Southern blacks had their first large-scale encounter of the war. There were two groups of Northerners: army personnel, and Northern missionaries who came to help care for the blacks and prepare them for freedom. A few in both groups liked the area so much that they chose to settle there after the Civil War. There were also two groups of blacks—slaves and free Negroes—though neither the missionaries nor military paid much attention to this ante-bellum distinction. After 1863 a third black group, slave refugees from outside Hampton, entered the picture.

It is important to note that another group—native white Southerners who played a vital role in structuring ante-bellum black life and did so again after 1865—was largely absent during the war. Because the Union held Hampton throughout the war, these whites abandoned the town. As a consequence, blacks in Hampton were able to define their relations with Northern whites and their notions of freedom without simultaneously having to cope with pressures from their former masters.

Out of the interaction between Southern blacks and Northern whites emerged the issues around which black freedom would be debated for the next forty years. Out of the relationship also developed the tension between freedmen and their Northern allies that produced the contrast between the black Hampton community and the white-run Hampton Institute after Reconstruction.

The blacks and the Northerners (at least the missionaries) were never very far apart except on one issue, but it was the crucial one: who would decide what was the best for the freedmen? Northerners assumed this right for themselves. The freedmen resisted. They wanted advice and help, to be sure, but slavery had meant following the dictates of others; freedom, therefore, meant—above all else—the right to chart one's own course. By war's end, the blacks

and Northerners were almost at loggerheads on this point. The events in Hampton between 1861 and 1865, and the attitudes which lay behind them, explain how
this strain developed.

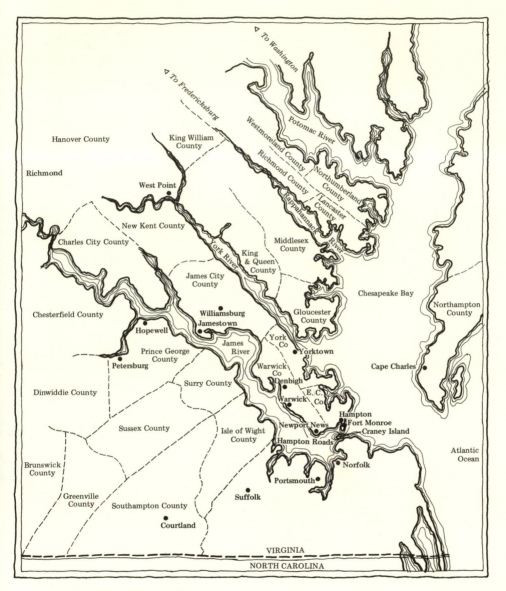

Eastern Virginia, 1848

Hampton on the Eve of War

Hampton is, at first glance, an improbable locale for major developments in America's racial history. Nothing in its past up to 1861 made it a place of importance. There were, however, two unnoticed distinctions about the village: its geographic location was of great strategic importance to any enemy with the power to attack the United States' southeastern seaboard, and its system of slavery was quite unorthodox for the American South. The Civil War unexpectedly brought both of these singularities to prominence, and thrust the town of Hampton into a major role in the evolution of post-bellum American race relations.

Hampton sits on the northern entrance to one of the largest and finest harbors in the world, Hampton Roads.[1] It is also located at the southeastern tip of Virginia's Peninsula. On the southwest side, by the city of Newport News, the James River completes its course into Hampton Roads. To the northeast, the York River terminates in Chesapeake Bay. Seventy-five miles northwest of Hampton, alongside the James River, is the city that would preoccupy Northerners for more than four years—Richmond. Across the Roads from Hampton are the cities of Norfolk and Portsmouth. At the entrance between Hampton Roads and Chesapeake Bay sit Hampton and Fortress Monroe. The fort's cannons guard the five-mile gap that provides access to Hampton Roads.[2]

The first British settlers to mainland America gave the name "Hampton Roads" to the area. It was a good choice. The rivers and tributaries that led from the harbor were quite literally roads, the only ones available to the early European residents. Traveling up one of those "roads"—the James River—British immigrants to North

America founded their first permanent colony in Jamestown in 1607.

The first black settlers to the colonies followed the same route, although they did so involuntarily. In 1619 the first Africans in British North America passed through Hampton Roads on their way to a future of slavery in Jamestown.

Over the next century Hampton village, founded in 1610, was county seat of Elizabeth City County, and a stopping off point for white and black settlers. Few of them stayed permanently, however, and for good reason. The land in the counties up the James or York Rivers was richer than that of Elizabeth City. Moreover, those upper Peninsula counties—Warwick, York, James City, and Charles City—were less exposed to tropical storms that periodically inundated Hampton.

Hampton village was a port of some importance in prerevolutionary days, serving as gateway to the wealthy plantations along the James and York Rivers. In the eight decades after the Revolution, history and commerce largely bypassed Hampton. Norfolk soon overshadowed it as a port. Agriculture, which had once flourished in Elizabeth City County, began to decline. The sandy soil of the environs around Hampton was rapidly depleted through over-cultivation of tobacco.[3]

In the nineteenth century the entire Peninsula above Hampton was not as prosperous as it had been in earlier days, largely because of soil exhaustion. Although studies on soil economy by Edwin Ruffin had taught the area's farmers to rotate their crops and to grow other plants besides tobacco, the Peninsula did not approach the wealth enjoyed by the residents of a century earlier. By the early 1800s Hampton had become a pleasant village of 700 surrounded by Elizabeth City County. It served primarily as the port to which the Peninsula's grain and truck farmers brought their crops. From Hampton, this produce was transported across the Roads to Norfolk and then north to New York or across the Atlantic to England.[4]

Besides agriculture, Hamptonians earned their livelihoods by fishing, oystering and tourism. Each of these industries was tied to the village's peculiar locale—it was surrounded by water on three sides. The rivers and the Roads were a bountiful source for seafood of all sorts. The water also provided the town with a scenic quality enticing to Northerners and foreigners as well as to native Virginians. Tourists in search of cool breezes and pleasant vistas vacationed at the Hygeia Hotel along the waterfront at Old Point

Comfort which was southeast of the village. Many of these tourists had first visited Hampton as members of the United States military when stationed at Fortress Monroe. The wages of troops at the Fortress provided a small but steady source of additional income for residents of the town.[5]

Only once between the Revolution and the Civil War did history impinge on Hampton: that occasion was the War of 1812 when the British invaded and pillaged the town. By 1860 Hampton had been rebuilt, and few remembered the disaster of almost fifty years earlier. The residents certainly bore no grudge against the Englishmen who had once destroyed their town. The two main streets were still named "King" and "Queen" after the British monarchs William and Mary. King Street ran north to south from the town limits to Hampton Creek; Queen Street ran west to east from the town's western limits to that same Hampton Creek as it joined Hampton Roads. Spanning the Creek was Hampton Bridge which led from the village to Old Point Comfort and Fortress Monroe.[6]

Drawing of Hampton village before its burning in May 1861. (Courtesy of the Hampton Institute Archives)

Northwest of the juncture of King and Queen Streets were mostly farms and forests. In the settled portion of the village, around the intersection of these two streets, there were only two buildings of distinction: the County Courthouse, and St. John's Episcopal Church. Across Hampton Bridge, and outside the village proper, was the Hygeia Hotel with its classically Southern verandas supported by white columns. At the tip of Old Point Comfort was Fortress Monroe, the military bastion that would make Hampton a crucial part of American history between 1861 and 1865. Its red brick buttresses looked out upon the Roads and protected its harbor ports from invasion.[7]

In 1860 there were 5,798 residents in Elizabeth City County. The 3,180 whites were in a majority for the last time until 1890. They enjoyed the somnolent life of the area. Most of them were small farmers who made an adequate living from their grain and vegetable crops. Others were craftsmen, fishermen, and boatmen. There were also some merchants, traders and hostelers who catered to their neighbors or, more profitably, to the soldiers and vacationers passing through the village. On Sundays, Hampton's whites gave thanks for their uncomplicated lives at St. John's or Hampton Baptist Church. During the week, those who could afford to do so saw to the education of their children: their daughters at Chesapeake Female Seminary near Old Point Comfort, their sons at William and Mary College in Williamsburg.[8]

The whites could luxuriate in their lifestyle because much of the labor needed to sustain it was performed by the other half of the county's population—the blacks. In 1860 there were 201 free blacks and 2,417 slaves in Elizabeth City County. They were compelled to work hard, but even their labor was less burdensome than it was for blacks elsewhere in the South. Both free blacks and slaves shared many occupations with the whites, and few suffered from the harshness of treatment prevalent in some other areas of the South.[9]

Hampton's blacks enjoyed two advantages: they lived in a county where labor intensive crops like tobacco no longer predominated, and they frequently had white relatives in the county. The latter advantage was particularly characteristic of the town's free black population. Though they were not entirely "free," they were not entirely "black" either. Most of them were mulattoes, and many of them shared family names with the whites responsible for their complexion. The intermixture of races and the sharing of last names was not peculiar to Hampton, Virginia, but the

cordiality between black and white sides of families was. As a consequence, free blacks and slaves were permitted more privileges
than were common in the ante-bellum South—and more than a
prudent slave master would tolerate. Hampton's whites had forgotten or never learned Frederick Douglass's warning that superior
conditions did not increase a black's fondness for slavery; it simply
made him more desirous of freedom.[10]

The lax attitude of Hampton whites especially benefitted the
201 blacks who comprised the "free colored" population. They
were permitted to own property; they lived dispersed throughout
the white community, and they could come and go as they pleased.
In 1860, seventeen of them owned property worth a total of
$15,000. Some probably had acquired their land in the same manner
as Cary Nettles, one of the county's largest black landowners.
Nettles bought his eighty-two acres from Christopher Nettles, the
son of his former owner —and possibly his half-brother as well.[11]

*St. John's Episcopal Church as rendered prior to
its burning in 1861. The entrance to the right is
that photographed in 1863 (see photo p. 28).
(Courtesy of the Hampton Institute Archives)*

The other sixteen blacks with real property typically owned only the lots upon which their homes stood, but a few had larger holdings. Along with Nettles, there were the heirs of Thomas Francis who owned eighty-two acres, and Samuel Dewbre who owned eighty-five. David Carry had seventeen and a half acres; Richard Hambleton, fifteen acres. James Bailey owned fifty-five acres and several town lots through his wife, Nancy. She was daughter of Cesar Tarrant, a black veteran of the Revolutionary War, who had been given freedom and a land grant by the state of Virginia in gratitude for his services. In addition to their real property, the free blacks of 1860 Hampton were taxed for personal property worth $1,100 including simple items like watches, clocks, household goods, but also—in the case of the larger landowners—farm animals. Two of Hampton's free black men paid an additional $3.60 in taxes. They were Hampton's only black slave owners. William Taylor paid $2.40 for his two slaves, who were also his wife and daughter; Jim Lester paid $1.20 in taxes for his slave, who was also his wife. Under Virginia law, these slaves usually could not be emancipated without permission of the state legislature.[12]

The members of Hampton's "free colored" community were a remarkably resourceful group. They made a great deal out of the opportunities they had, and, as a result, provided the nucleus of the post-bellum black community that evolved over the next thirty years.

The free black family most illustrative of the subtleties and complexities of Negro life in Hampton was the Peakes. Thomas Peake and his wife Mary were both very light-skinned mulattoes. Thomas was described as "fair-skinned" with black wavy hair and blue eyes. He was so Caucasian in appearance that he was arrested as a rebel spy during the Civil War. Union pickets refused to believe that he was a "black" man. Thomas was, in fact, a spy, but he served on the Northern rather than the Southern side. His white appearance deceived rebels as effectively as it did Yankees. Peake was a former slave who had been freed by his master in 1846. His wife Mary had been born free. She was the daughter of a mulatto woman and a Frenchman. Her father provided for her education, but he could not marry her colored mother under Virginia law, and he chose not to take her back to France where biracial marriages were possible.[13]

Thomas Peake met and married Mary during his service as a wardroom boy with the merchant marine between 1846 and 1850. When he returned to Hampton in the latter year, he brought his wife and mother-in-law, Sarah, with him. Sarah later married Thompson Walker, a slave who became a prominent spokesman for Hampton's freedmen after the Civil War.[14]

In Hampton, the Peakes lived in a modest house a mile from the Hygeia Hotel where Thomas worked as a servant. Their small house amidst similar white homes was the most valuable black-owned property in the county; it was worth $2,200. Mary did not allow her education to go to waste. She taught reading to free blacks and slaves alike. Teaching slaves was, of course, against Virginia law, but, like so much else in ante-bellum Hampton, it went unchallenged by white residents so long as it was done discreetly and caused no problems. Mrs. Peake continued her school openly after the war began and was one of the first teachers of ex-slaves in the Civil War South. Thomas was equally active; after his wartime work as a Union spy, he served as a constable and as overseer of the poor for Elizabeth City County.[15]

Joining the Peakes as a leader of the free black community in ante-bellum Hampton was William Taylor, formerly Billy Colton, slave of Samuel Colton. Born at the turn of the century, Taylor was already sixty years old when the war began. He had "hired his own time" and managed to purchase his freedom. For Taylor, the dignity of freedom required the dignity of a "freeman's name," so he renamed himself William Taylor. Few white Hamptonians were willing to acknowledge the change—the tax records to his death refer to him as Colton—but blacks and Northerners invariably called him "Reverend Taylor" after the war began. Taylor sought freedom not only for himself but for his family. This goal he accomplished in 1859 by purchasing his wife and daughter, although he could not legally emancipate them until the Emancipation Proclamation in 1863. Taylor was a home owner, a carpenter by trade; he was also literate and a "fiery exhorter." In 1863 when Hampton blacks organized their first independent church—First Baptist—they chose Taylor as their pastor.[16]

In 1860, along with Thomas Peake and William Taylor, there were thirty-four other free black men who were heads of families and liable to taxation in Elizabeth City County. Six of these were farmers with sufficient land to make an adequate living. Several others pursued the same occupations as their white counterparts; they were craftsmen, fishermen, oystermen or boatsmen. Among the craftsmen, Samuel Herbert was a bricklayer; another, appropriately named Hercules Savage, was a blacksmith. The remaining free men were common laborers or waiters, cooks, and attendants at the Hygeia Hotel.[17] Many of Hampton's free blacks appear to have been literate, although it is impossible to determine the exact number. Certainly, Thomas and Mary Peake, William Taylor, James Bailey, Cary Nettles, and Samuel Herbert, the village's free black elite, were.

Hampton's 2,417 slaves were denied many of the privileges enjoyed by "free coloreds." Nevertheless, they were considerably "freer" than bondsmen elsewhere in the South. Three major factors allowed for these circumstances: the county's patterns of slave ownership, the nature of slave occupations, and the treatment accorded slaves by whites.

In 1860, only 247 of the County's 3,180 whites owned slaves. The twenty-five largest slaveholders, with nineteen or more, owned a quarter of the county's slaves; the largest owned eighty-three. Most of the county's slaveholders had ten or fewer slaves. These figures, however, do not accurately portray the extent to which the white population was involved with the slave system. Several hundred whites besides the 247 slave owners regularly hired slaves. In fact, the 1860 census identifies almost a thousand slaves in Elizabeth City County who were hired out in that year.[18]

As a result, bondsmen enjoyed wide latitude in occupations open to them. Many performed the same skilled crafts as free whites and blacks. Others were in occupations that were potentially undermining to the slave system: some were fishermen and boat pilots with access to vessels that could carry them to freedom. Many slaves in these categories "hired their own time," paying only a set fee to their masters at the end of the year. Indeed, so relaxed was the system of supervision in Elizabeth City County that the 1860 census taker identified over a hundred such self-employed slaves without bothering to record names of their owners.[19]

The lax attitude toward slave control in Hampton extended to the slaves' personal lives. From sex and age groupings in the census, most slaves were allowed to live as families.[20] These figures tend to confirm Gutman's findings in the *Black Family in Slavery and Freedom*. Marriages between slaves of different owners, and between slaves and free blacks, were permitted. Laws against slaves learning to read and write were widely ignored. Bondsmen were an integral part of the community's religious life, as well, joining their free black and white neighbors in the congregations of the village's two churches. In fact, blacks outnumbered whites in Hampton Baptist by 900 to 100.[21]

Slave life in Hampton was different from the rest of the South in degree rather than in kind. Slaveholders were still masters, firm believers in the innate inferiority of the black race. As elsewhere in the South, slaves were sold from master to master as required for convenience or economic necessity. Despite diversification of slave occupations, life for many bondsmen was often hard. Their hours were long, diet poor, clothing scanty and often inadequate for winter.[22]

A few masters were harsh and unfeeling. Slaves of men like William Corsey and John Wood later recalled that sometimes they had only wild huckleberries and cow peas to eat, and that once they were forced to work until midnight only to be driven to the fields again at 3 A.M. Their children were given no clothing until old enough to work. Such practices were frowned upon by many whites; nevertheless, some masters were brutal, whipping and torturing their slaves for every infraction.[23] The story of George Scott, a runaway, illustrates both the severity and laxity inherent in the slave system around Hampton. For two years immediately before the Civil War, Scott evaded attempts to capture him without ever leaving Elizabeth City County. He had fled from his master, a Mr. Graves, who was reputed to be a cruel and harsh man. During his years of hiding, Scott lived in a cave near Hampton and was kept in food and supplies by other village slaves. Scott, on occasion, hired himself to white merchants and farmers around the town. They apparently shared the low general opinion of Graves, and so ignored Scott's fugitive status and refused to help recapture him.

Scott went freely among the slave population, visiting his friends on nearby farms. Despite Graves' diligent attempts to capture him, Scott remained free, always informed beforehand by other slaves that Graves was on his way. Once, when cornered by Graves, Scott outfought his owner, relieving him of both a pistol and Bowie knife. In another instance, he escaped from Hampton jail by dodging past the waiter bringing him his dinner, leaving only his shirt tail in the waiter's hand. Scott's reputation as a powerful and swift-footed man made even bounty hunters reluctant to pursue him. When the war began, Scott became one of the first "contraband" and served with the Union Army as a scout—a job for which he was well-equipped.[24]

Thus while slavery on the Peninsula was certainly less harsh than in the cotton and sugar states to the South, it was far from idyllic for the black man. White masters still remembered Nat Turner of Southampton County; in 1860 they remembered John

Brown and Harper's Ferry even more vividly. They worried that abolitionist literature might reach their bondsmen. On the other hand, it seems to have been the unknown black that gave whites concern. With their "own negroes," they felt relatively secure. This was particularly true of a village like Hampton in which most blacks and whites knew one another. There were ties of long association and even mutual ancestors to bind whites and their slaves together.[25]

The most important consequence of this relaxed slave regime in Hampton was the creation of a remarkable group of ante-bellum slave leaders, many of whom were closely tied to the free blacks of the county through blood or marriage. Together they proved such effective leaders that in the decades that followed, when the area's black population quadrupled, they were able to maintain their positions of authority and to command respect from blacks and whites alike.

One such leader, who had helped shelter George Scott, was Thompson Walker, slave foreman of the Wood's Farm near Hampton. Walker was the stepfather of Mary Peake, and a literate, articulate man who later became a speaker for the American Missionary Association and a founder of Zion Baptist Church, Hampton's second black church. William Thorton, who became the first pastor of Zion Church in 1863, was a slave carpenter who hired his own time. Like Walker, he was literate and a powerful orator. After the war, he became one of black Hampton's most respected figures.[26]

Fully as important as Walker or Thorton was William Roscoe Davis, nominally slave of Mrs. Shields, mistress of the "Little England" estate in Hampton. Davis was the son of a Madagascar slave woman smuggled into Virginia in the 1830s, twenty years after the American slave trade was outlawed. His father was a white sailor aboard that slave ship who raped his mother during the voyage. Davis was born and raised in Norfolk where he learned to read and write from his master. As a young man, he was articulate and puritanically religious with an imposing physical presence that would later serve him well as a spokesman for Hampton's post-bellum black community.[27]

After Davis was sold to Shields in Hampton, he served for a while as their foreman, and is reputed to have beaten the former white overseer before being given the job. During the five or six years before the war, Davis hired his own time as operator of a pleasure boat at Old Point Comfort. He married Nancy Moore, the sister of Thomas Peake, and was father of seven children. His wife had been emancipated by her master, but the master's heirs refused to grant her freedom. With savings from his pleasure boat, Davis contested the issue in court, through white intermediaries, of course, until war unexpectedly settled the question.[28]

Men like Walker, Thorton, and Davis were outstanding representatives of the enslaved portion of Hampton's black community, but they were far from unique. Many others, invisible in the antebellum records, would forge to prominence during the Civil War and Reconstruction. Together they represented a solid foundation upon which to construct the black man's freedom.[29]

Hampton's whites and blacks enjoyed their unusually harmonious life, in part, because no one paid much attention to what went on there. The Civil War brought an abrupt end to this neglect. Hampton was once again of strategic importance to Virginia's enemy—in this case, the United States. And Hampton's blacks were well prepared for the opportunities of greater freedom that Virginia's defeat might bring them.

The tensions built slowly in Hampton during the winter of 1860 and the spring of 1861. Virginia had watched other Southern states secede from the Union in January and February, but had taken no action of her own. Lincoln's call for troops on 14 April 1861, after the Confederate capture of Fort Sumter, pushed Virginia over the brink. She joined the Southern cause and her citizens had to decide whether their first loyalty was to state or Union.

The decision was especially difficult for the whites in Hampton. If they chose for Virginia, they would, in all likelihood, have to abandon their homes and farms. The Union army made it clear that Fortress Monroe would be held at all costs. Two regiments of Massachusetts troops had been rushed there and soldiers from other areas quickly followed. By May 1861, the garrison's strength had increased from 400 to 12,000 men.[30] The hastily organized rebel units on the Peninsula could not hope to challenge such numbers. In mid-May, Colonel Benjamin Ewell, commander of Confederate forces on the Peninsula (and until recently President of William and Mary College), concluded that Hampton could not be defended. "It is difficult to manage Hampton," Ewell reported to headquarters in Richmond. "The people are excitable and brave even to rashness and are unwilling to seem to give way. It might, on the approach in force of the Federal troops, be evacuated by the military and the remaining citizens ought to make terms." Hampton civilians could either flee with the Southern troops or accept federal occupation.[31]

The choice facing Hampton's black residents, especially its slaves, was very different. They already sensed what Lincoln would not acknowledge for two more years, that is, this war was over black freedom. Should the slaves accede to their masters' demand that they accompany them in flight, or should they remain in Union-held territory and gamble for true freedom?

With rebel evacuation of Hampton imminent, the blacks chose to gamble. On the night of 24 May 1861, three slave men fled across the causeway that led from Old Point Comfort to Fortress Monroe and appealed for sanctuary. The following morning, Major John Cary of the Virginia Artillery appeared at the Fort under a flag of truce. He demanded the return of the three escaped slaves as required under the 1850 Fugitive Slave Act. Cary further requested permission to evacuate the residents of Hampton to the southside of Hampton Roads and northward up the Peninsula. Both the escaped slaves and Major Cary were interviewed by the Fortress commander, General Benjamin Butler, who had arrived only two days before.[32]

Butler was a man of some military experience through his ante-bellum leadership of the Massachusetts militia. He was also a prominent Democratic politician with aspirations to the Massachusetts governorship or higher. At that moment in the spring of 1861, Butler was both an asset and liability to Abraham Lincoln. He was a nationally known Democrat vocally loyal to the Republican administration; but if he broke with the administration, many other Northern Democrats might follow him.[33]

Butler had already demonstrated his potential to create divisiveness. He had used armed federal troops to occupy Baltimore against the wishes of the Union's commanding general, Winfield Scott. Lincoln and Scott had feared such action might propel Maryland into secession; Butler felt occupation might be the only way to prevent secession. For his initiative, Butler was reassigned to Fortress Monroe, which both he and the administration mistakenly thought of as an out-of-the-way post.[34] The problems raised by the presence of three fugitive slaves and Major Cary from the opposing army were early indications that Hampton would be at the center, not the periphery, of events during the war.

Butler had first to decide whether the three slaves, Shepard Mallory, Frank Baker, and James Townsend, should be returned to their master, Colonel Charles Mallory. His decision could have major national implications. President Lincoln had formulated no policy on escaping slaves. Lincoln and other more conservative Republicans still hoped to draw the South back into the Union with little further bloodshed. Any Northern undermining of the South's slave system would destroy such hopes and might cause the border states to bolt to the Confederacy as well. The radical Republicans were more inclined to see the war as an assault on slavery. They wanted escaping slaves welcomed into Union lines whenever they appeared.[35] On the one hand, Butler dared not exceed his instructions again, as he had in Baltimore. On the other, he did not wish to offend Northern abolitionists, especially since so many were residents of his home state, Massachusetts.

Colonel Charles K. Mallory (CSA), owner of the first three "contraband." (Courtesy of the Hampton Institute Archives)

Butler questioned the three fugitives and found they had run away because their master meant to take them along in his flight to North Carolina with the Confederate army. The three slaves would have to leave their wives and families behind. After pondering this information, Butler struck upon a shrewd plan which turned Southerners' insistence that slaves were chattel property— just like pigs or cows—upon its head. The three fugitives, Butler decreed, were "contraband of war," enemy property which could be employed in waging war against the Union. Under his wartime powers, Butler had the right to seize such property so as to deny its use to the enemy.[36] It was a novel solution that fired the imagination of Northern abolitionists when word reached them. Butler was soon acclaimed all over the North for his initiative. Lincoln was uneasy both over the "contraband" theory and the fact that Butler had thought of it; but the policy did sidestep the issue of the slaves' status after the war, and Lincoln did not countermand it.

Having decided the status of the fugitives, Butler was ready to meet Major Cary. To the major's request that the slaves be returned, the general responded with an emphatic "No." The Fugitive Slave Law of the United States could hardly apply if Virginia was, as it claimed, a foreign nation. He added, however, if Colonel Mallory, their owner, would come in and take an oath of allegiance to the Union, he would gladly return his human property. Cary's second request, that Hampton residents be allowed to evacuate across Hampton Roads, Butler flatly refused. The guns of Fortress Monroe guarded that escape route. Butler offered no objection, however, to evacuation northward up the Peninsula as the roads in that direction were "in the hands of his [Cary's] friends."[37]

The interviews with Butler marked the end of the harmonious interracial world of Hampton. The blacks and whites had been forced to take a dispute between them to an outsider, to a *Yankee*, and the blacks had won. Nothing in Hampton would ever be quite the same again.

That afternoon of 25 May the village was abandoned; the majority of its residents fled north to the Confederate lines drawn from the northern edge of Elizabeth City County across the Peninsula to Newport News.[38] The Hamptonians going north, however, were mostly white. The blacks refused to believe their masters' stories of Yankee cannibalism or of selling kidnapped blacks to Cuba. Rather than accompany their owners, they went into hiding in the fields and woods around the village.[39] News of sanctuary to

*Butler and the "Contraband," 1861. (Courtesy
of the Syms-Eaton Museum)*

be had at the Fortress spread rapidly. On the day of evacuation, 8 more slaves crossed the causeway to the Fort; the next day 47 more came. This stream rapidly became a flood. Intermittent skirmishes between Union and Confederate troops and Union capture of Newport News made escape easy. By July over 900 contraband had found protection around the Fortress.[40]

These were freedom's first opportunists. In the ensuing three decades, they and the thousands who would join them in Hampton would test freedom's meaning with a determination and sophistication that at once surprised and dismayed many whites, including erstwhile allies. Yet to these blacks each action that followed their initial escape was as logical as the first. Freedom had to be something one could go to, lay hold of, and use, or it had no meaning.

Drawing of black "contraband" fleeing to Fortress Monroe after the first three contraband found sanctuary. Over 900 arrived during the month of July. (Courtesy of the Hampton Institute Archives)

Slaves at Fort Monroe Gate, 1861. From Leslie's Illustrated Newspaper. *(Courtesy of the Casemate Museum, Fort Monroe, Va.)*

Surviving Freedom: The Contraband and the Union Army, 1861-65

The relationship between the Union army and Hampton blacks during the war is significant for two reasons. First, many of the Union policies on escaping slaves originated in Hampton. Secondly, the strains between Northern whites and Southern blacks that led to sharply different visions of the blacks' postwar future first emerged in Hampton.

Northern policy on escaped slaves quickly became a national issue as other blacks in the South, most notably in South Carolina and Louisiana, followed the lead of Hampton's contraband and fled to Union-held territory. Ultimately it was Lincoln and his cabinet who determined what approaches should be taken with escaped slaves. Nevertheless, it was in Hampton that the strategies on slave care, employment, and settlement, many of which proved disastrous, first emerged. Unfortunately, many of these same strategies were implemented, unchanged, elsewhere in the South.

The hostility exhibited by many Union army troops toward escaping slaves was precursor of generalized Northern antipathy toward blacks that became more apparent during Reconstruction. The army's first concern was always control of, rather than assistance to, blacks. Blacks were deemed incompetent, unfit to determine their own best interests. Though some Northerners tempered this attitude with paternalistic concern for black well-being, the underlying belief of incompetency remained.

Blacks, understandably, had an opposite view. They had escaped from their Southern owners in hopes of gaining the rights and privileges of free men. Refusal to grant these benefits created a strain between blacks and the army that lasted throughout the war and Reconstruction. It also produced growing black demands for autonomy in their lives which many Northerners came to define as black arrogance and ingratitude.

Union army policies, and the army's strained relations with escaping slaves, emerged in the context of a brutal war. Until at least mid-1863, it was not at all clear that the North could win the war or that the status of blacks would change significantly. Hampton, major staging area for some of the war's bloodiest campaigns, was hardly an advantageous setting for the development of methods to handle the collapse of the Southern slave system. Neither blacks nor the military had the opportunity for careful appraisal of issues and events. Both were preoccupied with the issue of survival in wartime Hampton.

The North, unprepared for war, was even more unprepared for the burden of caring for thousands of fleeing bondsmen. The only organization which could perform this monumental task was the Union army. But to most army men, freedmen were at best a nuisance. At worst, they were representatives of the despised race for whom Northern white men were being asked to kill or be killed. As a consequence, army assistance to blacks throughout the war came grudgingly and ineffectually. Even after emancipation became a Northern goal, freedmen were frequently mistreated by their emancipators and many died as a result of army neglect. These problems of physical survival for the freedmen, of the military's inability to provide adequate services, and most of all, of the open hostility of many Northern soldiers toward blacks, did much to determine attitudes and actions of Hampton blacks during the war and the decades that followed. By 1865, Hampton freedmen had already learned many of the bitter lessons about Northern racial attitudes that other freed slaves would discover during Reconstruction.

In the summer of 1861, the exuberance many blacks felt at escaping was reflected in their ability to cope with the wartime situation. Many of the 900 contraband at the Fort or in the now abandoned village of Hampton proved themselves as resourceful in their new circumstances as they had been in the old. Mrs. Mary Peake began to teach her school openly, and by September of 1961 she had fifty pupils. Peter Herbert, an escaped slave, also started a school and attracted an equally large student body. William Davis gave up his pleasure boat to take a job as dispenser of rations to the other refugees at Fort Monroe. Some blacks found jobs as servants with Union naval and army officers, including one named Fred who charmed his employers with renditions of "John Brown's Body" and made good money in tips for his efforts. Their ante-bellum maritime experience served Hampton blacks well. Twelve contraband signed on as crew aboard the Union steamer *Minnesota;* they were reported as the only men who could be trusted to go ashore without an officer and still return on time and sober. A handful of contraband like perennial runaway George Scott took advantage of the situation and left the Peninsula entirely with some departing Union troops.[1]

But most of the Hampton refugees did not fare as well. The area outside the village limits was vulnerable to rebel raids, so blacks could no longer farm. Many of them were women, children, or elderly people who could not support themselves. A system of employing the able-bodied and caring for their dependents was needed. General Butler appealed to Washington for instructions, and in July he was given permission to employ blacks in strengthening the breastwork around the Fort and in other military projects. Edward Pierce, a private from Boston, and an abolitionist, was placed in charge as supervisor. Pierce put his black employees to work felling trees, digging trenches and ditches. Young Pierce reported the blacks to be hard-working and well behaved. The major difficulty, he complained, was superior officers who felt use of force would make blacks work harder. This was the first warning of many difficulties to come between the army and the blacks. Already some Union officers saw themselves more as unwilling overseers than as emancipators.[2]

The task of caring for the contraband in July of 1861 was a difficult one; other events that summer soon made it overwhelming. The most serious problem was the mounting number of escaped slaves. Elsewhere on the Peninsula, particularly near Newport News and Yorktown, there were frequent skirmishes between rebel and Union troops. Because slaves often assisted the Union forces as spies or guides, the Confederate command ordered removal of all slaves from plantations in the disputed area. This proved impossible. Blacks, one Southern officer warned his supervisors, "have been constantly in communication with the enemy and evinced the strongest dislike to being taken." Rebel attempts to get slaves behind Confederate lines only hastened the growing exodus to Fortress Monroe.[3]

Just as the pressure of black refugees became most severe, Confederate General Magruder burned the village of Hampton so that empty houses could not be used as billets for Union troops.

This act destroyed the buildings in which many contraband had found shelter, further aggravating an already severe housing shortage.[4]

At the end of the summer, Ben Butler was replaced in command at Hampton by General John E. Wool; the Third and Fourth Regiments of the Massachusetts Volunteer stationed at Fortress Monroe completed their enlistments and returned home. These troops, from the North's most abolitionist-inclined state, were more sympathetic to the contraband than were most of the soldiers who replaced them. In addition, Edward Pierce, charged with caring for escaped slaves, was among the departing Massachusetts troops. Pierce would continue his advocacy of the contrabands' cause in articles in the *Atlantic Monthly*, but his departure and

The southeast entrance of St. John's Episcopal Church after its burning in 1861. Photograph taken ca. 1863. (Courtesy of the Hampton Institute Archives)

that of General Ben Butler left no one sympathetic to the freedmen's needs at the Fortress.[5] Clearly some more defined and permanent method of freedmen's aid was required.

Shortly before his departure, General Butler found a possible solution through correspondence with Lewis Tappan, abolitionist and treasurer of the American Missionary Association. Tappan wrote Butler from New York offering the aid of his Association in caring for the contraband. Butler accepted with alacrity and the Association commissioned the Reverend Lewis Lockwood of the YMCA as its first worker among the black refugees of the South.[6]

That the American Missionary Association was the first Northern benevolent organization to send aid to Southern contraband was hardly a coincidence. The Association was already fifteen years old by 1861 and, from its inception, had been dedicated to "preaching the Gospel free from all complicity with slavery and caste." Though officially a nonsectarian evangelical society, the Association was closely allied with the Congregational and Presbyterian Churches; it was this form of evangelical Christianity that it sought to spread to the South. Its leadership had strong ties to the abolitionist movement and was deeply committed to the uplift of the black man, whether slave or free. Nor did the AMA demonstrate any timidity in pursuit of its goals. Even before the war, it sent missionaries into the South, and in 1855 established Berea College in Kentucky with an integrated student body.[7]

The coming of the war and the influx of contraband to Fortress Monroe in 1861 offered an opportunity for which the AMA had long been preparing. Here, at last, was a chance to provide spiritual and physical succour to Southern blacks, truly free from "complicity with slavery or caste." Over the next ten years, the Association would send scores of missionaries and teachers to the South to achieve these ends. The Hampton area, already abandoned by Southern whites hostile to the AMA, seemed an ideal laboratory in which to prove that black people could and should be free. As a result, the Virginia Peninsula became a major focus of AMA efforts during the war and Reconstruction. Over fifty Association workers, including a few Northern blacks, served in the area during these years.[8]

Lewis Lockwood, when he arrived at Fortress Monroe on 3 September 1861, was well aware of the potential significance of his work. "On the contraband, under God," he wrote, "perhaps hinges the destiny of this Republic. Without them this rebellion may not be suppressed."[9] Lockwood's premonition would prove correct, but in 1861 he could find few other Northerners in Hampton who shared his feelings. Hostile Southern whites may have fled, but many hostile Union men remained, and more arrived every day. Although missionary and educational work among freedmen would make great strides during the war, the first duty of Lockwood, and of missionaries who joined him, proved to be protecting the blacks from their supposed allies in the Union army.

Army procedures for caring for contraband were makeshift from the start; with the departure of Edward Pierce in September of 1861, they collapsed completely. The army was not entirely to blame for this state of affairs. There was a war going on, and the Virginia Peninsula was one of the few Southern areas still held by the North. Its proximity to the Confederate capital at Richmond made it an ideal staging ground for battle. Nonetheless, winter was rapidly approaching; constant skirmishes outside of Hampton made it impossible for blacks to harvest their crops. In a few weeks, the refugee settlements would be faced with wholesale starvation unless the military acted.

In response to this crisis, General John Wool, who had replaced Butler at the Fortress, issued a Special Order in October of 1861 to formalize procedures for the care of escaped slaves. All able-bodied blacks were to be put to work; those not hired as officers' servants were to be employed in the Quartermaster's or Engineer's Departments. Wages were set at eight dollars a month for men and four dollars for women, plus full rations for workers and half rations for their dependents. The blacks, however, were not to receive their wages in cash. Payment was withheld to buy their clothing, and the remainder was put in a fund to provide food and clothing for those unable to work.[10]

It was no accident that the army struck upon a system of treatment that was hardly distinguishable from the slavery blacks were seeking to escape. Many Union officers had served in the South; this was apparently the only procedure of caring for blacks they could conceive. Even officers not familiar with the South shared the basic assumption that underlay the employment scheme, i.e., blacks were not competent to care for themselves.

The ironies of the proposed system were apparent to Hampton blacks. It made no distinction between those legally free before the war and those who were, in fact, "contraband of war." Even those who hired their own time before the war would have earned more under the old system than under the new. As a consequence, many of the blacks did everything they could to avoid dependence on the army dole. Especially lucky were those who had been oystermen or fishermen; they now had an even larger potential market, and they insisted upon payment in cash.[11]

The abuses possible under General Wool's plan were being fully exploited within weeks. Officers charged with carrying out his program had none of the sense of responsibility for one's own property nor of benevolence built from long acquaintance that had helped to ameliorate a similar system during bondage. They did, however, share with ante-bellum masters the strong desire to make large profits. They accomplished this by cheating blacks in every way they could conceive.

The Quartermaster's Department, charged with keeping pay records and with distributing goods to blacks, robbed them at every turn. Clothing and rations were credited to refugees but actually sold on the black market. The quartermaster, a Captain Tallmedge, pocketed the profits. Initially, rations were distributed at the Fortress and at Camp Hamilton, a large refugee settlement established across Mill Creek from the Fort. Tallmedge ordered an end to distribution at the camp, thereby denying nearly half of the freedmen rations to which they were entitled. These excess rations Tallmedge also sold on the black market. By Christmastime, 1861, Tallmedge's dishonesty and greed had produced many of the consequences the Special Order was implemented to avoid: hundreds of blacks were left without food, clothing or the means to purchase firewood in the midst of winter.[12]

The Reverend Lockwood appealed to General Wool for redress, but freedmen's aid was not high on the general's list of priorities. His promised directives to the quartermaster were either never sent or ignored when received. The few blacks who went directly to Wool with their complaints were given requisitions for food and clothing but Tallmedge refused to honor them and often threw the offending blacks in the guardhouse. David Billips, one of the original contraband who would survive the war, experienced such confinement for his efforts to receive some pay. He had the temerity to appeal to General Wool a second time. In return he received a pair of shoes and two dollars for five and a half months' labor at the Fort. Hiring his own time as a slave, he had cleared six dollars a month after paying ten to his master.[13]

Lockwood began to despair of improving conditions through negotiations with the army. In December he took William Davis and Thompson Walker, two of the original contraband, on a speaking tour of Northern cities to raise money for the AMA. During

the tour, all three men denounced the harsh treatment that escaped slaves were receiving. Reports of their comments reached
Quartermaster Tallmedge; when Lockwood returned to Hampton,
he was refused permission to enter the Fortress. The school and
church for freedmen there were forced to close temporarily.[14]

In the end, Lockwood's outspokenness proved effective. Complaints about the mistreatment of freedmen became so widespread
that General Wool was forced to appoint a commission of investigation, but only after George Whipple, Corresponding Secretary of
the AMA, appealed personally to Secretary of War Stanton. The
Commission report, submitted in May 1862, substantiated the
freedmen's complaints in every particular. Wage payments by the
quartermaster were $10,000 in arrears; food and clothing rations
were inadequate, the bulk of them having been sold by the quartermaster for his own profit. Incredibly, Captain Tallmedge and
his assistants were not court-martialed, but merely relieved of their
responsibilities for care of freedmen. Cash payment of wages was
instituted and the withholding of wages to care for sick and indigent was discontinued. A hospital for freedmen was ordered built
at the Camp Hamilton refugee settlement next to the Fort, and
the freedmen's school at the Fortress was ordered reopened. To
guard against further abuses of blacks, the office of superintendent of contraband was created at the Fortress.[15]

The AMA was anxious that an officer truly sympathetic to the
freedmen be appointed to the superintendency. They recommen-
ded, and the secretary of war appointed, Captain C. B. Wilder of
Connecticut. Wilder was an abolitionist and closely tied to prominent Congregational families in New England. His nephew, John
Wilder, was appointed to assist him in his duties.[16]

The morale of the blacks and the missionaries was greatly improved by these actions. They were especially pleased with the
new superintendent. John Linson, one of the newly arrived missionaries, described Wilder as "zealous, prompt, and busily engaged
in setting things in order."[17] It quickly became clear, however,
that the army was more interested in quieting missionary complaints than solving freedmen's problems. Wilder was viewed with
disdain by his brother officers who considered him more a missionary than an army man, and he would be constantly harassed
by them throughout his years in Hampton. Mistreatment of freedmen continued unabated, and in some instances grew worse. Wilder complained that "as the colored people increase in numbers,

so does the hostility to them and their advancement." C. P. Day, a missionary teacher, added that "some officers and soldiers here seem to have lost sight of the rebellion and are fighting the ex-slaves, determined if possible to prevent them from making an honest living."[18]

General Wool promised his "utmost support" for missionary work with the freedmen, both before and after the Commission's investigation, but his subordinates clearly did not get the message. Military doctors forced the blacks and missionaries to vacate the old Chesapeake Female Seminary two miles west of the Fort. They had been using that campus as a school and living quarters. The excuse was that the doctors wanted the blacks "out of the way" in case the buidings were needed as a hospital for soldiers wounded in General George McClellan's Peninsular campaign. Mc-Clellan's plan was to attack Richmond from the south by marching up the Peninsula. His campaign, however, did not begin in earnest until May, so the buildings stood vacant for several weeks. Meanwhile, blacks were forced to live in tents along the Mill Creek Swamp. Appeals to General Wool brought only the curt response that the missionaries had been "teaching school long enough." In fairness to the general, it should be noted that many of his troops were little better housed than the refugees during that winter of 1861-62.[19]

April of 1862 brought the spring thaw and somewhat improved conditions. Blacks were given lumber to construct their own houses. Together with the missionaries, they renovated the burned-out courthouse in Hampton to use as a school and church. Doctors were appointed to care for sick freedmen.[20] But the spirits of blacks and AMA workers had been buoyed only to be dashed a second time. In June, General Wool was replaced by General John Dix, and the struggle for fair treatment of the freedmen, which seemed partially won two months earlier, began anew.

Many freedmen still had not received their wages. Captain Tall-medge and his cronies attempted to regain their lucrative posts as paymasters and ration dispensers for the blacks. John Oliver, the black AMA worker in Newport News, reported that the quartermaster there, R. G. Wormsley, had gotten rich during his few months of service. He was "made of the same quality of material out of which all Quarter Masters [sic] are made. Ask for nothing and you gets [sic] nothing." Oliver left out one important characteristic of the quartermasters who served on the Peninsula: they were vindictive. When Wormsley got word of Oliver's criticisms, he cut off supplies for the missionary school and denied rations for their pupils.[21]

Once again protests were made to Washington. George Whipple came from New York to negotiate a new agreement on freedmen's care and missionary work in Hampton. Nevertheless, in July, Wilder submitted a report to General Dix repeating many of the same allegations made in the Commission report four months earlier.[22]

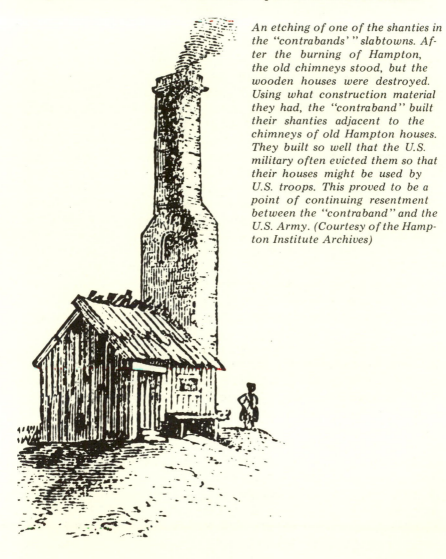

An etching of one of the shanties in the "contrabands'" slabtowns. After the burning of Hampton, the old chimneys stood, but the wooden houses were destroyed. Using what construction material they had, the "contraband" built their shanties adjacent to the chimneys of old Hampton houses. They built so well that the U.S. military often evicted them so that their houses might be used by U.S. troops. This proved to be a point of continuing resentment between the "contraband" and the U.S. Army. (Courtesy of the Hampton Institute Archives)

General Dix attempted to correct the abuses reported, but many of the most severe problems were beyond his control. Union troops on the Peninsula by the summer of 1862 numbered over 100,000. Most of these soldiers were under the command of General McClellan, whose campaign against Richmond was meeting disaster after disaster. John Oliver described McClellan's army as "demoralized beyond redemption," and he may well have been correct. They had spent the spring in relative idleness and were now suffering huge losses. When not in battle, these troops engaged in repeated rampages of pillaging, looting, and rape in freedmen's settlements. Blacks who started farms on abandoned land had their livestock and crops confiscated by the soldiers as "contraband." C. B. Wilder feared wholesale starvation among blacks unless these practices could be stopped.[23]

General McClellan and his officers did little to halt the outrages. Instead, they were frequently responsible for them. McClellan himself was well known for his antipathy toward blacks and his troops apparently shared his feelings. Several times during the summer of 1862, soldiers under his command descended upon black settlements and impressed every able-bodied man for work with the army. General Dix usually became aware of these incidents only after blacks brought their complaints to him. When Dix tried to stop the raids, McClellan's officers simply ignored his inquiries. A provost judge was appointed to investigate the problems but no significant improvement occurred until the Peninsula campaign collapsed in July of 1862 and most of McClellan's army was withdrawn from the area.[24]

The spring and summer of 1862 proved devastating for army-black relations. A reservoir of distrust had been created that no effort at corrective measures could eliminate entirely. By the summer of 1862, blacks were even refusing to establish homesteads on abandoned land. The war seemed to be going badly for the North. Blacks feared that the South was about to win and that they would soon be "restored to slavery." They saw no reason to farm only to have their land and crops taken from them at war's end.[25] Nor were blacks alone in their mood of despair. William Coan, an AMA Missionary in Norfolk, came to see the Union army as a greater enemy of blacks than the rebels. Speaking of the Northern army he said, "Let it be understood that there is nothing left...undone, by the enemy [the Union army], that shall be to injury of the colored race."[26] C.B. Wilder agreed with Coan; on the eve of the Emancipation Proclamation he counselled educating blacks as quickly as possible. Once educated, he reasoned, blacks "would not be worth much to slavery" no matter what the outcome of the war.[27]

Hampton's blacks and missionaries were being overly pessimistic. The war was not about to be lost. Although conditions in Hampton did not change significantly during the fall of 1862, decisions were being made nationally that would affect the lives of all Southerners, black and white.

Congress, in its Confiscation Acts of 1862, provided for the freedom of slaves escaping from rebel owners. In the summer of 1862, Lincoln decided that he would issue a preliminary emancipation proclamation providing freedom to slaves still in rebel-held territory after 1 January 1863. He delayed announcing his intentions until a major Union victory so that the proclamation would not be interpreted as a sign of Northern desperation. His opportunity came in September after the Battle of Antietam. Although military historians disagreed as to whether McClellan actually defeated Lee in that battle, the Union army did stop the first Southern invasion of the North and force Lee to retreat back to Virginia. That was sufficient for Lincoln's purposes and on 2 September 1862, he issued his proclamation. In fact, the president's Emancipation Proclamation was more limited than the Congressional Confiscation Acts; it freed slaves only in territory under rebel control. Slaves in Union-held areas like Hampton were excluded from its provisions. Nevertheless, blacks and missionaries in Hampton interpreted the Proclamation as a promise of eventual freedom for slaves.[28]

January 1, 1863, Emancipation Day in Hampton, produced a grand celebration sponsored by the missionaries. To them, the main issue had been resolved, that is, blacks were henceforth and forever free. Blacks were of less certain faith. They participated in the celebration, but with reserve. They already were much imbued with cynicism concerning proclamations from Washington and Northern expressions of concern. They had learned to be cautious, to expect little and thus avoid disappointment.

Despite black skepticism, there was a marked, though temporary, improvement in treatment by the army after the Emancipation. The most severe military outrages against blacks ended. Now that blacks were officially free, the government finally established policies on how they were to be treated. A Bureau of Negro Affairs in the War Department was created, and C. B. Wilder made superintendent for Hampton. More importantly, General Benjamin But-

Emancipation Oak at Hampton Institute. (Courtesy of the Hampton Institute Archives)

ler, having outraged the white citizens of New Orleans, and shocked the sensibilities of many Northerners as well, with his infamous "Ladies of the Street" order, once again was posted to Fortress Monroe.[29]

Butler's return proved a perfect illustration of a reality that freedmen elsewhere in the South would not learn for several years: far more important than national policy in determining treatment of blacks was the sympathy of the Union commander in the area in which they lived. Butler supported Wilder's efforts, listened to complaints of blacks and missionaries, and, when possible, acted in their behalf.[30] But by 1863 the problems of blacks in Hampton were considerably less susceptible to resolution through political flourish and basic good will than in 1861. The Emancipation Proclamation settled the issue of whether the army would *permit* blacks to survive; whether it had the ability to *enable* them to do so was a quite different matter.

McClellan's Peninsula campaign of 1862 and further Union conquests in 1863 and 1864 proved a mixed blessing for the thousands of black refugees in Hampton Roads. Rapid expansion of Union-held territory and removal of the freed population to the security of the lower Peninsula produced enormous increases in the black population. The first wartime census of freedmen, conducted by the army in December of 1863, and published in February of the following year, reported 10,499 black refugees in the four counties of the lower Peninsula. Of these, 9,500 were concentrated in the refugee camps of Elizabeth City and York Counties. Even by the date of its release, the census was inaccurate due to great increases in the number of refugees during January 1864.[31] Once emancipation became Northern policy, each Union victory produced a huge influx of blacks seeking the relative security and promised freedom of Hampton.[32]

General Butler did all he could to encourage this flight to freedom, issuing an order welcoming all freedmen into Union-held territory. Unfortunately, the army was unable to cope with the resulting flood. Refugees sometimes arrived in groups as large as 1,200; no quarters were available and rations were often in short supply. Albert Howe, later treasurer of Hampton Institute, reported that blacks were housed in an old tobacco barn with chalk lines drawn on the dirt floor to delineate assigned living spaces for each family. Other freedmen were housed in dilapidated sheds and barns in an area west of Hampton known as "Slabtown" because the houses were constructed from old packing crates. They lacked clothing and firewood; few could find work of any sort. There were frequent deaths from disease, exposure, and hunger. But even in these dire circumstances the freedmen showed great capacity to care for themselves; of more than 10,000 refugees believed to be in the area, only 5,401 were drawing army rations and many of them were wives and children of black soldiers.[33]

By 1864, Wilder, as Superintendent of Negro Affairs, was becoming increasingly desperate. He lacked the ability to provide the necessities of life for blacks, and, despite the policy of both the local commander and the government in Washington, he could gain little cooperation from army quartermasters and subordinate officers. Initially he had supported the enlistment of Negro soldiers in hopes this would change attitudes among his colleagues; instead he discovered that recruitment often increased the number of black wives and families that the government had to support.[34]

To help relieve the pressure of excess population, Wilder developed schemes for placing refugees in Northern homes as servants and for resettlement of others on outlying plantations. Both of these measures proved to be fraught with difficulties. The problems encountered in placing blacks in Northern homes were illustrative of the growing gap between Northern white and Southern black definitions of freedom. Wilder and the missionaries knew many Northern families that were as committed as they to black freedom and uplift. They were convinced that the placement scheme would enable many of the most promising black refugees to receive an education "in the atmosphere of freedom." Blacks would go North to work and learn; they would then return better equipped to help their own people. Even among these most faithful allies of the freedmen, there was no expectation that the blacks would stay permanently in the North.[35] Moreover, there was a happy practical coincidence in the placement idea. Northerners most desired young women or children who could do housework. As it happened, these were the two groups most burdening army relief rolls. In December of 1863, of the 5,401 receiving government rations, 4,917 were unemployed women and their children.[36]

None of these nuances were lost on the increasingly perceptive blacks. If Northerners did not want them to stay permanently, why should they go in the first place? And why, particularly, should they go if they were to do the same work they had performed as slaves? That was hardly what freedom meant to them. Nor did the opportunity for education entice them. Missionaries in Hampton already offered schooling, and it could be had in AMA schools where blacks could learn in the company of their own people. Refugees discovered they had sought freedom from Southerners only to find many Yankees as prejudiced as their former masters. It defied common sense to expect that one could find more freedom by moving to a world with even more Yankees. Perhaps most important in the reasoning of black women, but overlooked by many missionaries and army men, was the fact they were wives of soldiers. They would not leave Hampton because it was to Hampton that their husbands would return if they survived the war.

Lieutenant J. B. Kinsman, the officer charged with carrying out the placement scheme, was infuriated by the black women's refusal to avail themselves of the "opportunity" to go north. He proposed, as a solution, denying rations to all women unwilling to go. General Butler quickly vetoed this choice of emigration or starvation. Unfortunately, his successors in postwar Hampton would not find the proposal so repugnant.[37] It ultimately became clear even to Lieutenant Kinsman that it was wisdom rather than stupidity that determined the black women's choice. Many of the Northerners who promised to arrange homes for black emigrants were of exactly the character these women feared most. A few Northern recruiters were undoubtedly reputable men like John Truman, a Philadelphia Quaker who placed over 100 women and children in Pennsylvania homes. Others, like Oliver St. John of the "New York and Brooklyn Freedmen Employment Bureau" were of both doubtful integrity and dubious humanity. St. John wrote Kinsman claiming ability to place a thousand freedman a week in his area. The blacks would be placed in good homes and taught to read and write before being returned to the South.[38]

The true nature of St. John's scheme became apparent, however, when he described the method by which blacks would be distributed upon their arrival in New York. Prospective employers would contract with St. John, then "at the appointed time, the parties will be supplied with tickets to go onboard the boat...and select and take home the freedwoman or boy wanted immediately. In this way a vessel load of two hundred could be disposed of in three or four hours."[39] St. John was apparently unaware of the similarity of his method to the "scramble" used in the slave pens of America and the Caribbean during the heyday of the slave trade. It was a similarity that would hardly have been lost on the freedmen; nor did it escape C. B. Wilder and Kinsman. During the war, black laborers transported to the North from Hampton were accompanied by an army officer to guarantee their fair treatment.[40]

The proposal to settle freedmen on abandoned farms in secure areas proved more attractive to both blacks and the Bureau of Negro Affairs. But when this idea was put into effect, the refugees most in need of such opportunities were denied land, and the areas designated for settlement were not really secure.

In parcelling out land to the freedmen, the Hampton Bureau of Negro Affairs held close to the concept that it hoped would triumph in the post-bellum South: the creation of black family farms. Men with families or groups of men allied together were given plots of land on which to raise a crop. Rent for the land was to be paid to the Bureau in either cash or kind. The produce from the land was to be used to feed the farm residents; any surplus after rent was paid could be sold for profit. In exchange, the Bureau provided rations until the first crop was harvested. It was a fine idea which many of Hampton's original contraband accepted immediately. They knew the land and how to farm it. They also were convinced that, once the war ended, they would be allowed to keep the land as their own. Unfortunately, the idea did little to relieve the army of its burden of women and minor dependents. The Bureau believed that it took a man to run a family farm, so no land was assigned to the nearly 5,000 most needy refugees, women and children.

The experiment worked well on properly run and truly secure farms. Settlements were established at "Newtown" in York County, at "Slabtown" in Elizabeth City County, on scattered farms in Warwick County, and across the Roads in Norfolk. Assistant superintendents for Negro affairs were appointed in each county to help the freedmen and oversee their labor. On the best organized farms, land was divided into small plots, usually eight to ten acres, which each family farmed independently. Trees on the land were cut down to build houses. The mansions on large estates were used by the missionaries as their residences, schools, and churches.[41]

Unhappily, these refugee farms, particularly those in York County, were often plagued with difficulties. One serious problem was the continuing dispute between the Bureau of Negro Affairs and the regular army officials stationed in the same area. The battlefront commanders tended to look upon the Bureau as a rival command in their district. They complained that black settlements impeded the free movement of their troops and that Bureau officers overstepped their bounds in moving blacks about without their permission. In addition, many camps were plagued with shortages of food and fuel, and most were in areas exposed to sporadic rebel guerilla activity. In a few instances blacks were kidnapped and sold into slavery in rebel-held territory.[42]

Neither black placement in the North nor settlement on abandoned farms proved effective solutions to the refugee problem because neither actually helped the bulk of the refugees who were women and children. Many of the women, of course, were married and victims of yet one more ambivalent Northern attempt to cope with black freedom. They were soldiers' wives who resented the manner in which their husbands had been forced to "enlist."

Permission to enlist Negro soldiers, which was granted in August 1862, inspired Union commanders to impressment raids on the black settlements around Hampton. The men captured were dragged away to army encampments and ordered to enlist. They were not told that they had a choice in the matter, and those who steadfastly refused were confined in ball and chain. The men were taken away without regard to their health or the needs of their family. One freedwoman, Jane Wallis, in appealing for the return of her husband, pointed out that she, her husband, and their three children were all in very poor health. Mr. Wallis' trade as a shoemaker was their only source of income and without him they would starve. Many other freed families who had survived independently were thrown on government rations because the husband was taken away.[43]

On the issue of forced enlistments, the freedmen had more justice at the hands of the army than was usually the case. Ben Butler once again proved himself to be the most stalwart friend of the blacks to command in Hampton Roads. He ordered a thorough investigation and his officers ultimately compiled more than fifty pages of testimony from freedmen and others documenting the abuses. Impressment was ordered halted and was, at least by troops under Butler's command.[44]

The impressment scandals had a devastating effect upon black and missionary attitudes. Noting that blacks felt forced labor and enlistments to be very strange ways of treating "free people," C. P. Day complained that "it is destroying their [blacks'] confidence in Brother Wilder as well as in all the whites." Some of the original residents of Hampton, like Thompson Walker and Peter Herbert, became so embittered that they began to advocate black emigration to Haiti. At least there, they reasoned, blacks could at last be "free from arrogance."[45]

Impressment was but one of many abuses freedmen suffered at the hands of the Northern military, but it was final proof that not even emancipation and black participation in the war effort could change army attitudes. The tragedy of this first encounter between the Northern military and the freedmen is one of opportunities lost. The Hampton experience offered the chance for Northern whites and Southern blacks to learn about each other, to learn how to work together. But the moment passed unutilized.

The years between 1861 and 1865 clearly demonstrated the army's unwillingness to care for the freedmen or to do the job with any degree of good will. Even in circumstances as opportune as Hampton, with its variegated and skilled black community, the army proved incapable of approaching blacks other than from preconceived notions about black inferiority and incompetence. The army ignored free or slave status before the war; blacks with skills were put to the same tasks as those without them. The possibility that cooperation rather than force might improve the blacks' circumstances and ease the army's burden was seldom entertained. Even after emancipation, the military at Hampton treated blacks as free people only to the degree forced upon it by orders from Washington and by the actions of sympathetic local commanders such as General Butler.

Army policy toward Hampton blacks was disastrous: blacks suffered enormously and grew increasingly suspicious of Northern whites. Yet the Union military did not learn. The worst features of these same specious policies, heavily tainted with antipathy toward blacks, were applied in every ensuing encounter with freedmen throughout the South. This hostility reflected the ambivalence of the rest of the North on the question of black freedom. The ideal of black freedom was much espoused, but the reality of blacks who possessed it and wished to use it was quite another matter. The Union army was merely the first element of the North to demonstrate that it could not cope with this new reality. Its failure boded ill for the future.

Hampton was the first and one of the most important centers of American Missionary Association work during the Civil War. Although a few Methodist, Baptist, and Catholic missionaries passed through Hampton Roads during these years, and Quakers established a small mission up the York River at Yorktown, the area was clearly AMA territory. The successes and failures of missionary work with Hampton's freedmen were almost solely the product of AMA efforts.

The AMA's work in Hampton never involved the numbers of missionaries nor the influence on government policies that resulted from the Port Royal "Experiment" in South Carolina, begun in 1862.[1] Nevertheless, the Association invested a major portion of its meager resources in the Hampton area. More than fifty missionaries served in Hampton Roads during the war; after the spring of 1862 there were usually twenty-five to thirty-five there at any one time. Most of these were on the Peninsula in or near Hampton. The majority of missionaries were white, although at least three black AMA workers served in the area between 1862 and 1865. Most of the missionaries were young, from New England, New York, or Ohio. They belonged to the Congregational or Presbyterian Church, and were deeply committed to evangelical Christianity and to the Calvinist vision of salvation advocated by those two denominations.

The AMA missionaries served in an area that, by war's end, contained more than 40,000 blacks, 25,000 of whom were in refugee settlements on the lower Peninsula near Hampton. By 1865 they had established six mission schools around Hampton and twice that number across the Roads in

Norfolk. These schools also served as churches which on Sundays offered services for all who wished to attend. The churches would ultimately prove a major stumbling block in missionary-black relations. Most of the blacks who professed Christianity called themselves Baptists while a handful more identified themselves as Methodists. This difference in denominational affiliation of the missionaries and blacks was not a problem at first. Over the four years of war, however, when the future of blacks as free people became the issue, this difference took on ramifications far beyond denominational or even theological distinctions.

The workers of the American Missionary Association came to Hampton with high goals and considerable trepidation. They meant to prove to a doubting North that blacks were indeed human beings like themselves, that blacks could and should be free. But the missionaries were also well aware of the difficulties they might encounter. Their previous experiences had largely been confined to work with free blacks in the North. They had never sought to aid such large numbers of blacks before, nor had they confronted as many so potentially different from themselves. It was possible that these Southern Negroes, newly escaped from slavery, might demonstrate themselves unfit for freedom as white Northerners defined it.

The Hampton missionaries, however, were people with great determination and commitment to their ideals. They were the first white Northerners to volunteer aid to Hampton's freedmen, and they stayed long after the less stalwart had abandoned blacks to their uncertain fate among white Southerners. The missionaries created the freedmen's schools and their successor institution, Hampton Institute. But their efforts were marred by many frustrations and mistakes. The missionaries provided crucial assistance in showing that blacks were ready for freedom, but, in the end, they often did not care for the manner in which blacks used their newly won liberties. In the missionaries' minds, freedom brought with it a defined set of responsibilities. The missionaries' definition of those responsibilities was one that freedmen would not readily accept, not only because they were not whites or Northerners, but also because they were not missionaries. These differing perceptions about the responsibilities of freedom led to increasing frustration in relations between blacks and missionaries.

Cooperation between blacks and missionaries obviously proved most successful when both parties were in agreement upon goals. Thus the two groups could work together in opposition to army mistreatment of freedmen. Likewise, blacks and the AMA workers joined together in establishing schools. There was even agreement between them in creating black churches. It was, unfortunately, on disputes over religious content, not the religious edifice, that the experiment in interracial cooperation foundered. Such disputes often arise only when people have the leisure to argue and so it was among the missionaries and freedmen. It was, ironically, only when the AMA effort at Hampton had become a demonstrable success that the quarrel between the two groups became serious.

Had the missionaries ended their wartime work at Hampton in the same spirit of tolerance as they began it, this conflict might never have occurred. Lewis Lockwood, their first worker in Hampton, had such a spirit. He proved an ideal choice as the pioneer missionary to Hampton's contraband. Lockwood possessed a sensitivity for a different kind and race of people, a spirit of Christian acceptance, and an energy and endurance in harsh conditions that made him singular among the missionaries who served in Hampton.

Lockwood's first action after arriving in Hampton in September 1861 was to go among the contraband and learn their needs. "I want, as soon as possible," he wrote, "to visit the people in their dwellings, ascertain who are Christians, combine them together, and labor...for their spiritual edification and the conversion of sinners."[2] Lockwood was very impressed by what he saw. "I find them a religious people," he reported, "and remarkably intelligent, considering their circumstances." All who professed to be Christians he addressed as "brothers" or "sisters." He met Thompson Walker and William Davis, two of the original contraband, whom he singled out for special praise, suggesting that they would make excellent "exhorters."[3]

Lockwood began his work by supporting efforts that blacks had started on their own initiative. He learned of Mary Peake's school which was being held in Brown Cottage, next to the abandoned Chesapeake Female Seminary. He visited there "with great satisfaction." Forty-nine pupils were enrolled at that time with more expected. Lockwood gained permission for Mrs. Peake to run her school openly from General Wool, who had replaced Butler at the Fortress. With the missionary's help, Peter Herbert also expanded his school for blacks. Mrs. Peake was able to reorganize her school with classes in the mornings for children and in afternoons for adults.[4]

The blacks of Hampton were anxious to have their own Sunday schools and churches. When Lockwood arrived, blacks were attending services held in the army hospital chapel, seated in the rear as during slavery. "You can readily see that they need a church constructed for them expressly," Lockwood advised his superiors in New York. "They can enjoy full religious freedom only by themselves." Blacks readily agreed; by December they had contributed seventy-five dollars toward the construction of their own church with fifty dollars more pledged by the end of the month.[5] Though construction of the church would take some time, "Sabbath" schools began immediately. Lockwood was assisted in the schools by some of the Union soldiers stationed at the Fort and by black exhorters such as Davis, Walker, and William Thorton.[6]

The Reverend Lockwood spent all of his time among the freedmen or in pleading their cause with army officials at Fortress Monroe. He came to know the blacks intimately. Though the army provided him with living quarters, he was forced to find his own board among blacks, which he did with the family of William Davis.[7] He not only sought to preach and teach but also became something of an amateur historian, recording life histories of many of the ex-slaves and free people that he encountered. He thought of blacks as fellow Christians, but was also sensitive to how different they were from himself. Not only did he feel that they should have the freedom to worship in their own way, but also urged that the Association produce a new primer, "expressly designed for them." He was reported by John Oliver, the black missionary, to be teaching "on the early history of Africa and her learned men" because "this people...know nothing of the history of their ansistry [sic]."[8]

The blacks of Hampton responded enthusiastically to Lockwood's efforts. Within a month, three Sabbath schools were in operation. A third day school, taught by a Mrs. Bishop, a free colored woman, and two contraband assistants, was opened at the Fortress. It served forty to sixty students. In December a fourth school was started at Mill Creek Bridge north of Hampton; it was also taught by a local black man, Wilson Wallace. Even those who could not attend school sought to improve their educations. Lockwood distributed a large number of "Union Primers" among the blacks, and found that working men took every moment of leisure to study their books and teach each other to read.[9]

By Christmas Day, 1861, Lockwood and the black community

of Hampton were ready to join together to celebrate the progress made during these first few months of freedom. The students of Mary Peake's and Peter Herbert's schools gave concerts and recitations for Northern visitors. The Northerners brought small gifts for the children and all were impressed at their rapid learning. Lockwood, ever an enthusiast, even theorized that "these black children are brighter than white children."[10]

The promise of freedom at Hampton attracted ever increasing numbers of escaping slaves into Union lines on the Peninsula. Increasing the numbers of missionaries to aid these refugees proved more difficult. There were many anxious to come, but few accommodations for them. In March 1862, Lockwood wrote to New York proposing that only men be sent, particularly black men, who could cope with the harsh conditions. Though there was much work that women missionaries could do in teaching colored women sewing and other aspects of "good housewifery," Lockwood felt it would be impossible to find suitable lodgings for them.[11]

In the year 1862, eleven missionaries, including two blacks and a woman, joined Lockwood in Hampton.[12] One of the first of these, George Hyde, took over the school taught by Mrs. Peake. She was ill with consumption and died in late February at the age of thirty-nine.[13] Hyde himself found conditions in Hampton too harsh and was forced to leave before the year was out because of ill health.[14]

Other missionaries fared better though they often found the tasks confronting them to be overwhelming. C. P. Day, who arrived in April, reported that his pupils were "more advanced than I had supposed," but that "in order to do justice to the children it will be necessary to have more teachers." He had ninety students in one room![15] John Oliver, the black missionary assigned to Newport News, soon had two schools in operation with seventy-five students in one and fifty in the other. He taught at each on alternate days. He devoted the rest of his time to caring for the many sick among the ex-slaves. Army doctors refused to treat the blacks unless Oliver went for them personally. Destitution among the freedmen was terrible, many women had "nothing but an outside dress, and that full of holes." Oliver could not understand "how our civilization can bear the shocking sight."[16]

Hyde, Day and Oliver were followed by the brother and sister team, Porter and Mary Green, children of AMA missionaries in Hawaii. They were precursors of another Hawaiian, Samuel Armstrong, who, five years later, would drastically alter the nature of AMA work in Hampton. Porter preached to the contraband at the Fortress and in Hampton; Mary taught in one of the primary schools in the village. John Linson, who arrived at the same time, also taught school in Hampton. In the fall, Palmer Litts and a Mr. King arrived and were assigned to the large contraband camp on Craney Island in Hampton Roads near Norfolk. With them came Thomas DeSota Tucker, another black, who assisted at C. P. Day's school in Hampton.[17]

The new missionaries generally concurred with Lockwood on the importance of their work and on the remarkable nature of the contraband. The Reverend S. Jocelyn, who briefly replaced Lockwood when the latter fell ill in December 1861, reported: "I have found their love of freedom strong. Their desire for learning and the aptitude of children and adults to learn are remarkable.... The religious knowledge, experience, character, unusual intelligence and gifts of numbers among them, have surprised the missionary teachers, and visitors."[18] The special nature of Hampton's ante-bellum black community was partially responsible for the missionaries' surprise. To some degree, however, they were victims of their own abolitionist propaganda. In the effort to promote anti-slavery sentiment in the North, the abolitionists may have overdrawn the brutalizing effects of bondage upon black people, at least upon those who lived in places like Hampton.

As more blacks and missionaries arrived in Hampton, descriptions of the contraband, while still positive, became less euphoric. As early as September 1861, Lockwood had cautioned that he found the blacks from the back country "generally inferior in intelligence" to those who had lived near Hampton. C. P. Day, when he arrived, noted that he found in his school "children such as slavery makes—quarrelsome, thievish, and seemingly inclined to every species of wickedness." The children learned quickly, however, and within a month Day could comment, "you hardly ever saw 150 children more cleanly in their persons and apparel. Their lessons are in the most cases quickly...learned and their behavior is kindly affectionate to each other." George Hyde, teaching in Mrs. Peake's school, said he saw no reason why his students "may not go on and master the sciences which children do in our schools at home. Yet that can only be certainly known by trial."[19] Hyde condemned those whites who used a double standard in judging blacks: they discovered that ex-slaves had many of the same vices as some white people, and then concluded that "modified slavery" would be best for blacks.[20]

The American Missionary Association and its field workers were very much on the defensive during the early days of their work at Hampton. Emancipation of blacks was still in doubt. Hampton was envisioned as the "Chef d'ouvre [*sic*] — the model development of the independent capabilities of the colored man."[21] The missionaries made every effort to emphasize the black man's achievements and potential. As a consequence, even the mildly precautionary comments of Day and Hyde were never published in the *American Missionary Magazine*.[22]

The official attitude of the AMA, in the field and in the home office in New York, was that the black man had emerged from slavery with a religious spirit and a great desire to learn. "The want of many sources of knowledge" was "compensated by a strange fullness and richness in spiritual revelation of the knowledge of God." Any deficiencies from which the blacks might suffer resulted, not from race, but rather from the demoralizing effects of bondage. The contraband were downtrodden fellow Christians to be uplifted through the missionaries' efforts. Their future could be the same as any other "earnestly inquiring" Christian.[23] The missionary attitude was clearly more benevolent than that of white Southerners and of many white Northerners. Nevertheless, it was also clearly paternalistic—missionaries would decide what was best for blacks. It made no allowance for the possibility that blacks might have their own ideas about uplifting themselves.

The early group of AMA workers continued Lockwood's practice of addressing the contraband as "brother" and "sister." They prayed together, ate together, and often had to live together. They also envisioned Hampton as exclusive AMA territory. The missionaries were incensed when a Southern Baptist minister visited Hampton and complained that the blacks were becoming "saucy and impudent." He refused to eat with them, was outraged at being addressed as "brother" by them, and steadfastly refused to shake hands with them. He was, Lockwood remarked bitterly, "a man...entirely unfit to meet the wants of that people."[24]

To prove the importance of their work in Hampton and to convince the North of the justice of emancipation, the AMA sent its workers on fund raising tours in the North. As during the abolitionist movement, the most effective speakers were often victims of slavery themselves. In Hampton, the AMA found a number of men ideally suited for the task. William Roscoe Davis was sent on an extensive speaking tour of Massachusetts, New Hampshire, and New York. William Thorton and Thompson Walker lectured in Philadelphia and New York City. Of Davis, Lockwood said, "his natural abilities and uncommon eloquence...have surprised his numerous hearers, and inspired in them new feelings in relation to American slaves."[25]

One major reason for the AMA's intense campaign in the North was the obstruction they continually faced in Virginia. Even after the issuance of the Emancipation Proclamation, the army still resisted expansion of the missionary effort beyond the confines of the Lower Peninsula. Norfolk fell to the Union in May of 1862, but missionaries were denied permission to start schools there. Unlike the residents of Hampton, most white citizens of Norfolk remained in the city after its capture. When Lockwood visited there shortly after the surrender, he found blacks still treated as slaves by both the white military and civilian population. The white ministers of the three black churches, many of whom had been slaveholders, continued to admonish the blacks that faithfulness to their masters was the first criterion for being a good Christian. These ministers curtly refused Lockwood's request that he be allowed to preach to their congregations. Nonetheless, the Norfolk black community appeared, in many ways, to be as resourceful as that of Hampton. Black Sabbath schools, independent of the white-controlled churches, had been established immediately after the Union takeover. Within weeks, day schools were started in the homes of literate blacks.[26]

It was, however, not until April 1863, when General Butler returned to take command of the district surrounding Hampton Roads, that day schools under white missionary teachers began in Norfolk. Two schools were opened in the black churches of Norfolk and later were moved to two of the four unused white schoolhouses in the city. Other schools were started in the adjoining city of Portsmouth, on Craney Island in the Roads off Norfolk, and on outlying plantations. The mansion of former Virginia Governor Henry Wise, near Norfolk, became one of the largest freedmen's schools on the south side of the Roads.[27]

There were now twenty-five missionaries at work on the Peninsula and half that many across the Roads, but they were unequal to the tasks. The day school of Brute Street Baptist Church in Norfolk had 550 students within three days of its opening, 700 within a month. The evening school had an enrollment of 1,100 with an average attendance of 375.²⁸ Responding to the need, the AMA sent additional teachers to Norfolk. By September 1863, the Association had twenty-one teachers in eleven day and evening schools in the area, teaching over 3,000 students. There were, in addition, at least an equal number of Sabbath schools in which these AMA workers also taught.²⁹

The main reason for the tremendous success of the schools was the enthusiasm for learning demonstrated by the freedmen. They attended school readily, and in Norfolk and Hampton, helped construct or repair their school buildings. Despite the thousands attending school, many more would have come if they had had clothes to wear. The Reverend W. S. Bell on the Wise Farm in Norfolk lamented that, "We are obliged to clothe many of the children before they can come to school." Even those who did not attend classes attempted to study on their own. AMA Secretary Jocelyn reported the distribution of thousands of primers to adult

Butler School House, Hampton, Va., ca. 1870.
(Courtesy of the Casemate Museum)

freedmen. They tried to teach themselves to read and asked help from their children attending school when they needed assistance.[30]

By the end of 1863 the situation in the freedmen schools of Hampton Roads had stabilized to the degree possible in a war zone. The structure of the schools was much the same throughout; all were based on the common schools of the North. The goal was to provide each student with "a good English education" and to make each a "good Christian," but many road-blocks stood in the way. Classes were very large, usually from 60 to 100 students in a single room. One teacher taught all subjects; the oldest and most advanced students were appointed as monitors to keep order and to aid younger pupils. The curriculum of most schools consisted exclusively of primary material: reading, spelling, the rudiments of arithmetic and geography. The books used were the standard texts of primary students in the North, the *Union Primer*, *National Primer*, and the Bible; instruction was by rote. The missionaries interspersed education with Union politics; they meant to teach freedom as well as the "three Rs." The teachers at Wise Farm, Norfolk, held classes in the former governor's dining room. "Here, where treason was talked over, and toasts drunk to the success of traitors," exulted one teacher, "we every day hear sung the famous John Brown song." They lacked only a picture of "the old hero"; the children very much wanted to see one.[31]

The most advanced school in the area was in the restored courthouse at Hampton. Its 250 students progressed so rapidly that it was necessary to divide it into "Primary" and "Higher" Departments. C. P. Day presided over the more advanced pupils. He taught multiplication, division, penmanship, and elementary reading to the upper level students. His classroom was on the second floor of the courthouse. On the first floor, the Misses Green and Martindale taught another 100 students at the primary level. Day administered corporal punishment in both rooms. Major problems in all the schools were discipline and the transient population. The freed children tended to be unruly, and often order could be maintained only through generous applications of the rod. Day complained that the constant influx of refugees and the forced resettlements of freedmen by the army hampered the progress of his school.[32]

All of the freedmen's schools were plagued by shortages of supplies. Assistance from the military remained minimal; Northern charitable organizations were poorly organized and impoverished. Hampton teachers often complained of receiving empty boxes or old copies of the *American Missionary Magazine* rather than the clothes and school books they had ordered. On one occasion, George Whipple curtly reminded the home office in New York that it would be "months if not years" before most of the pupils could read the *American Missionary* and by that time, "they will undoubtedly want new ones."[33]

Despite these problems, the missionary teachers were ecstatic at the progress of their schools and optimistic about their future. Day reported of his school that, "as a whole, it is not to be beaten by any other of the kind on the continent." Other teachers made similar claims for their schools. The blacks displayed not only a great facility for learning, but high ambition as well. Many of the black youngsters expressed a desire to go to college; men of all ages were interested in becoming teachers and ministers. The blacks progressed so rapidly that by 1864, C. B. Wilder believed "a larger portion of the colored population of Eastern Virginia can read than of the white."[34]

The missionaries conducted their religious work in concert with their efforts in education. In fact, the conversion effort in each mission station was the center around which all other work of the Association developed. The ministers visited among the adult freedmen to discover which were Christians; they prayed with the sick and preached in the black mission churches. They were surprised and pleased that so many of Hampton's original contraband professed to be Christians. Their purpose, however, was not merely to make the black man a Christian.

The missionaries appear to have conceived their religious task in two parts: one-half inculcation of Northern, middle-class rules of behavior to one-half conversion to Northern, Presbyterian Christianity. In both, the mission schools played a large role. Like other reformers of their day, the missionaries considered *moral* instruction the most important part of education. Students in the freedmen schools heard the Bible read at length each day; they were taught prayers and the Presbyterian catechism. That latter document, with its insistence upon orthodox Calvinist doctrines of predestination and a small community of the "saved," must have seemed especially alien to the freedmen. Few of them appear to have been formal members of churches prior to the war. Those who were, like the 900 slaves who attended Hampton Baptist Church, shared with white Baptists the less austere belief that the individual could earn salvation by leading a godly life while on earth.[35]

For this reason, and others, the missionaries were not notably successful in converting blacks to their brand of Christianity. The freedmen readily attended the missionary churches, because they trusted the missionaries, and because these were, at first, the only churches available to them. But they refused to become Presbyterians, and instead began to form churches of their own.[36] This disappointed, and even angered, some missionaries. It would not have, had the missionaries been more perceptive *and* tolerant of the freedmen's religion. On almost every question of faith, i.e., the role of doctrine, the nature of God, of sin, of salvation, the nature of worship, the relation between religious and social behavior, missionaries and blacks were in sharp disagreement. Conflict over these issues seriously disrupted missionary work in Hampton and brought about marked changes in missionary attitudes toward blacks.

The heart of the problem was that the missionaries had a clear, and inflexible, concept of what the true faith was. They were the products of three hundred years of evolution in Calvinist thought both in Europe and America. It was not, however, the intricacies of that theology (which in 1860 continued to befuddle many white Presbyterians, not to mention blacks) that was the source of conflict between blacks and missionaries. Rather, it was that evangelical Presbyterians like the missionaries had developed an elaborate set of norms for both religious and social behavior. People who did not share the missionaries' world view found these rules difficult to accept.

The problem can be seen in the difference between the missionary and black understanding of God. To the missionaries, God was the Omnipotent Creator. He was the Stern Rule Maker who knew in advance what sins men would commit, and who had already decided what punishment He would mete out to sinners. Those who earnestly desired to be saved and lived godly lives were likely to find salvation, but there always remained an element of uncertainty. The missionary's God was always a Being as much to be feared as loved.[37]

The God of the slaves could hardly be more different. He was an understanding and all-forgiving Father. He knew the trials his people had suffered and was prepared to tolerate transgressions made in ignorance or sincerely regretted after the fact. Moreover, the blacks' God was less remote and austere. Men could negotiate and reason with Him. His mercifulness was limitless and a good argument might convince Him of one's repentance.[38]

These contrasting visions of God quite naturally produced markedly different styles of both religious and social behavior in the two groups. Missionaries attended church to pray, to reflect on past sins, to acknowledge the glory and power of God. The blacks' purposes in church were not necessarily different, but the ways in which they demonstrated them were. The missionaries' services were marked by quiet refinement. Blacks seemed to go to church to "make a joyful noise unto the Lord." They enjoyed shouting, clapping, being "seized by the Spirit." They looked forward to fiery sermons from their preachers, and to singing the spirituals that had eased life on the plantation. This lack of decorum in black services offended the missionaries, and they, on manifestly inadequate evidence, assumed it offended God as well.

From the very beginning of the work with freedmen, missionaries had found the blacks' faith somewhat unorthodox. At first, however, the Northerners found explanations that satisfied them. As one white teacher wrote to the *American Missionary Magazine*: "Once I looked upon their peculiarities as the result of ignorance and superstition; now I believe that God, in his infinite goodness, has condescended to reveal Himself unto these children of darkness in ways that they can understand—even if it be in visions."[39]

As time passed, the missionaries became less tolerant. They were increasingly puzzled and a bit dismayed by the zeal and peculiarities with which blacks took up the faith. Their efforts to convert the blacks led to a spontaneous revival in Hampton in 1866. The freedmen deserted their classrooms in droves to attend to the more important, and more enjoyable, task of saving their souls. Missionaries who tried to conduct normal services at the churches could not make themselves heard over the commotion in the black congregations. Describing one such experience, a minister reported:

> Such a strange, weird scene as I beheld never met my eyes before. At the altar were about a dozen men of all shades, sizes and forms. Some were ragged and so dirty that their appearance was wild in the extreme. They were holding each other by the hand, and singing some of their old plantation songs, and as they sung kept time with their bodies....Down the aisle came rolling a man in such terrible agony because of his wickedness. In another part of the church were men and women jumping up and down, throwing up their hands, screaming "Glory to God. Oh what a Savior I have found!"[40]

It was not merely the blacks' religious style but also the manner in which they interpreted Christian doctrine that shocked the missionaries. In one instance, a black minister, instructed on the sanctity of marriage by the missionaries, had himself married to three different women! White ministers left over from ante-bellum days did little to alleviate the problem. In the winter of 1864 the entire black community of Portsmouth was thrown into an uproar when the Southern white pastor of the colored church there advised his congregation that all blacks living as man and wife were damned for living in adultery, there being no laws which permitted black marriages. It was only with considerable effort that the missionaries and the Bureau of Negro Affairs convinced the minister to recant.[41]

Disagreements between missionaries and blacks over religion inevitably extended into the way blacks conducted their secular lives. The reserved, orderly format of the missionaries' religious services fit well with the restrained life they had lived in the North. The spontaneous, often boisterous, services of the freedmen matched the uncertainty of life they had known in slavery. Many blacks, especially the original contraband of Hampton, shared some of the missionaries' values, particularly concern for family and desire for education. Not all, however, agreed with missionaries that drinking, dancing, card playing, and other earthly pleasures were sinful. To blacks, these were justified relaxations from the rigors of everyday life and labor. But the missionaries tended to measure the depth of one's Christianity by adherence to their own norms for social behavior which were more restrictive than those of ordinary Northerners. They were also, of course, alien to most freedmen. By missionary standards, the blacks were inveterate sinners; they were, as one missionary unhappily concluded in 1866, "sadly deficient in *practical piety.*"[42]

Of equal importance was the fact that the missionaries judged the readiness of blacks to be free and equal citizens by these same rigid standards. When they first came to Hampton, they were pleasantly surprised by the blacks they met and were quite optimistic about their potential; by the end of the war, however, their views were increasingly negative. In neither instance did the missionaries look at the black man as he really was, but rather as they expected and wanted him to be.

The first missionaries to Hampton found the original contraband not as "brutalized" as abolitionist propaganda had led them to expect, but they had another set of preconceptions upon which to fall back. They came to Hampton imbued with what George

Fredrickson has described as "romantic racialism," an attitude held by many Northern abolitionists. To these people, the black man was distinctly and permanently different from the Caucasian race, but not necessarily inferior. At its extreme, as in *Uncle Tom's Cabin*, this school of thought conceived of the black man as the perfect Christian—humble, docile, forgiving, and patient in suffering. These were all attributes that the more aggressive white race lacked, but ones which would ultimately lead the black race to create, one advocate of this theory argued, "a later but far nobler civilization."[43] The emphasis was on the word "later."

Many of the freedmen whom the missionaries met at Hampton seemed to fit this stereotype perfectly. Comparison of the freedmen with the wandering tribes of Israel seemed to come naturally to the missionaries. The blacks were in a "transition state," wrote H. S. Beals, "which...is truly a wilderness of suffering." But there was much reason for hope; like the Israelites the freedmen were sustained by God. George Hyde wrote that the blacks had a "strange fullness and richness in the spiritual revelation of the knowledge of God." The Reverend J. B. Lowery of Yorktown added, "They listened to the gospel with an interest seldom seen among those more highly favored....They are not as degraded as I expected to find them. They are quite intelligent, naturally."[44]

Like the Uncle Tom of abolitionist lore, the freedmen exemplified the virtues of forgiveness, patience, and fortitude in dire conditions. "The fiery trials through which they have passed," wrote a Norfolk teacher, "have taught them patience and long suffering. I have seen many homes of extreme wretchedness and destitution...yet I have [heard] not a word of complaint." Best of all was the freedmen's forgiving nature. Mrs. Peck, also of Norfolk, reported:

> It might be expected that privations and sufferings would engender a feeling of bitterness toward their former masters, but it is not so. We are often deeply affected by their fervent prayers for their old masters, prayers breathing a spirit of forgiveness "til seventy-times seven." Since we find they have some of the Christian virtues, faith, hope, forgiveness, patience, etc., so largely, we can but believe there is some motive for them, for "To he that hath, shall be given."[45]

Robert Harris of Providence spoke for many of his fellow missionaries when he concluded that, despite problems of superstition and "extravagance," "I believe these long oppressed millions will eventually become the most religious people on earth."[46]

As the AMA effort in Hampton evolved, however, its missionaries became increasingly uncertain in their assessment of blacks. The first missionaries knew the freedmen as individuals. Those who followed showed less ability, and less inclination, to do so. The provision of housing and rations by the army made it unnecessary for blacks and missionaries to live and eat together. The vast numbers of freedmen to be assisted made intimacy more difficult. The missionaries themselves were a very transient group, few had time to come to know individual freedmen as well as their predecessors had. Few continued the practice of addressing Christian blacks as "brother" and "sister," in part because they were no longer convinced the blacks really were Christians.

Later missionaries do not appear to have felt the need to know individual freedmen well; they had not only the stereotyped expectations of romantic racialism, but also the detailed reports of their predecessors by which to make judgments. If the freedmen did not automatically meet their expectations, the missionaries often tried to force them to do so. When one missionary lady discovered that the freedmen with whom she was working were not at all inclined to forgive their former master for past injustices, she lectured them that they must do so! Lockwood complained of the growing impersonality in missionaries' relations to blacks and of the unrealistically high expectations many had of the freedmen. He condemned men like C. B. Wilder who "yankee-like, expects more of the people here than they can possibly do, just out of slavery."[47]

The freedmen, too, were changing. By 1864 the vast majority of the freedmen on the Peninsula were not the relatively urbane residents of Hampton but ex-slaves from back country plantations. As early as 1861, Lockwood warned of the differences between the two groups; within a year these differences were making themselves felt. The missionaries found the freedmen from the country to be "very excitable" in nature. It was necessary to train them carefully to "understand the difference between sense and sound."[48] These blacks required far more help from the missionaries, but they were less responsive and cooperative than their predecessors.

The crux of the problem was that the freedmen were "sinners." And the crux of *that* problem was the missionaries' own rigid moral code. Hampton's AMA workers were extraordinarily circumspect in their discussions of the blacks' misdeeds. Few details were given. "Open sin," as C. P. Day called it, could mean licentiousness, but it could also mean simple Sabbath breaking. Those who did give details painted a dire picture. John Bebout, missionary on Craney Island, was most critical. "I could...get any of them to agree to do a *month's* work for me, tomorrow," he explained,

> and perhaps they would commence it right away, but as soon as I was out of sight, they would go off and leave it...I have no more confidence in the religion of 9/10s of them than I have in the squealing of a pig...I have heard them lay there [*sic*] plans to steal, and saw them start to do it, after being at prayer meeting, praying and singing, and exhorting till midnight.[49]

Despite their professed Christianity, another missionary wrote, the blacks were "course [*sic*] and rude in their manners" and were "imprudent and turbulent in their behavior toward us."[50]

The freedmen also had a predilection toward alcohol. Abbie Guile, a missionary teacher, appealed that a "good temperance man" be sent to Hampton because it was "becoming a very wicked place.... It strikes me that we are losing ground daily." C. B. Wilder also saw the situation as out of control and urged George Whipple to dispatch more preachers to the village. "Such preaching as we get from colored men with few exceptions is but little better than nothing and in some instances worse." Miss Smith, in Norfolk, summed up a growing conviction among the missionary workers when she wrote of the freedmen, "They seem to have been systematically taught that the only thing which made sin to be sin was causing inconvenience or loss to their masters."[51]

Even as the missionaries became more pessimistic about the freedmen's religious and moral values, they tried, as best they could, to phrase their criticisms in ways that stressed the probabilities for improvement and avoided overt racial distinctions. Thus C. P. Day wrote, "these people are not better than white people, for they will lie sometimes." The faults of the black man were the results of bondage and could be overcome. The Reverend Samuel Hunt, newly appointed superintendent for education of the AMA, expressed the new caution of the organization by the end of the war. He warned that many had been viewing the freedmen through a *"rose-colored medium."* Reporting on his investigative trip to Hampton, Hunt concluded:

> I had known how wonderfully the negro had deported himself since the war commenced—grateful to friends, and refraining

from violence towards his enemies, docile and tractable under the drill, firm and courageous in battle.... Closer inspection, however, revealed that the iron of slavery had entered deeply into the soul of the poor bondsman.... With many bright examples of personal excellence,...it still remains true that many Freedmen are ignorant, vicious and degraded.[52]

As years passed in Hampton, the missionaries increasingly came to see their religious work with the freedman as a failure. But the problem was perhaps as much sociological as theological. Not for the first time, nor the last, the moral and social values of the Christianizers had become inexorably linked to their understanding of Christianity. Most freedmen considered themselves Christians, but few of them shared the missionaries' vision of Christianity or their other values. Certainly, they did not act upon those values in the same fashion.

The missionaries came to doubt the blacks' professions of Christianity and to see them in need of far more "civilizing" work than first thought necessary. Their new caution about the nature of the black man was phrased to inspire redoubled effort, not to admit defeat. Nonetheless, their dependence upon stereotypes and generalizations to understand the freedmen, their failure to inquire into the black man's alternate style of religious and social behavior, and their tendency to lose sight of individual freedmen in their effort to help all left the door open for a far less "romantic" racialism should the blacks continue to resist reform. Most important of all, the missionaries never conceded that blacks had the right to pursue life with values different from their own unusual ones. They would not abandon the blacks, but they would also not permit them perhaps the most basic of freedoms—the right to make their own mistakes. On the contrary, blacks like those who abandoned the mission churches to found their own were seen as "lost." Black impudence, about which the missionaries complained, might have been simply black independence. If missionaries were objecting to such behavior, they did not sound very different from the Southern Baptist who refused to shake hands with blacks or, indeed, from the blacks' former masters!

The growing pessimism over the black man's character contributed to decline in missionary morale. The novelty of work among the freedmen wore off quickly for the missionaries, leaving behind only the difficult, frustrating tasks to be accomplished. The expansion of the effort to Norfolk and Portsmouth on the south side of the Roads, and especially to the Sea Islands of South Carolina removed Hampton from the center of national interest and concern. Just when the missionary effort seemed to be taking coherent form, the AMA officials in New York were dismayed to find their Virginia workers embroiled in incessant conflicts among themselves.

While Lewis Lockwood complained of C. B. Wilder's harshness in handling the blacks, Wilder was continually condemning Lockwood for his ineptitude in handling AMA funds and his chaotic manner of distributing relief goods from the North. "I can certainly have no confidence in a society that employs, knowingly, such incompetence and imprudence and waste of funds contributed," Wilder warned George Whipple. Lockwood was forced to relinquish control of missionary funds for Norfolk and was ultimately transferred to the Sea Islands of South Carolina in October 1862.[53]

Lockwood's departure did little to ease tensions in Hampton. The remaining teachers and ministers showed little ability or desire to work together. There were continuing squabbles between the Norfolk and Hampton workers over the distribution of funds. Those in Hampton all lived together in Tyler House, the mansion of former President John Tyler, and quickly developed all the hostilities and jealousies that can come from living in such close quarters.[54] Each teacher demanded clarification of authority from the home office, usually insisting, of course, that he be put in charge. C. P. Day complained of having responsibility for five schools and demanded the title "superintendent of schools" for Hampton. When this was granted, the Reverend R. D. Stone, who had taken over many of Lockwood's duties, demanded delineation of his own role. He was duly made "superintendent of *missionary* work" at Hampton. This, however, only heightened the conflict for, as we have seen, there was no clear division between educational and missionary activities. Day complained that he could do nothing about Sabbath breaking among the adult freedmen "unless I step upon the toes of a brother," and Stone argued he could not do his job because some of the missionaries sent to Hampton would not abjure entirely card playing and dancing.[55]

In addition to these problems, many of the missionaries were unable to work effectively with the freedmen. C. B. Wilder was the harshest critic of such missionaries, stating that many who came down were more interested in an "overseer's berth" and making money than in helping the blacks. He was instrumental in the removal of John Bebout, the missionary who had complained so bitterly about the blacks on Craney Island. Of Porter Green, the son of Hawaiian missionaries, Wilder remarked, "he is too indolent except to eat or sleep for anything." He found John Oliver, the black missionary who had moved to Craney Island, overwhelmed by the number of students and behavior problems he encountered in his one room school. Other teachers echoed Wilder's criticisms. Mrs. J. W. Coan and C. P. Day complained that Thomas Tucker, another black missionary, was "of no particular use except to wait on the colored ladies.[56]

The difficulties of the Virginia missionaries were disheartening and confusing to the AMA leadership in New York. Their workers seemed in danger of losing sight of the freedmen's problems because of preoccupation with their own. George Whipple became a regular commuter on the New York to Hampton steamer, trying to pour oil on the stormy missionary seas in Hampton Roads. In an attempt to stave off further problems, the AMA implemented more rigid selection standards for its missionaries and teachers. Teachers were to be healthy and energetic, and experienced—especially as "disciplinarians." "Singularities and idiosyncrasies of character" were unacceptable. All workers were required to abstain from the use of tobacco and liquor. Above all, they had to have "the missionary spirit." They should be prepared to do hard work, and "to subordinate self to the cause *and* acquiesce cheerfully in the directions and supervision of those...in charge."[57]

During the years of war in Hampton, the American Missionary Association workers achieved spectacular success in educating freedmen. They also played a valuable role in convincing a doubting North of the propriety of black emancipation. But their achievements were purchased at considerable cost to themselves and to their understanding of the freed slaves. Their evolving disillusionment cast a pall over the future of Northern white cooperation with the freedmen.

The missionaries came to Hampton with the expectation that the blacks were different from themselves and in great need of assistance, which they would willingly provide. They only gradually came to understand that, in aiding black development, they meant for the blacks to develop along the same lines as themselves in both religious and social behavior. That the blacks might not wish to do so surprised and dismayed them. The missionaries were the first among white Northerners to fully realize within themselves the racial, cultural, religious, and even regional prejudices that would ultimately doom America's first effort at racial justice and equality. Having discovered these prejudices within themselves, the missionaries could not close their eyes to them nor overcome them, though they tried harder and longer than most of their white contemporaries. The tragedy of the Hampton missionaries was that they could not connect the right to be free with the right to be different. They too proved guilty of that arrogance from which blacks sought freedom.

Black Hampton's New Majority

The years of war made Hampton's original black residents ever more suspicious and hostile toward the Union military; these years also made native black Hamptonians increasingly resistant to the culture and religion that their missionary allies tried to force upon them. There was, however, a third factor—as important as either the military or American Missionary Association —in shaping the nature of post-bellum black Hampton. With each passing day after the spring of 1862, Hampton's original contraband were becoming more and more of a minority in their own black community. By the first wartime census of blacks in 1864, they were already outnumbered by more than two to one.

The newcomers had also been slaves, but they were from counties throughout much of eastern Virginia. As it had been since colonial times, the best "roads" in Virginia were its rivers, and it was by these routes that the thousands of new black refugees entered Elizabeth City County. Of the more than 20,000 who came, many thousands stayed after the war to make the county their home. They came in search of the same things that had inspired the escape of the original contraband, i.e., freedom and the chance to use it, education, the right to practice their faith as they wished. Their departure from bondage, however, was considerably more difficult than it had been for Hampton natives. The blacks of the village had only to decide to stay; these new refugees had to decide to escape and to succeed at it. They were, moreover, less accustomed to the possibilities and pitfalls of freedom than were Hampton's black natives. But like Hampton's freedmen, they proved to have clear ideas about the meaning of freedom and what to do with it. Despite many mistakes along the way, these new black emigrants soon became a part of the developing black community, and many, in the post-bellum era, became some of Hampton's leading citizens.

Like the original contraband, the first goal of slaves from up-country Virginia plantations was freedom itself. Word of the freedom to be had behind Union lines seemed always to precede the arrival of Northern troops. Confederate officers who brought their slave valets with them to the front soon discontinued the practice. Too many of the blacks bolted to freedom at the first opportunity.[1]

Once the war began in earnest, the slave system in eastern Virginia began to disintegrate. Even slave owners not at the front faced major problems. On Gwynn's Island in Chesapeake Bay, Mrs. Mary Hunley complained on 12 May 1862, that two young slaves, Isaac and "her" Henry had "run off to the Yankees," carrying with them all of her son's clothes. Seven days later she noted that her slave Maria escaped on a Union gunboat, leaving behind her children and clothes. "Thursday, just at day, she returned, carried off one." Mrs. Hunley added, "I have carried the others out of her reach but expect my house to be burned down every hour."[2] Maria did not burn down the Hunley house, but early the next month her mistress lost all of her slaves. Captain Andrews of the Union forces arrived and announced that her slaves were to be confiscated. Closing her brief diary, Mrs. Hunley remarks: "As soon as he was seated he told me he was ordered to take all my people away. I added again what crime I had committed to be treated so cruelly." (A question Maria might also have asked—with considerably more justification.) "He said I was found in bad company (harboring Confederate troops)....In one half hour's time the land was swept of every negro I owned."[3]

Just proximity of Union troops inspired the defection of the slaves of Edwin Ruffin, Jr. On 24 May 1862, he recorded in his plantation book:

> Strong proof of the effect of the presence of the enemy this morning—Eight of my men left last night and went off to the enemy—generally young and likely—one of them was my carriage driver, one the house boy—and one a young carpenter whose apprenticeship ended last Xmas and who had just returned home—with eight others employed on the fortifications near Richmond.[4]

The slave "stampede" continued for the next month. On 24 June 1862, Ruffin took his remaining fifty-nine slaves, all women and children, to Petersburg and sold them south. The next day he ceased all farming operations. Altogether he had lost "119 of [my] best negroes." He ended his wartime entries with the comment, "Shall sell everything I can—and remove my family to a place of safety."[5]

It was not always the promise of freedom but rather desire to escape more oppressive bondage and separation from family that inspired Virginia slaves to flee from their masters. Early in the war, Stafford Cook had removed his slaves from York County across the York River to Confederate-held Gloucester County. Cook took eight of his men slaves, all of whom had wives, to Richmond and sold them. When he told a neighboring planter that he intended to take his remaining slaves further South, the slave foreman of that plantation quickly alerted the slaves on Cook's own farm. That night, Cook's slaves stole a boat and, with thirteen other black escapees, rowed back across the river to freedom in Union-held Yorktown.[6]

Because Union troops attacked and retreated along the Virginia rivers, most slaves fled in the direction of the nearest major river. Often they were pursued by rebel troops and their former masters. The bitterness engendered by slave disloyalty made these white Virginians ready to kill; it did not much matter to them whether their victims were Yankee soldiers or fleeing bondsmen. Many escaping slaves and those who, while content to stay where they were, helped others to flee, lost their lives.[7]

The most fortunate slaves managed to reach a Union encampment along a river. There they were assembled in convoys, usually a line of longboats tied behind a sidewheeler or Union gunboat. The convoys then moved down tributaries until they reached the James or York Rivers, and proceeded from there southward to Fortress Monroe. Even this riverine part of the journey was hazardous. The trip usually took two days and the boats were constantly subject to sniper fire from the shores. The Union troops who oversaw these convoys were, ironically, considerably more solicitous of the slaves' well-being than were some of their comrades at Hampton. They shared their rations with the blacks, gave them what clothes they could spare, and began indoctrinating them with Union propaganda. As they proceeded down the rivers, the new freedmen were taught to sing such Yankee doggerels as:

Abe Lincoln is a gentleman
   Jeff Davis is a mule
Abe Lincoln is a gentleman
   Jeff Davis is a fool!

Shout, boys, Shout
for I am a Union man
Oh Yankey [*sic*] doodle dandy
Hurrah for Uncle Sam

But the slaves also had songs of their own that more poignantly described the meaning of escape to them:

Christ does not care for the King bright throne
   the noble and the great
He'll bring the proudest sinner down
   to beggar at his feet

Come over now
Slavery chain done broke at last,
Broke at last,
Broke at last,
Praise God till I die[8]

Whether the slaves reached Hampton aboard Union riverboats or through an even more perilous overland journey, the pattern of their departure from the plantations remained similar throughout the war. First the most privileged, and therefore the most knowledgeable, would leave; they were the house servants, the artisans, the slave foremen. In most cases, the fifty-nine women and children left behind on Ruffin's plantation being a notable exception, once the possibility of successful escape was established, the blacks who fled took their families with them or returned for them as soon as possible. This mass exodus from the upcountry plantations left no question that many slaves, given a choice, would risk their lives to be free rather than stay on the plantations. More uncertain was their understanding of freedom. Having had far less opportunity to exercise certain degrees of freedom than native blacks of Hampton, would they use it wisely or abuse it and prove the long-standing claim of white Southerners that the black man without slavery was a savage?

The last years of the war in Hampton were harsh ones for the new freedmen. They would often dismay their missionary allies through their errors, and, by war's end, they would prove that what whites really feared in their talk about "savagery" was, indeed, the case: The black man, without slavery, could not be readily controlled by white men.

What these newly escaped freedmen found when they reached Hampton was a world gone amuck. All the old rules governing life on the plantation no longer applied. Authority was dispersed among different groups of whites who often seemed in contention with each other. There was much destitution and hunger among the blacks; yet other blacks, by the way they lived, carried themselves, and the kind of work they did, seemed to think themselves as good as whites. The old personal relationship between master and slave had collapsed. In its stead was a new, impersonal relationship between army and freedmen, between employer and worker.

There were more people, black and white, assembled together than these refugees had ever seen. There was frantic activity everywhere—at the army and contraband camps, in Hampton village, at the Fortress, and on the wharves. Opportunities abounded for activities strictly forbidden on the plantation. On the other hand, the basic necessities of life—food, clothing, and shelter—were far from assured. To cope with these new circumstances, the freed slaves naturally fell back upon their experiences as bondsmen.

Foremost in the minds of the freedmen in these unknown circumstances was the reconstruction of their families. C. P. Day heralded that "mothers are having restored to them children whom they never expected to see this side of eternity." Those not so fortunate advertised for missing family members through the Bureau of Negro Affairs, and after the war through the Yankee-sponsored newspaper, the *True Southerner.*[9]

Like many families caught in war, desire for reunion does not guarantee the ability or, in some instances, even the desire to care for one's dependents once reunited with them. Most freedmen who came to Hampton, according to missionary reports, were organized in family units. But these units sometimes reflected a plantation lack of morality shocking to Northerners. The family unit was frequently difficult to separate from the over-all plantation group. For example, one group escaping from Ruffin's planation included only one man and twenty women and children. Many such units were brought to Hampton aboard Union gunboats. Sometimes, a single slave might be the father of children by more than one slave woman or, even more distressing to the missionary ladies, the slave mother might not know which of several possibilities was the father of her children. To this was added the equally baffling problem of women and men who had been sold from plantation to plantation, taking a new mate at each place and then, after escaping to Hampton, having to choose among former husbands or wives who had also escaped.[10]

The unorthodox familial patterns which the later refugees brought from slavery created more problems for blacks, and for missionaries, than simply determining which wife belonged to which husband. Freedwomen willingly accepted the responsibilities for caring for their children and for keeping proper homes, but not all knew how to do so. On many plantations, one "black mammy" was charged with the care of all slave children. The missionaries continually called for a school to teach the women the habits of "good housewivery [sic]," to teach the care and *discipline* of their children. Black freedwomen lacked many of the skills considered to be essential by the missionary ladies. They did not know how to sew, or to cook, or to keep a clean house. More importantly, they lacked knowledge of infant and child care.[11]

The missionaries' concern for propriety, however, sometimes obscured the sound advice these newly freed mothers needed to hear. Though they did discuss the nursing of infants or the sicknesses of children, the Northerners frequently tended to give more attention to the social behavior of the freed children. "Your children, as soon as they are old enough to go should be sent to school," remarked "Anna," a columnist for the *True Southerner*, "and never allowed to play any length of time in the streets...children who are educated in the street will eventually become bad men and women." She added pointedly: "I have seen colored children stand at the windows of white people and look in to see what they could see. They should be taught that this is impolite even to do so to a colored neighbor, more so to a stranger."[12] Good manners are important, no doubt, but to black parents like those living in barns with only chalk lines to delineate one set of family quarters from another, Anna's advice must have seemed singularly irrelevant.[13] Once again, New England decorum had come face to face with Virginia reality, and, once again, reality was ignored.

While black children were not learning the behavior the missionaries deemed proper, all too often their parents were having difficulty unlearning behavior the missionaries found abhorrent. The adult freedmen expressed a desire to shoulder all the responsibilities of freedom, even the codes of moral and social behavior advocated by the missionareies, but old habits were hard to change, and the new ones being urged upon them did not always make sense in light of their experiences. Marital fidelity and continuity did not come naturally to all freedmen. There were frequent missionary complaints of the "unfaithfulness" of black partners in marriage and of much casualness in the making and dissolving of marriages. Too often, one member of a black couple accepted the custom of monogamous marriage before the other. Such disputes led to numerous complaints to C. B. Wilder about the desertion of a husband or wife. Many of the acts of violence within the wartime refugee communities centered around problems of infidelity.[14]

Closely related to these problems were the questions of support for dependents, particularly the elderly and sick. Once again the experience of slavery contradicted the requirements of freedom as defined by the missionaries. The freedman's comprehension of the relation between wages earned and the provision of food, clothing, and shelter for himself and family developed only gradually. Their understanding was, no doubt, retarded by the army's policies of rations and of withheld or unpaid wages. The situation was similar to that on the plantation where the black did labor for the master in exchange for food, clothes, and a shack to live in. What money he received, he could spend as he saw fit. Thus, on the rare occasions when blacks were paid their just wages by the army, the money was not always wisely spent. The opportunity to use money frivolously in wartime Hampton was infinitely greater than it had been on a plantation or in a rural village. Missionary complaints of drunkenness and improvidence among the freedmen indicate blacks took great advantage of these opportunities.[15]

The problem involved setting priorities and understanding the value of money rather than a rejection of basic responsibilities. The missionaries complained more of the general destitution among blacks than of the failure of the breadwinner to support his family. Husbands and fathers tended to support their families on whatever meagre resources they had. By 1866, it was primarily fatherless families, the crippled, and the elderly who remained on the government dole.[16] These groups suffered severely during the war. The plantation system had its own methods of coping with such people. The lack of a father presented no problem as long as the mother and children could work; the elderly or crippled were sometimes neglected with the hope that they would die, but, more often, they were supported out of the general resources of the plantation. The individual family groups that the freedmen were being encouraged to develop made little provision for such incapacitated people, particularly if they could not claim relationship to a family of able-bodied freedmen. Even when this was not the case, an old person's family was not always willing to accept the burden of his care. Throughout the war and Reconstruction, the primary means of support for these unfortunates was the government dole.[17]

The opportunity and ability to work, however, did not necessarily help black emigrants understand freedom nor change their old habits of working. They took readily to the idea of working for themselves when they first came to Hampton, but their enthusiasm was quickly tempered by the harsh treatment they received in their labor for the army and by the irregularity of their wages. Many, especially those assigned to labor gangs with the military, maintained the habit of doing as little as possible. They were good "eye servants," as John Bebout called them, working whenever a white supervisor was around but slackening their pace or stopping entirely whenever the white overseer was absent.[18]

The army's failure to pay on time gave the freedmen little incentive to work hard or well. Approaching the problem from the point of view of the frustrated employer rather than the defrauded laborer, H. S. Beals remarked about the freedmen, "I have long been convinced that one important branch of their education is to disabuse their minds of the idea that they work for nothing and are thus entitled to gifts." Blacks denied "gifts" were liable to steal, and, despite Beals' counselling, since the freedmen did not receive their promised wages, many of them did steal. The problem continued throughout the war. Still denied the rights of property and seeing their own homesteads raided with impunity by gangs of Union soldiers, many freedmen showed little respect for the property of others.[19]

Those freedmen who had the opportunity to rent farms from the Bureau of Negro Affairs, which became possible in the last year and a half of the war, fared better than the others and did much to prove that blacks could support themselves if given the chance. In 1865, William Thorton joined with three other freedmen to rent "Oakland Farm" for $210. William Thompson and others rented "Buckroe Place" for $500. In York County, 41 black families combined to rent the 357-acre farm "Leansdowne" for 311 barrels of corn. Thirty-three other freedmen and their families rented

196 acres at "Briarhurst" for 93.5 barrels of corn. In Elizabeth City County in 1865, 37 farms were rented to 138 tenants and their families. All the farms were reported in good condition and none of the tenants defaulted on their rent payments.[20] Unfortunately, most of the freedmen on the Peninsula never had the opportunity to rent and farm land independently during the war. Those who did were primarily the original contraband from Hampton village. The majority of blacks spent their first years of freedom in wretched poverty, confined to inadequate housing in refugee camps, and barely able to subsist on irregular government wages or scanty government rations.

Given the dire circumstances of the newly arrived blacks, it was not surprising that their settlements were soon plagued by theft, unruliness, drunkenness, and what the missionaries called "licentiousness." The missionaries, however, were not much given to sociological explanations for misbehavior. They defined the problem as sin by individuals. To them, harsh social conditions did not excuse transgressions by those who professed to be Christians. But the upcountry refugees proved even more resistant to missionary definitions of Christianity than were native black Hamptonians. Moreover, these new refugees brought with them experiences in black-white relationships that were markedly different from those that had prevailed in ante-bellum Hampton. This new wave of blacks did not perceive its treatment by whites in Hampton to be so different from that on the plantation. They were, therefore, reluctant to abandon patterns of behavior that had sustained them in bondage. It was on these two grounds—the nature of their Christianity and the nature of interracial relationships—that the new refugees evolved their definitions of freedom. In so doing, they helped determine the directions in which post-bellum black Hampton would move.

The religion of the new emigrants were neither as formal nor institutionalized as it had been for ante-bellum Hampton blacks. Few of the former had attended church services with their masters. Their church had been an informal, often secret, institution. The slave church had been, nonetheless, the only aspect of their lives in which they had enjoyed considerable autonomy. It was one of the few places in which slaves had had some opportunity to assert leadership and relative independence from the master. The church also provided an outlet for the creative urges of the bondsmen in the music of their spirituals, the prose and poetry of the exhorter's sermons, and in the folktales based on the Old and New Testaments. Thus the slave church was, in many senses, as central to the lives of the bondsmen as their own church was to the lives of the missionaries. The differences were in the content of the religious teachings of the two churches.[21]

The missionaries' faith taught them how to live their daily lives in a godly manner; the blacks' faith served more as an escape from the daily oppressions of bondage. Its emphasis was emotional, otherworldly, apocalyptical; it stressed not so much the avoidance of sin on earth as the deliverance from earthly burdens in the afterlife. As we have seen, the blacks' religion had no coherent theology as white Christians would define it. The revelations of God were made known to the blacks through visions, and through the interpretation of what little knowledge they had of the Bible that fit their own circumstances. The blacks, as well as the missionaries, found special meaning in the story of the Jewish exodus from Egypt.[22]

The black religion of the new refugees contained a mysticism and "excess of emotion" which the missionaries found increasingly distasteful, particularly since neither element seemed to help blacks lead what the missionaries defined as "more Christian" lives. The black church before emancipation *was* notably weak in the social and moral imperatives it could require of its adherents. Under slavery, these had been the prerogatives of the master and overseer. The slave church was designed to help sustain the blacks in bondage; it could tolerate the petty deceits and thefts of the slaves in relation to their masters because these acts helped the blacks maintain a sense of their individuality and humanity. From the missionary point of view, however, the result was that the black Christians frequently behaved in very unchristian-like manners. The missionaries were also convinced that the black preachers were doing little to improve the situation.[23]

The freedmen, on the other hand, seemed satisfied with the nature of their religion. One of their first cooperative acts was to institutionalize it in separate churches under their own control. In 1863 they founded Zion Baptist Church at Hampton with William Thorton as pastor, and First Baptist Church of Hampton with William Taylor, another of the original black residents, as pastor. In Warwick County the next year, they rebuilt the old Denbigh Baptist Church for their own use.[24] During the war and Reconstruction, these churches became the chief social and political as well as religious organizations of the black community. The ante-bellum black leaders of Hampton retained their ascendancy by becoming the ministers and deacons of these churches.

The creation of all-black churches was a reflection of the racial attitudes dominant in the black community. Throughout the war there was a tendency of freedmen to seek independence from white supervision and authority. The new black emigrants intensified this trend toward racial exclusivity. The missionaries were so preoccupied analyzing the blacks that they seldom perceived that blacks might be doing the same to them. There are clues, however, that suggest this was the case. Like the missionaries, blacks depended on previous experience and preconceptions to understand the whites they encountered in Hampton. For the emigrants, this appears to have meant trying to fit Northern whites into the master-slave dichotomy they had known in the past.

From this perspective, most of the army officials whom they met were the easiest for the freedmen to understand. They told the blacks where they were to work, assigned them to a shanty, or bare piece of ground where they were to live, instructed them about rations and clothing distribution. The blacks were promised pay, but little was forthcoming; those who complained were punished. It was not difficult for blacks to view these whites in the context of master or overseer. They knew they could expect little from such men, nor would they work very hard for them. A few army officials like Benjamin Butler and C. B. Wilder were more difficult to fit into preconceived positions. They were more solicitous of the blacks' well-being; they attempted to aid them and to protect them from more hostile whites. A friendly, protective master, however, was not an unknown concept to the former slaves. These men, too, could be understood in an ante-bellum frame of reference.[25]

The missionaries undoubtedly presented the biggest problem to the new freedmen and were instrumental in breaking down simplistic analogies the blacks might draw between Northern whites at Hampton and their ante-bellum masters. The missionaries encouraged the freedmen to become educated and to express their religious convictions. These were symbols of freedom that the blacks recognized immediately. The missionaries were continually reminding the blacks that they were free and must learn the ways of free people. All that they did was in an attempt to aid the blacks. There was no parallel to this type of white person in slavery. But old habits change slowly. The relationship of black to white in slavery was that of the powerless to the powerful; whatever the missionaries' intentions, to the freedmen they were, most emphatically and importantly, white. Because of the missionaries' assistance, the blacks were more willing to do what was asked of them. Probably these black attempts to please the missionaries in return for their kindness did much to perpetuate the latter's myths of black docility and acceptance of Northern values, thereby creating even greater frustration when blacks failed to live up to these values.

The blacks resisted, however, the presumption of the right to interfere in their private lives. They had learned as slaves that they had certain obligations to white people, i.e., to labor for them and to obey them when under their supervision. In the use of their own time, some of the freedmen appear to have had the freedom to do whatever they pleased so long as it did not threaten the master. Others appear to have been closely supervised at all times by master, overseer, or drivers. For those in both groups, freedom meant escape from the constant scrutiny of whites. The blacks saw no necessary correlation, therefore, between going to missionary schools and churches and changing their habits when the missionaries and other whites were not around. Freed children were eventually made to behave well in school, but continued to be unruly at home and in the streets. Adults prayed fervently in church, but did not give up all the old habits which the missionaries defined as "sins."[26]

As the freedmen grew more accustomed to their freedom, they showed a growing tendency to define their own priorities and to structure their lives as they wished. Even the most independent freedmen, however, did not reject missionary assistance. They turned to the missionaries for the education of their children and for help in their conflicts with unfriendly whites. At the same time, blacks grew increasingly insistent that their rights as free men be respected and that they receive equal treatment from white civilians and officials. Freedmen protested against discrimination in public facilities and on public transports. They were also increasingly ready to protect themselves against white abuse. Many expressed themselves ready to fight not only the rebels but prejudiced Union men as well. When Union sailors attempted to rape a black girl in Yorktown, one of the sailors was shot to death by the black mob that had assembled to protect her. Blacks wanted white help, but they also wanted an equal voice in the kind of help and the manner in which it was given.[27]

Samuel Hunt was right when he noted that "the iron of slavery had entered deeply into the soul of the poor bondsmen," but like so many missionaries before and after him, he did not really understand that which he described.[28] He correctly observed that the refugees from the upcountry plantations had brought with them all the attitudes and styles of behavior they had learned in slavery. He did not understand, however, that many of these attributes were the very things that had helped blacks to survive slavery, that had given them the strength to flee once freedom was within reach. Nor did he or other missionaries understand that the new refugees retained these forms of behavior in part because of what was being done to them by Northern whites. Far more strongly than William Thorton and other natives of Hampton could have felt it, these men and women wanted freedom from the arrogant whites who had controlled their lives. To them, white arrogance had no geographic definition. If they were treated in the same fashion, they would behave in the same fashion.

But like the original contraband, the refugees knew what they wanted from freedom. The fact that they had not enjoyed small pieces of it, like the native black Hamptonians, did not diminish their taste for it. Freedom meant the right to control one's own life, to pray in one's own way, and to suffer the consequences of one's own mistakes. Perhaps because these new freedmen were more different from the missionaries than were the original Hampton contraband, they were more insistent upon defining such things for themselves They were more distrustful of whites, and made mistakes in the post-bellum era that the missionaries may have been able to help them avoid, but like their fellow blacks who were native to Hampton, they learned from their mistakes. Not only did many of them become leading citizens of postwar Hampton; they also became leading advocates of the adoption, in the black community, of many missionary values and styles. Like so many other things in Hampton, however, black acceptance of those values came only after most missionaries had departed and blacks could make the choice because of their own needs, rather than because of needs imposed upon them.

Reconstruction: Freedom Deferred

By the end of the war in 1865, the ex-slaves of Hampton had produced a record in which they could take some pride. It mattered little that few of their white allies were unreservedly enthusiastic about it. The freedmen had proven that they wanted freedom, that they would risk their lives to find it, that they would fight for it, and that, like other Americans, they would insist upon their right to define how best to use it. Had they been permitted, like other Americans, to take full advantage of freedom, the freedmen's accomplishments in the ensuing years may have been spectacular indeed. But the freedmen were black. Neither they nor their white fellow countrymen could forget that fact. White Americans used the black man's race to take back with their left hands the freedom they had given with their right. The freedmen of Hampton remembered the importance of race as well. Slavery had taught them the virtues of patience, caution, and solidarity. The war taught them prudence in dealing with even those whites who claimed to be friends.

Both of these lessons proved essential, for Reconstruction on the lower Peninsula of Virginia proved as complex and chaotic as the preceding four years of war. Although Hampton remained the focus of affairs, events in all four lower peninsular counties—Elizabeth City, James City, York, and Warwick—combined to determine the freedmen's future in the area.

Blacks, who had encountered many surprises and disappointments in their association with the Union army and missionaries during the war, learned that Reconstruction had equally unpleasant shocks in store for them. The freedmen had high hopes for the Bureau of Refugees, Freedmen and Abandoned Lands created by Congress in

March of 1865. They were especially happy at the promise that land confiscated from former rebels would be distributed among them as family farms. Both the Bureau and the land redistribution plan, however, quickly fell victims to Andrew Johnson's lenient policy toward ex-Confederates. Johnson had little regard for the freedmen and would never permit Bureau officers sufficient authority to protect blacks from hostile Southerners. Moreover, Johnson's wholesale pardons to former rebels carried with them restoration of confiscated property. As long as Presidential Reconstruction prevailed, the freedmen of Virginia received no free land from the government and precious little assistance of other sorts.

The coming of Radical Reconstruction and provision of suffrage for black men in the South in 1867 buoyed freedmen's spirits. But the utility of the vote for blacks on the Peninsula, as elsewhere in the South, was severely restricted by their dependence on whites for their livelihoods. In addition, blacks could exercise their vote as they wished only so long as there was a sufficient federal military presence to protect them. Even by 1868, that presence was too limited to be effective on much of the Peninsula.

The blacks of Hampton were not alone in experiencing these disappointments. Although the chronology differed somewhat from state to state, all freedmen encountered this piecemeal betrayal of Reconstruction promises. Nevertheless, Hampton remained unusual among Southern black communities of this era. Building upon their wartime experiences, Hampton's blacks gradually began to evolve the pragmatic strategies needed for even modest advancement in the post-bellum South. While they might not trust most white Southerners, they learned they would have to work with some. While they might resent the paternalistic attitudes of their Northern white allies, they understood that forbearance was the price of progress in education, politics, and economics.

By the end of Reconstruction in Virginia in 1870, Hampton blacks knew that their freedom in the post-bellum South was inevitably going to be circumscribed. They sought to make those compromises most advantageous to themselves. In so doing, they made Reconstruction the foundation for continued progress rather than merely an era of bitter disappointment.

Freedman's Village, Hampton, Va. (1865). This is a copy of a photograph by Alexander Gardner or assistant, Washington, D.C., who came to Hampton accompanying President Lincoln in 1865. Original photograph is at the Library of Congress. Print is from Harper's Weekly. *(Copy courtesy of the Casemate Museum)*

The Chaos of Peace

The formal end to hostilities did not bring peace to Hampton Roads. Hundreds of additional black refugees invaded Hampton. Along with them, two irreconcilably hostile groups returned to the village: bitter whites who had lost a war, and newly self-confident black soldiers who had helped to win one. At the beginning of the war there had been only 2,600 blacks in Elizabeth City County and just under 10,000 on the Peninsula as a whole. By 1865, 40,000 freedmen were concentrated on the Peninsula; 7,000 were in the village of Hampton alone. The already overburdened relief agencies in Hampton could not meet the additional needs for assistance among both blacks and whites. The unclear division of authority between military and civilian agencies fostered the breakdown of civil order. Lawlessness was rampant and clashes between the races were almost daily occurrences.[1] In these circumstances the conditions of many blacks actually deteriorated as a result of peace.

Many of the hardships encountered by the freedmen on the Peninsula resulted from the simultaneous rapid increase in the black population and sharp decline in available jobs. Most government facilities in Hampton were hastily deactivated at the end of the war, eliminating many jobs. As many as 5,000 blacks who lost their jobs were unable to collect back wages owed them by the government. Particularly serious was the closing of the government hospital where many husbandless black women had worked as laundresses and chambermaids. These women and their families were forced to subsist on government rations. Black troops were hurriedly mustered out of service, further increasing the ranks of the unemployed.[2]

By the winter of 1865-66 the conditions of the Peninsula's freedmen had become desperate. That winter was especially cold. Most blacks had no means of obtaining firewood to heat their shanties. Food from the small crops some blacks had been able to raise during the summer had been exhausted. Postwar inflation had driven food prices beyond the reach of those few freedmen with money. In an effort to force blacks to return to their home counties, the newly formed Freedmen's Bureau in Hampton issued only half rations to the indigent. Typical of the freedmen was one black veteran who had managed to support his family of eight for several months on his savings. By January 1866 these savings were exhausted; there was no work to be had and his former owner re- fused to take him back even for work without wages. He and his family were reported starving to death. The missionaries told of hundreds of other freedmen in a similar plight. "There are so many suffering and destitute here," wrote Ellen Benton in Hamp- ton, "...little children crying all night with the cold, they have no clothing to keep them warm and could not afford to keep a fire."[3]

Sickness and death are the natural consequences of such condi- tions, and both began to plague Hampton during that cold winter. Adding to the devastating effects of pneumonia and malnutrition were outbreaks of smallpox in Warwick and York Counties and an epidemic of cholera in Elizabeth City County. C. B. Wilder, who had been appointed assistant subcommissioner of the new Freed- men's Bureau, complained of three and four deaths a day in War- wick County, many resulting from the lack of doctors and medi- cine. The daily ordering of coffins—often the smaller sizes appro- priate for children—became one of Wilder's most onerous duties.[4]

Sickness and poverty were not the only enemies attacking blacks after the war. Their human opponents seemed determined to do to the freedmen whatever disease could not. Hampton vil- lage remained relatively peaceful, primarily because of the strong Union military presence there, but in the rest of Elizabeth City County and in adjoining areas of Tidewater, white masters returned reconciled to military defeat, nothing more. To find their former slaves serving in the Union army and farming their plantations were facts that these ex-Confederates could not accept. Whatever the consequences of war, the former rebels were determined to re- main masters in fact, if no longer by law. "That the negro is or can be made equal to the white man," the Richmond *Whig* argued,

the world will never be convinced....There must be a mudsill to society. In the South that mudsill is, or was, the negro....

These people are negroes, they are free, and let them continue free—but let them be *free negroes*....The negroes' happiness and safety are best promoted by...conformity to his manifest destiny and that is social and political inferiority to whites.[5]

To enforce this conception of the freedmen's role in postwar society, former rebels resorted to violence and intimidation. Many blacks who tried to return to their plantations were driven off at gunpoint, particularly those who had served in the Union army. Freedmen who tried to return to their homes in Surry County, across the James, were stopped at the docks on the Surry side by whites who did not wish their blacks to know they were free. Whites there were hiring and binding out black laborers and using the whip just as in prewar days. Blacks still received no wages and were given no clothing either.[6] Whites on the lower Peninsula engaged in the murder and looting of blacks with near impunity. Bands of white guerillas raided black houses along the James in Warwick County, stealing food, livestock, and often killing the inhabitants as well. The civil authorities did nothing to halt these outrages. Instead local justices often conspired in the harassment by issuing orders for the arrest of blacks on the slightest grounds and by refusing to punish white criminals. Elihu Brittenham, for example, murdered a freedman and was arrested but allowed to go freely about Hampton with one unarmed guard. Another white man, Julius Hall, was convicted of murdering a colored woman in his employ and her three children. He was found insane by the circuit court and confined to Williamsburg Insane Asylum. Three months later he was released as cured.[7]

Peninsula whites directed their fury against Northern whites as well as the freedmen. Incendiaries burned black schoolhouses in Norfolk and Yorktown. Violence began to occur in Hampton village as well. Assassination attempts were made on C.B. Wilder and missionary workers. Shots were fired into the Butler School near Fortress Monroe just missing Miss Campbell, one of the teachers. Missionaries learned to be careful about travelling after dark. One evening in January 1866, a white mob attacked and beat C. C. Paine, superintendent of missionary schools. His companion and fellow teacher, Mr. Booth, had his jaw broken in two places.[8]

The hardship and violence of postwar Hampton was too much for some black refugees. A few, like Isabella Sourstan, appealed to their former masters for help in returning home. "I am cramped here nearly to death and no one ceares [sic] for me heare [sic]," Mrs. Sourstan wrote her master, "I don't care if I am free. I had rather live with you. I was as free while with you as I wanted to be."[9]

But most of the Peninsula's freedmen disagreed with Mrs. Sourstan. They preferred the hardship, the violence, even near starvation of the refugee camps to life on the old plantation. In Hampton there was an opportunity to give their freedom full meaning. Haphazardly but nonetheless stubbornly, they set out to build a black community. To C. B. Wilder's assurances that they would be well-treated if they returned home, blacks replied sagaciously, "We knows old master better'n you do."[10]

The first necessity for the blacks who remained on the Peninsula was to safeguard the rights they had already gained against the onslaught of "secesh" violence. To the consternation of Hampton's unreconstructed rebels, freedmen showed no intention of remaining "mudsills" of society. Not only did they meet white violence with violence of their own, they also began to manifest an aggressive spirit of racial pride.

At first the black response to white violence was purely defensive. Whites who committed depredations in black settlements risked "instant justice" from black residents if captured. White Union soldiers who staged a raid on Slabtown in Hampton were hung up by their thumbs. Three white men who caused a disturbance in the Freedmen's Store in Hampton were whipped in the street by a black mob.[11] Most freedmen generally tried to avoid violence despite considerable provocation. The Norfolk race riot in April 1866 resulted from a freedmen's parade to celebrate the passage of the Civil Rights Bill. Tensions had been building in the city for months with whites promising brutal suppression of any black disturbances. The parade, which included units of the Negro militia, was at first peaceful despite verbal harangues and barrages of bottles and brickbats from white onlookers. Then one black marcher was shot by a white man. The white was captured and killed by blacks, whereupon shots were fired into the crowd from houses along the street. A general melee followed which ended only after white Union troops were called in. Three whites were killed and four blacks were wounded.[12]

White and black violence escalated rapidly on the lower Peninsula as well. Much of it could be better described as criminal violence with racial overtones rather than as strictly racial clashes. Blacks robbed and murdered whites with a frequency approaching such white crimes against blacks. Lieutenant Massey, Freedmen's Bureau officer in York County, complained that "freedmen who are illdisposed ... feel that they can commit crimes with impunity."

To the attitude that blacks had no rights that whites needed to respect, freedmen seemed to be replying that Southern whites had no laws blacks needed to obey. "Freedmen of the county are easily governed by U. S. Authority," Massey continued, "but to the civil authorities they appear to entertain the most bitter hostility."[13]

Blacks in the area, particularly in York County where they most outnumbered whites, seemed convinced that Union victory put them on a par with or a level above whites who had been rebels. Arguments between blacks and whites on the merits of their respective races were frequent and heated, particularly if fired by alcohol. On 22 May 1866, court day in York County, such an argument ended with Robert Lewis, black, striking his white antagonist. Lewis was arrested and jailed, but the next day made his escape. The whites who pursued were met by "at least two hundred freedmen...fully armed [and] prepared to keep at any cost." Lewis was not recaptured. So belligerent had York County's freedmen become that the next month Robert Powers, the presiding justice of the York County Court, appealed to the Freedmen's Bureau and army for help. "It is in my opinion at the present time," Powers wrote, "not only impractical but I believe impossible to execute the civil laws satisfactorily unless officers of the civil law be assisted by the strong arm of the military."[14]

While the freedmen were demonstrating their determination to defend their rights even in defiance of civil authorities and Bureau officials, they continued to expand their conception of what freedom meant to them. The form of community organization centering around the churches, which had begun before the peace, continued during Reconstruction. To the three black churches founded during the war—First Baptist, Zion Baptist, and Denbigh Baptist, Warwick—a fourth, Baptist Church, Churchill, was added; this one was also pastored by one of the original contraband, William Roscoe Davis. Another black Baptist church, under Alexander Dunlap, a freedman, was founded in Williamsburg. And in Hampton, the Bethel African Methodist Episcopal Church was founded with Peter Sheppard as its pastor.[15]

In York County, with its high concentration of refugees, community leadership took a different form. Its focus was straightforwardly political. Daniel and Robert Norton, black natives of the county who had gone north before the war, returned to become chief spokesmen and advocates for freedmen there.[16]

To the freedmen of York County and the rest of the lower

Peninsula, the priority, second only to defense of freedom itself, became greater social responsibility and stability within their communities. Most freedmen appear to have been supporters, if not active participants, in the armed defense of black settlements and black rights. At the same time, they seemed equally near unanimity in opposing the criminal element among them, black or white. Much of the theft and violence within postwar black communities was perpetrated by blacks. Black church and political leaders joined forces with the Freedmen's Bureau and even the civil authorities to bring peace to their settlements.[17]

At meetings in the black churches, the freedmen testified to their willingness to live in peace with white people, so long as their rights were respected. Black ministers conducted revivals wholesale and performed scores of marriages each week, legitimizing bonds made in slavery and sanctifying liaisons made in the postwar period. Because of refusal to admit black members by the national temperance organization, the Sons of Temperance, leaders of freedmen on the Peninsula allied with the Bureau in creation of the "Lincoln Temperance Society" to help stem excessive drinking among the blacks. The frequency and the intensity with which appeals to abstinence were made, however, suggests that black leaders were no more successful than the missionaries in curbing the consumption of alcohol among the freedmen.[18]

Along with the immediate issues of defense and tranquility within their communities, freedmen also committed themselves to more long range goals. Those goals, and the manner in which blacks went about achieving them, were best expressed in two political meetings held at First Baptist Church, Hampton, in 1865. At the first meeting, in August, blacks testified to their determination to acquire property, arguing that farms they then held under the aegis of the Freedmen's Bureau produced bigger, better crops than had ever been the case under slavery. They appealed to the national government to forbid the return of these lands to their rebel owners. At the second meeting, in November 1865, they passed a series of resolutions defining their stand on political equality for blacks:

> Resolved: That...we most earnestly pray to our friends, the Republican Party, at the North, that no Representatives be admitted to Congress from this State, until the colored men of Virginia are allowed the privilege of voting [and] Resolved. That we return to Almighty God many thanks for the blessings

he [*sic*] has bestowed upon us, and we pray that our conduct may be such that his [*sic*] bounties may continue until the colored people of America may stand equal with the white race in all political rights and privileges.[19]

To achieve these goals of property and suffrage, the Peninsula's blacks struck out on two fronts: they sought to acquire land and, through petition and protest, to gain the right to vote. In the first they experienced little immediate success. They established a "Freedmen's Store" in Hampton with an initial investment of $4,000. The store was controlled by an association and "filled with groceries and goods of all sorts, purchased with our own money," proclaimed one of their ads. Other blacks established independent businesses in hostelry, transportation, and fishing. The "Lincoln Land Association," also created by the freedmen, managed to purchase a few hundred acres of farm land which was worked collectively by several black families. A guiding light in this last venture was the pastor of Zion Baptist Church, William Thorton, who, along with the purchase of land, acquired a sawmill for one of the farms to increase the freedmen's and the Association's profits.[20]

Most freedmen, however, lacked capital to acquire property. For them, political activity seemed the most likely avenue to full equality. As a result, political meetings in the four counties of the lower Peninsula were frequent and, if gauged by the number of petitions produced, productive. Meetings were conducted with the utmost of decorum. Freedmen of the Peninsula had a penchant for parliamentary procedure. Prayers were read, presidents of meetings were elected, secretaries duly appointed and resolutions duly passed; permanent organizations were formed and reformed. Throughout this process, the same names emerge as leaders: William Taylor, William Thorton, William R. Davis, and Thompson Walker of Elizabeth City County, Daniel Norton of York County, and Alexander Dunlap of Williamsburg and James City County. John Oliver, formerly a missionary teacher in Warwick County and later of Norfolk, was also frequently present. Calvin Pepper, and D. B. White, two white men, who for varying motives had cast in their lots with the freedmen, were also usually present.[21]

The resolutions passed by these meetings of Peninsula freedmen reiterated the goals of property and suffrage. Delegations were sent to Washington to appeal to national authorities when blacks became convinced that local Bureau and military officials were too much in sympathy with the former rebels. The most important of these delegations represented the Peninsula chapter of the National Equal Rights Association led by Frederick Douglass. Thorton, Dunlap, Pepper, and White, as well as the Reverends Thomas Baine and R. H. Hill of Norfolk, made up the Hampton Roads delegation. The Virginia group succeeded in meeting Colonel Woodhull of the Freedmen's Bureau, General O. O. Howard, bureau commissioner, being unable, and Thorton accompanied Douglass on his disastrous interview with Andrew Johnson in which the last clearly delineated the primacy of the white people in the Reconstruction of the South.[22]

On the one hand, the freedmen of the Peninsula quickly learned the procedures through which they might demand their rights from the federal government. On the other hand, they did not grasp certain realities about national affairs which caused their desires to be ignored. Repeatedly they exercised the right of petition, only to find their appeals completely disregarded. They had learned to approach their government through the devices provided by law for all citizens. They failed to perceive, however, that very few of their white fellow citizens, Northern or Southern, saw them as such. From the freedmen's point of view, the war had been fought over their destiny; having won their freedom, they were content to follow the rules of the democratic process in attaining further gains. They were convinced, moreover, that their rebel enemies would soon be forced to accept the reality of their freedom and citizenship. But blacks tended to confuse form and substance, political procedures and the reality of political power. They did not yet understand the nature nor the power of the political forces combining to suppress them.

Sustaining Peninsula blacks in these trying circumstances was their faith and their apocalyptical view of life. For many ex-slaves, the will of God, not the machinations of men, had brought about their sudden emancipation. God, in his own good time, would also see that black men received all the other rights due to them. William Davis, as quoted in the *True Southerner*, postulated this vision most clearly:

(Davis) said that the whites had land and the colored people had labor and that they were willing to work for their living. He said that the negroes had no idea of insurrection, that they did not rebel when they were in slavery and would not do it now. They had waited patiently upon the will of the Lord to free them and they would wait patiently upon the will of the Lord to grant them their other rights as freedmen.[23]

As their appeals continued to fall on deaf ears in Washington, Hampton's freedmen began to sense that "the will of the Lord"—particularly as they understood it—might be advanced by their own efforts. They also realized that they would require assistance from whites. In choosing their white allies, the freedmen tended to pay more attention to whether or not the potential comrade agreed with their goals than to his real ability to assist them in the accomplishment of those goals. As elsewhere in the South there were a number of such men drawn to the Peninsula during Reconstruction, and blacks soon found themselves saddled with self-proclaimed allies of often questionable integrity.

Two newspapers were founded in Hampton to appeal to the freed population. *The American Palladium and Eastern Virginia Gazette* proclaimed in its first edition: "The freedmen will be an incubus, clogging forever the wheels of good government, maiming the harmony that should exist between sections of the common country, until trained in the principles of morality and religion." The *Palladium* announced itself in favor of schools, churches, workhouses, and moral and social reform for the freedmen. In asking black support for the paper, it promised to "lead off the van... in establishing a spirit of moderation and feeling of Christianity among you."[24] The freedmen apparently did not take kindly to the harshly paternalistic tone of the *Palladium.* They denied their support and no further issues were published.

More successful was the *True Southerner* edited by D. B. White, formerly a lieutenant colonel of the Eighty-First New York Volunteers. The paper was published from November 1865 until mid-April 1866. White presented himself as a staunch defender of the freedmen's rights. Whatever faults the freedmen might have, White blamed on slavery.

> Having no use for an education beyond the limits of his master's plantation, the slave has been brought up in ignorance, having no power to hold property, he has never learned how to obtain it, and having no security for any of the goods of this world, he has never learned those first important lessons to the freedmen—industry, energy, and economy.[25]

White promised to advocate the equality of the freedmen before the law, his right to suffrage, and the right of his children to education. In the five months that the paper lasted, White proved good to his word, and won endorsements for his paper from the black leaders of both Norfolk and Hampton. He carried announcements and reports of all black meetings in Hampton Roads, advertised their churches and businesses, provided space for their protests and criticisms of their treatment. He was fierce in his condemnation of the returned rebels.[26] Though he was generally supportive to the Bureau, White harshly criticized many of its policies, particularly those forcing blacks off the land and requiring them to work for their former masters. White demanded to know why in the eyes of the government "a negro who does not work [is] any more a vagrant than a white man who does not work, or why it is necessary that a colored man should have more visible means of support than a white man." White also argued that blacks were more willing to work; the real problems were former rebels who seemed likely to "idle around and grumble until they starve." Even though they had been rebels, White continued, they were still human beings. The government should intervene and the whites "put to work and cared for."[27]

Despite White's advocacy of the blacks' causes and their support for his paper, the *True Southerner* was never able to make ends meet. In February 1866, White moved his paper to Norfolk in hopes of a more profitable market. Norfolk whites proved more intolerant than those of Hampton, however. The larger black community of that city never had a chance to show its support for the *True Southerner.* In April of that year, White's offices were attacked by a white mob; his presses were dumped in the Roads and no more issues of the paper were published.[28]

Of the Northerners who came to Hampton as promoters of the freedmen's rights, the most outspoken, and most infamous, was Calvin Pepper, a lawyer with an uncertain past. Pepper arrived in Hampton shortly after the war and falsely presented himself to the blacks as a close friend of the president, O. O. Howard, and Orlando Brown, bureau subcommissioner for Virginia. Much to the dismay of C. B. Wilder, who was unwillingly implementing the policy of returning abandoned lands to their owners, Pepper promised blacks that they would all receive land and encouraged them not to pay rent. Bureau attempts to halt Pepper's activities only further strained relations between its officers and the freedmen. Pepper was saying the things blacks wanted to hear. In fact, he was making the same promises in November 1865 that Bureau Superintendent Wilder had made only a few months earlier. Blacks wanted land; they had come to believe they deserved the land of their former owners. Choosing between the promises of Pepper and temporizations of C. B. Wilder was an easy matter.[29]

Pepper helped organize freedmen's protests against Johnsonian Reconstruction, led delegations of freedmen to Washington to demand land and suffrage. He rapidly became the white man most trusted by Hampton's freedmen.[30] His interest in freedmen, however, was far from entirely altruistic. Pepper began to exploit the freedmen's trust in him for his own profit, and his activities quickly came under closer scrutiny from the Freedmen's Bureau. Pepper's first illicit venture was assisting black veterans in receiving their Civil War service bounties from the government. For a small fee, Pepper took possession of a veteran's discharge papers with the promise to expedite payment of his bounty. As Pepper collected more and more of these discharge papers, he became increasingly difficult for the veterans or anyone else to find. The Freedmen's Bureau had official responsibility to assist blacks in receiving their bounties. As blacks began to suspect that Pepper had duped them, they turned to the Bureau for help.[31]

Pepper managed to evade Bureau attempts to halt his bounty collecting scheme. A more grandiose plot to defraud freedmen, however, led to his expulsion from the Hampton Roads district. Pepper was local agent for "The Land, Homestead, Settlement and Labor Agency of 10,000." This organization, headed by John Andrew, former governor of Massachusetts, was created to assist freedmen in obtaining land and jobs in the former Confederacy. Freedmen could become members of the organization upon deposit of fifty cents or more. The agency kept lists of land for sale and of available jobs. When a group of freedmen had accumulated sufficient capital, it could request that the agency purchase a plot of land for its members. Contributions by the freedmen were held, without interest, by the agency for three months; thereafter they would be deposited in the Norfolk branch of the Freedmen's Bank.

Under the peculiar method of bookkeeping which Pepper developed, he would credit to each account double the sum that the freedmen deposited. If a freedman contributed a sum equal to that Pepper himself had deposited, this double credit would be made permanent. If this condition were met, Pepper promised to deposit to a freedman's account in the bank double what he had subscribed, the additional money coming from Pepper's own funds. In the only published statement of the Agency's finances, Pepper had deposited $1,000; his closest rival was his wife who had contributed $225. The chance that a freedman would accumulate enough to receive this phenomenal 100 percent interest on his account was clearly remote, a fact which was obscured by the manner in which the process was explained. All that a freedman understood was that for every dollar he deposited with Pepper, he was given a receipt for two dollars.[32]

When Pepper's operation was discovered by the Bureau, Wilder ordered an immediate investigation, requiring Pepper to produce financial statements, proof of the security of freedmen's money on deposit, and a list of agency officials legally responsible for its holdings. Unable to produce such documentation, Pepper countered by denouncing the Bureau for persecuting him and appealed to the freedmen for support. But this time Pepper had gone too far. Leaders of the black community, like William Thorton, supported the Bureau's investigation and demanded a full exposition of the agency's finances. After evading military officials for several days, Pepper was arrested and transported to Richmond for hearings before General Brown. Still unable to demonstrate that his Agency was more than a device through which to defraud the freedmen, Pepper was prohibited from returning to the Hampton Roads district and his undistinguished career in the area was terminated.[33]

The blacks of Hampton had seriously misjudged Pepper's intentions. On the whole, however, they made some significant gains during the first, chaotic year of peace. They established their willingness to defend their new freedom; they created an increasingly stable black community, with its own churches, formalized family structure and growing economic resources. They saw to the education of their children and manifested the desire and potential to become responsible members of the American body politic.

Simultaneously, the weakness of their position and their inability to improve upon it became evident. They could not achieve their goals of property and political equality without active cooperation from the federal government. On this front they encountered only constant frustration. The freedmen sent petitions and made protests to Washington which they presumed to be their right as free men. They were ignored. They came to suspect that local officials of the federal government were misrepresenting them to Washington. Indeed, part of the reason blacks allied themselves with men like Pepper was his claim of close relations with the president and leaders of the Bureau. The freedmen did not realize that local Bureau officers like C. B. Wilder felt a frustration nearly equal to their own. It was not he who was betraying them; rather both he and they were being betrayed by the government in Washington.

The Freedmen's Bureau and Johnsonian Reconstruction, 1865-66

6

When the war ended, Hampton's blacks proclaimed their faith in God, the national Republican party, and the American political process. The will of the first of these three elements is unfathomable, but the behavior of the second two, by the fall of 1865, certainly weakened black faith in both.

Blacks were not the only ones whose faith was being tested. The new president, Andrew Johnson, seemed to be deliberately defying the intent of Congress and the wishes of most Northerners in his Reconstruction program. Before its adjournment in May of 1865, Congress had provided for the disfranchisement of prominent rebels, the confiscation of their property, and its redistribution among the freedmen as family farms. The president's policy of granting pardons to important rebels, which he insisted carried with them the restoration of property, was undermining congressional plans for reconstructing the South. Moreover, the president seemed to be encouraging the white South's efforts to reduce blacks to a condition that was slavery in everything but name through black codes and vagrancy laws.[1]

It was to avoid exactly such mistreatment of freedmen that Congress had created, in May 1865, a Bureau of Refugees, Freedmen, and Abandoned Lands in the War Department. The Bureau was to oversee the well-being of the freedmen and to carry out the distribution of land to them.

Of the agencies created to serve the freedmen during the Civil War and Reconstruction, the lower Peninsula's blacks and their missionary allies greeted the Bureau with greatest enthusiasm and expectation. Here was an agency which would protect the freedmen in their rights, oversee their education, and foster their development as a free, economically self-supporting people.[2] The original agents of the Bureau in Hampton Roads shared this enthusiasm. C. B. Wilder was appointed Bureau assistant sub-commissioner for the Ninth District of Virginia in June 1865. He understood the new agency in the terms conveyed by its shortened, informal title, "Freedmen's Bureau." Most of the more than forty thousand blacks in his district were refugee freedmen. He initially saw himself primarily as "advocate" for these freedmen; the abandoned lands within his jurisdiction were to be used to assist them in becoming productive, responsible members of free society.

The grand visions of the freedmen's future conceived by Wilder, the blacks, and the missionaries were short-lived. Bureau agents in the South soon found themselves caught between the orders of the president and the intent of Congress. If they obeyed Johnson's directives on land restoration and treatment of ex-slaves, they clearly violated the purpose of Congress in creating the Bureau. If they attempted to procrastinate in hope that Congress could reverse Johnsonian policies, they were disobeying direct orders from the commander-in-chief, the president. Since most were army officers, such disobedience could result in military court-martial.

For Bureau agents on the lower Peninsula, the requirement to obey presidential directives was especially repugnant. Many of these officials, particularly C. B. Wilder, had strong ties to the abolitionist movement and missionary groups. They had entered the army specifically to aid the freedmen and were more nearly missionaries in uniform than officers assigned to the not always welcomed duty of Bureau agent. These officers faced a hopeless dilemma. Under Johnsonian Reconstruction, they were required to carry out three major policies: restoration of rebel property to its owners, establishment of a contract labor system between white landowners and black workers, and removal of the excess black population from the lower Peninsula. In each instance they thereby violated the best interests of the blacks, the desires of the freedmen's Northern allies, and—in many cases—their own consciences as well. The true stalwarts of the black man's cause in the Bureau did not remain to carry out the Johnsonian program, but it was implemented nonetheless, and the high hopes of the area's freedmen were dashed as a consequence.

The Freedmen's Bureau came to Hampton with less fanfare than in other areas of the South. There were no dramatic changes;

Freedman, ca. 1870. (Courtesy of the Hampton Institute Archives)

C. B. Wilder, superintendent of Negro affairs since 1862, simply took on a new title and a larger geographic area of responsibility. His district now included not only the counties of Elizabeth City, York, Warwick, and James City on the lower Peninsula, but also the neighboring counties of Mathews, Gloucester, Charles City, New Kent, and King William.[3]

Peace and the return of the former rebels complicated Wilder's responsibilities considerably. The uncertain distribution of power among military, Bureau, and civil officials meant his office became the focal point for all business relating to freedmen. On the one hand he became chief adjudicator of the black community, resolving such family problems as the case of a blind freedwoman none of whose children wanted the sole responsibility of caring for her; he required each child to support the mother for two months of the year. On the other hand, he had to cope with imperious returning rebels, "replete with presidential pardons," demanding the restoration of their lands and the removal of black squatters.[4]

In his attempts to resolve disputes, Wilder invariably placed more credence in the word of a freedman than in that of a rebel planter, and often more than in that of a Union military officer. He was in constant conflict with army officers at Fortress Monroe over the nonpayment of wages to the freedmen. He suspected every request from a fellow Bureau officer upcountry for the return of a black refugee so that "he might properly support his family" as a ruse by a planter to force the return of a valuable worker. Wilder frequently admonished his subordinates, when investigating charges against the freedmen, to interview not only the white complainant but the accused black as well. Many of his reports on such cases were forwarded to Richmond with the notation about the black in question, "this man is known by me to be an honest and hard working freedman."[5]

Wilder's hard work and good intentions did not prevent a rapid deterioration of relations between the Bureau and the freedmen. Wilder, like the blacks, was a helpless victim in the process. The problem was land for the freedmen. He had taken the Bureau's Circular Order Thirteen of 28 July 1865 quite seriously. It laid out procedures for the distribution of confiscated land to ex-slaves. But before Wilder could implement the Order, O. O. Howard, bureau commissioner, advised his agents that Circular Thirteen was rescinded. In its place, Circular Order Fifteen, written at the command of President Johnson, was issued. The new Order directed Bureau agents to return confiscated land to pardoned rebels and encouraged these same rebels to permit small plots to the black laborers they employed. In short, freedmen would get no government land; they were to return to their home plantations and work for their former owners.[6]

Freedwoman, ca. 1870, clearly of Indian background. (Courtesy of the Hampton Institute Archives)

When the freedmen in Wilder's district were informed of the new policy, they were at first unbelieving, and then infuriated. They suspected that local agents like Wilder were lying to them. When Commissioner Howard and Subcommissioner Brown visited Hampton encouraging freedmen to return to their former homes and work for wages, the blacks began to realize the truth. It was the president and national government that were defaulting on Northern wartime promises.[7]

The blacks did not surrender meekly. They had remained loyal to the Union when their masters had rebelled. They had farmed the abandoned farms throughout the war; their black predecessors had done the same for several generations without pay. It was they, not the pardoned rebels, who deserved the land. Despite Union orders, the freedmen on the lower Peninsula refused to give up their land voluntarily. Nor would many of them pay rent for the land to their former owners. Instead, they armed themselves and threatened to respond violently to any effort to evict them. In such instances, white Union troops, many of whom had recently fought in the same army with these black settlers, were ordered to drive the squatters off restored land at gunpoint.[8]

It is no wonder that many freedmen began to wonder who really won the war, the North or the South? As Frances Cook of Hampton wrote to the *True Southerner:* "There are those who said we had better be with the Rebs 'cause we had not support and protection. The officers that the government placed here are throwing us outdoors or taking our mites of corn and we see no justice; if we beg for mercy, there's none for us."[9]

Many blacks in the area concluded that the North and its Bureau agents were as hostile to them as the former rebels. They determined that they had only themselves to depend upon and must therefore have a voice of their own in any council deliberating their future. The first major confrontation between the freedmen and their no longer trusted Northern allies came in December 1865, when the blacks of York County were ordered to elect their representative to the Freedmen's Court. These courts were established by the Bureau to adjudicate cases between freedmen and native whites. Each court had three members: a representative of the white civilian government, an officer of the Freedmen's Bureau, and a representative for the freedmen. Blacks took the term "their representative" literally and elected Daniel Norton, one of the two black brothers who had just returned to the county from the North.

Norton's election was disallowed by Orlando Brown who ordered a new election with the stipulation that a white man be chosen. Lieutenant Massey, Bureau officer for York County, called an assembly of freedmen, explaining that "the prevailing prejudice [in Virginia] prevented as yet any citizen from sitting on the same bench with a colored man" and that "a white man was more accustomed to the form...of a court of justice." The argument did not sit well with the freedmen; they petitioned Brown that Norton be allowed to sit on the court. This was again denied. At the next polling, the freedmen again unanimously elected Norton as their representative. When Massey lectured them on their responsibility to follow Bureau orders, they replied that "they were independent of the Bureau; they were now citizens and could take care of themselves." As if to prove the point, the freedmen left the meeting cheering loudly for their elected representative and fired off "volley after volley of arms...displaying that they were ready for any emergency." Massey reported rumors that the Nortons and others in York County had created a secret organization which had armed itself to defend blacks against both the rebels and the Bureau.[10]

The freedmen's sense of victory, however, was short-lived. If the freedmen would not consent to what the Bureau thought best for them, it would be done anyway. Samuel Armstrong, who had replaced Wilder as assistant subcommissioner, ordered Massey to appoint an appropriate (and white) person to represent the blacks on the court. He added, pointedly, "You are empowered to expel from the limits of your county any party whose influence is demoralizing to the people and tends to produce armed combinations for resisting proper authority."[11]

The court election incident further strained relations between the Bureau and the freedmen. It was also indicative of the Bureau's behavior once Johnsonian Reconstruction was under way. Blacks were to be controlled; they would not be permitted to develop their own initiatives and leaders. Petty semblances of democracy would be tolerated; but if the vote did not go as Bureau officials desired, the vote would be disregarded.

Blacks were not the only ones to rebel against the new Bureau policies on black land and labor. Agents of the Bureau, who had accepted their posts with the expectations of helping blacks to become a self-supporting, independent people, suddenly found themselves being required to serve as surrogate overseers for pardoned rebels. Many did not take the change peaceably. Those who did not were replaced, and at least one, C. B. Wilder, was court-martialed.

Wilder complained publicly about the new policy of land restoration, particularly its impact on freedmen: "The promises of the Government that land would be set apart for them...cheered and encouraged them in their struggle with destitution," he wrote to the AMA, "until it was announced that no lands would be allowed them, and no provision made for them...except to go to work for their former masters as best they could."[12] Blacks opposed that new policy and so did Wilder. In his efforts to subvert it, he approached—if he did not commit—disobedience to direct commands. (Although that was not, as we shall see, the grounds for his court-martial.)

To Wilder's superiors in the Bureau, who were again responding to desires of the president, the worst problem on the lower Peninsula, Wilder's district, was its overpopulation of freedmen. Labor-starved planters in more remote counties wanted the return of their former bondsmen; native whites in Elizabeth City, James City, York and Warwick Counties felt threatened by the overwhelming preponderance of blacks. The Bureau directed Wilder to see to the rapid resettlement of these black refugees in their home counties. Wilder pleaded with Richmond for a revision in this policy, arguing that the refugees were unwilling to leave, were unwanted in their home counties, and would be mistreated if they returned. He did all he could to retain abandoned lands in the Bureau's possession to support such freedmen.[13]

Wilder's reluctance to transport freedmen was not without cause. Many of the refugees came from what was then the Bureau's Second District of Virginia, which lay across the James River from the Peninsula and included the counties of Surry and Isle of Wight. There, Bureau agents permitted former slave owners the utmost discretion in their treatment of the blacks. Former rebels were reported hiring out freedmen on the same auction block used in ante-bellum days. The auctioneer was the former rebel sheriff of the county, who carried out the proceedings still dressed in Confederate uniform. The going rate was twenty-five dollars a year, excluding clothing, for men, twelve dollars to fifteen dollars for boys. At the same time in Wilder's District, the Bureau was requiring wages of five dollars to ten dollars a month.[14]

Mrs. Minnie Drew, a freedwoman of Surry County, appealed to her husband in Hampton for assistance, "I have been looking for you for sometime [sic]. I want you to come as soon as you can,

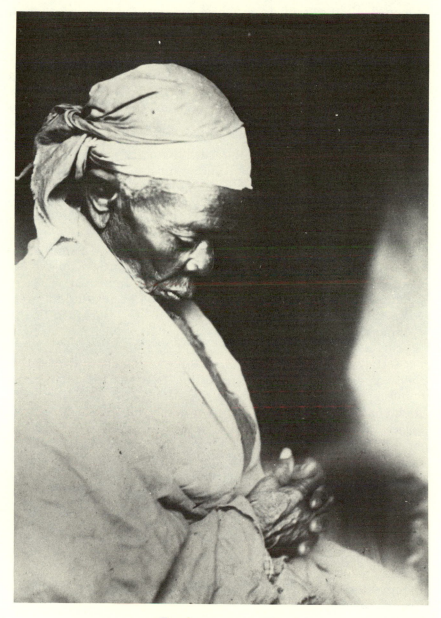

*Freedwoman, ca. 1870. Note hands. (Courtesy of
the Hampton Institute Archives)*

if you don't the Yankees will hire me out, for they say that all that have not homes by New Year's Day...will be hired out to the highest bidder. I am in a great deal of trouble and don't know what to do until I hear from you."[15] Whether Austin Drew was able to rescue his wife is not recorded. Many other freedmen from Hampton who undertook similar missions to Surry County were unsuccessful. The former rebels there drove off any freedmen from outside the county to prevent "their blacks" from understanding their newly acquired rights.[16]

Captain Stewart Barnes, Bureau superintendent in the Second District, steadfastly denied that hiring out by force had occurred in his district. R. M. Manly, Superintendent of freedmen's schools, admonished the *True Southerner* that publication of such false statements would do "great harm" to Bureau policies of resettlement.[17] Policy was already becoming more important than fact in the Bureau's public stance. A week before Manly and Barnes made their statements, Captain A. S. Flagg, inspecting officer for the Bureau, found evidence of public auctions of freedmen in Surry County and declared that all contracts made in such fashion were void. Even earlier, on 22 December 1865, the Bureau office in Richmond had found it necessary to forbid explicitly such practices by its local agents.[18]

C. B. Wilder's complaints about forced contracts and his use of them as excuses for not transporting freedmen to their home counties only further strained his relations with his superiors in Richmond and Washington. By the fall of 1865, he was already at loggerheads with Orlando Brown, assistant commissioner for Virginia in Richmond, and with military and civilian officials on the Peninsula. To retain land for the freedmen, Wilder designated many of their farms as "vital to Bureau operations." He continually complained to Richmond that white Virginians were being pardoned who had been "thick with the Rebels." When any owner was restored his land, Wilder insisted that the freedmen occupying it be allowed to remain until their crops were harvested or that they be reimbursed for any investments they had made. If white planters made contracts with their former slaves for labor, Wilder required that these contracts be reviewed and approved by the Bureau before taking force.[19]

Wilder was not without support in his opposition to new Bureau policy. The *American Missionary Magazine* condemned it and praised Wilder for his faithfulness to the freedmen's cause. D. B. White denounced the new policy vehemently: "old Virginia is reconstructing with a vengenance [*sic*]. If they cannot have slavery they will have land monopoly. How contemptible to withdraw the only chance poor freedmen have to get to mother earth without paying tribute to the noble blooded white Virginian."[20] But these defenders of the freedmen, like the blacks themselves, were without power in Richmond or Washington. Not only was Wilder unable to change Bureau policy, he found himself increasingly isolated and unable to protect blacks or his subordinates from the wrath of white planters and hostile military officials.

Of the four counties on the lower Peninsula, York County suffered the highest concentration of refugee freedmen. The need for living space was desperate. Nonetheless, all confiscated lands were rapidly being restored to the planters. Lieutenant Rodney Churchill, Bureau agent in York County, found himself thwarted at every turn in his efforts to aid blacks. Freedmen forced off restored land could not relocate; local military commanders refused to provide them with transportation. The blacks were often left with the choice between abandoning their standing crops and all personal belongings or squatting illegally on restored lands. The "rightful owners" of such property were quick to appeal for military assistance. Union commanders, though unwilling to help the Bureau, showed no reluctance at aiding former rebels in driving freedmen off their lands.[21]

Because he protested such injustices, Lieutenant Churchill quickly incurred the wrath of the military and such powerful civilian officials as Robert Powers, presiding justice of the York County Court. At Powers' insistence, Churchill was transferred to James City County, only to discover the Northern military there to be equally intransigent and the freedmen's condition equally dire. Military officials in James City were one with the planters. They endorsed the demand by the County's landowners that the Bureau be confined to seeing that freedmen followed contracts made and that it be denied the right to see that *planters* lived up to their contractual responsibilities. The commanding general in Williamsburg even refused to provide Churchill quarters at Fort Macgruder, the local Union army camp. Churchill asked Wilder for a transfer to an area in which he could be more effective, but the latter was powerless to help him. In March 1866, after two months of frustrated effort in James City, Churchill was mustered out of the service and returned to the North.[22]

Rodney Churchill was permitted to retire quietly. C. B. Wilder was not so lucky. His disagreements with official Bureau policy became increasingly clear-cut. Wilder saw his duty as the protection and improvement of the freedmen; Orlando Brown saw it as returning peace and productivity to the district. In his Circular Order of November 1865, Brown carefully delineated the functions of the Bureau as he saw them:

> The principal function of this Bureau is not to supply a channel through which government or private charity shall be dispersed, but to make the Freedmen a self-supporting class of free laborers, who shall understand the necessity of steady employment and responsibility...for themselves and families. Where employment is offered on terms that will provide comfortable subsistence of the laborers, removing them from idleness and from dependence on charity, they should be treated as vagrants if they do not accept it.[23]

The freedmen, Brown assured his subordinates, "must and will be protected in their rights." He added, however, that to earn this protection, the blacks had to "meet these first and most important conditions of a state of free men, a visible means of support and fidelity to contracts."[24] Wilder must have felt that Brown was putting the cart before the horse; from his perspective the problem was not that the freedmen would not work and take care of their families, but rather that by engaging in these contractual arrangements, they were almost invariably being defrauded and mistreated.

Wilder's intransigence on the proper role of the Bureau earned not only disfavor in Richmond, but the bitter enmity of the Peninsula's white natives and Union army commanders. As a consequence, in the fall of 1865, Wilder was charged with three counts of malfeasance in office and brought before an army court-martial. The three charges were selling cannon to blacks, allowing blacks to cut living timber on restored land, and speculating in land sales. By time of the trial, all save the last charge had been dropped. Wilder was acquitted because the prosecution could never prove that he had speculated in land, and, besides, it was not a crime. But the damage had been done. During the trial, the Bureau's records had been in the hands of the army quartermaster and most of them, including the records of wages owed freedmen, had somehow been lost. More importantly, Wilder's own effectiveness had been destroyed. He could get cooperation from neither the military nor civilian authorities on the Peninsula; the Bureau in Richmond refused to support his decisions. His assistants, particularly those who shared his concern for the freedmen, were mustered out of the service and not replaced. In one instance, four of his subordinates were discharged in one day![25]

Wilder's bitterness and disillusionment were clear when he wrote to the American Missionary Association: "This is the state of things forced upon this people under the pretense of leniency to rebels, but really robbing loyal, innocent men to feed...a tribe of treason plotters, and whoever complains or exposes this shameful pretense...is treated as an enemy of the President...and if an officer is threatened with dismissal."[26] "Was there ever," Wilder pleaded at the conclusion of his trial, "prostitution of plighted faith 'like unto this'?"[27]

Wilder's dismissal, in March 1866, came as a surprise to no one. D. B. White editorialized that Wilder's departure had been inevitable because he had been "an officer impartially devoted to justice in all his acts.... He endeavored to secure justice to all parties as it is secured under the best regulated governments, making no distinction in reference to color." It was the dismayed conclusion of the *True Southerner*, and no doubt shared by many freedmen and missionaries on the Peninsula, that this was not the kind of government presently in power at Washington.[28]

Given the unhappy circumstances surrounding Wilder's dismissal, however, the freedmen's allies were much pleased and surprised by the man who replaced him. He was General Samuel Chapman Armstrong who, in the years to come, was to have a greater impact upon the blacks of Hampton than any other Northerner. From the perspective of friends of the freedmen, Armstrong's credentials were impeccable. He was the son of AMA missionaries to Hawaii; he had taught in his father's manual training school there before entering Williams College under President Mark Hopkins. After graduation in 1862, Armstrong had joined the army and rose to command the Ninth Regiment of U. S. Colored Troops. With this background, Armstrong easily bridged the growing division between secular and religious efforts for the freedmen. To him, it was a "grand thing to be identified with this Negro movement." "What nobler work," he wrote his mother, "has been given to man since the [R]eformation."[29] Here was a man with whom the missionaries were certain they could cooperate. D. B. White spoke for many when he wrote: "The President, his servants, and his liberal co-laborers have chosen the wrong men for their purpose. The General is a man of much ability and too keen to be dupped [*sic*] by men whose hearts have so recently been in sympathy with secession."[30]

But White underestimated the sagacity of the opposition. If Armstrong had attributes which made him particularly attractive to friends of the freedmen, he possessed others which made him equally attractive to their detractors and to high Bureau officials. First of all, Armstrong was a man with demonstrated administrative ability and great personal charm. He won his appointment from Bureau Commissioner Howard himself, who confided to Armstrong that his was the "most delicate post" in the Bureau. His superiors were certain that Armstrong would know how to avoid the divisive confrontations between the Bureau and other military officials or restored landowners that had characterized Wilder's tenure of office.[31]

As important as Armstrong's innate ability and charm was his acceptance of the philosophy of freedmen's work espoused by Orlando Brown and other Bureau officials. Stability could return to the South only when the sanctity of property was once more assured and a stable working force restored to the land. Armstrong was not so naive as to believe that all Southerners had the best interests of the black man in mind, but he professed great faith in "men of property." Their interests and those of the freedmen were mutually compatible; they needed each other. They would be able to work together once the freedmen learned respect for contracts and acquired proper working habits.[32]

Armstrong's view of his role among the freedmen differed significantly from that of his predecessor. Both took a paternalistic view toward the freedmen and believed blacks must be made self-supporting. After four years of work with the freedmen, Wilder was convinced that blacks would take on this obligation willingly and competently if only given a chance. In contrast, Armstrong held firmly to the notion of black incompetence. Wilder was considerably less critical and, perhaps, more accurate in his descriptions of freedmen; he conscientiously documented both their successes and failures and distinguished among different groups of freedmen, for example, the original contraband and refugees from inland counties. Armstrong consistently prejudged the freedmen, referring to them as a monolith, and describing only those aspects about them that supported his conclusions, even though he was aware of their diversity and accomplishment. For example, throughout his long career in Hampton, Armstrong ignored the existence of the original contraband except when he needed them as evidence for his plans as Bureau agent or principal of Hampton Institute.

Like Wilder, Armstrong considered himself a great friend of the freedmen. It was not his feeling, however, that freedmen needed a voice in determining who their friends were and what these friends ought to do. Certainly, not all white men cared about the black man, but Armstrong never doubted that a well-intended white man could better determine what was best for blacks than blacks could themselves.[33]

These attributes no doubt made Armstrong more attractive to Orlando Brown and General Howard, but the quality which won him the assignment at Hampton was even more basic in their minds. Unlike C. B. Wilder, Samuel Armstrong was a true army man; he obeyed orders. Only twenty-six when he came to Hampton, Armstrong was idealistic enough to question the justice of the existing social order, particularly the prescribed inferiority of the black man. Nevertheless, he assiduously enforced the directives of his superiors, whatever his personal reservations might have been. He frequently sought to advise those above him, to caution them against actions he believed inappropriate for his district; but once the final decision was made, he followed it faithfully. Being a man of considerable political acumen, he did not always tell missionaries and freedmen the exact nature of tasks assigned to him, but he executed them successfully and, at the same time, maintained the good will of his superiors, the missionaries, and of Hampton's white hierarchy, though not always of its black one.[34]

Armstrong's belief in Bureau policies and his obedience in following orders served him in good stead during his four years as Bureau agent in Hampton. It is doubtful that a man of lesser talent or self-confidence could have carried out the many difficult, often onerous, duties that fell to him. Like his predecessor, C. B. Wilder, Armstrong had the responsibility of removing thousands of black refugees from the lower Peninsula, of overseeing the education of those who remained, and of keeping the peace between the races in his sprawling district.

Reminiscing years later, Armstrong would recall that at Hampton in 1866, "Friendliness between the races was general," and that Bureau officers were "gaining...the confidence of both races."[35] In fact, during his first year in office, Armstrong found conditions as unsettled as Wilder had a year before. Over half his district remained out of cultivation due to lack of capital and an unsettled labor force. Relations between landowner and laborer were acrimonious. Written contracts were still uncommon; whites complained, "Niggers won't work," with blacks retorting, "Whites won't pay." Wages were low, usually barely providing subsistence for the laborer and his family. Often even these paltry wages went unpaid, usually in the owner's attempt to defraud his workers, but frequently because the owner had no money with which to pay. In turn blacks were still refusing to pay rent. Many had farmed the land since early in the war and had never paid; they had come to see the land as rightfully theirs. Others clung tenaciously to the dream of "forty acres and a mule," convinced that the government would evict rebel owners by the end of the year. In fact, quite the opposite was true; most of the farms still under Bureau control were scheduled for restoration by 31 December 1866.[36]

Disputes over land only exacerbated already intense racial hostilities. Civil order still threatened to collapse. Passions were continually inflamed by partisan journals of both sides. As a result, "county court days bring trouble," Armstrong wrote. "Whiskey is plentiful, there is drunkeness [sic], rioting, and invariably 'a war of the races.' " In the aftermath of such confrontations, blacks were invariably punished and the whites allowed to go free. The suspension of the Freedmen's Courts in 1866 had deprived the blacks of any chance of justice in disputes with whites.[37]

Armstrong found the general condition of freedmen in his district very unsatisfactory. The refugee camps of Elizabeth City and York Counties were "a social disease" which had to be cured.[38] Ignoring the contraband who did not fit his analysis, Armstrong wrote:

> The freedmen as a class are destitute of ambitions; their complacency and filth is a curse; discontent would lead to a determined effort [for] a better life. Many cling to Hampton and stick to Virginia, apparently to lay their bones here when they have not more use of them. "Born an' bred here; bound to die here" is their supremely stupid answer when asked to go elsewhere.[39]

And many *were* dying. Hundreds of old men and women without homes or the ability to support themselves were reported in Hampton and York County. Local supervisors of the poor refused to admit them to county poorhouses. To prevent them from starving to death, Armstrong won permission from Orlando Brown to put them in the Chesapeake Army Hospital in Hampton. But there were thousands of other freedmen in hardly better circumstances; 1,300 families were still dependent upon army rations; almost all of them were women with many children. Still more families were without proper shelter or food and unable to find work. The only solution of which the Bureau could conceive was to deport these people to the counties from which they had come in hopes that they might find work there.[40]

The whites on the lower Peninsula agreed wholeheartedly with the deportation scheme. Second only to emancipation itself, the huge increase in the black population of the region angered them most. Robert Powers, the magistrate in York County, warned that if the government cut off rations to the estimated 25,000 black refugees in York, as it planned to do by October 1866, the County would have no way of supporting them. I. H. Barlow, mayor of Williamsburg, agreed emphatically, promising support of the black needy with civil funds only when "all those *not* belonging to the towns and counties *before* the war" had been removed "either by voluntary action or by Federal authority." White planters also joined in the efforts at Negro removal, refusing to rent land or hire black laborers until the population was reduced to prewar levels.[41]

The chief difficulty of this plan, as had been the case all along, was that the freedmen refused to leave. They feared mistreatment and loss of education for their children if they left the Peninsula. In an effort to reassure them, Armstrong polled his assistant superintendents, asking "to what extent these dependents can without real inhumanity be removed to the counties from which they originally migrated."[42] The replies were not encouraging. Depredations against blacks were increasingly common not only in surrounding districts but also in the upcountry counties of Armstrong's own district. Whippings, court injustice, and even wanton murders of freedmen were reported as close as James City County. The idea of scattering the schools upcountry along with the freedmen showed little promise. Back country whites remained immovably opposed to freedmen's schools with Northern white teachers. Those schools which were erected at any distance from a protecting Union garrison were quickly burned.[43] In explaining to Richmond the slowness with which the population dispersal program was being implemented, Armstrong argued that some freedmen justly feared the consequences of returning to their old homes; "some masters have threatened to shot [*sic*] returning ex-slaves who...left them, especially if they had joined the Army."[44]

But as orders from Richmond and Washington for removal became more insistent, Armstrong obeyed. Black families in over-populated counties were given only enough rations to prevent starvation, thereby encouraging them to leave. Strong and healthy women with families were to be denied rations altogether and "given tickets to anywhere they think they can find work." Black workers for the government were to be offered transportation to their home counties; those who refused were to be dismissed from their jobs. The new policy was so stringent that even self-supporting freedmen from outside the Peninsula were denied the right to have their families join them in Hampton.[45]

The fact that the Peninsula's black population was to be dispersed had been settled, but the questions of who would go and where they would go had not. On the second question, Armstrong proposed a three-part scheme: sending some to Florida and Texas where he believed land and work opportunities were great, sending others to the North, and returning the remainder to their home counties in Virginia. Armstrong tried to encourage commanders of black troops to migrate with their soldiers to Florida or Texas when their units were mustered out. The strong ties and acquired discipline of military experience would, he believed, make such regiments excellent colonization teams, particularly if led by their former commander.[46] He also encouraged the leaders of Hampton's and York County's black communities to investigate the opportunities for southward migration. But if freedmen were unwilling to return to their old homes, they were even more opposed to moving south to an entirely unknown region.

Armstrong proposed the selection of freedmen representatives to visit Texas and Florida as likely places for migration. Meetings were held in Elizabeth City, Warwick, and York Counties to elect such representatives. Still angry over the rejection of Norton as Freedmen's Court representative, this time the freedmen simply refused to select delegates. Finally, in exasperation, Armstrong appointed "three intelligent freedmen" for the project. "Those selected," he explained to Orlando Brown, "can, and probably will, reach a certain intelligent minority." But Armstrong reckoned without the growing solidarity of the Peninsula's freedmen. The three men selected refused to go.[47]

Armstrong had more success with the idea of sending some of the refugees to the North. He was particularly enthusiastic about this idea, arguing to Orlando Brown: "I think it right to get as many as possible into a land of liberty. Those that go into the interior will not get such treatment as the resident Negroes and such as free men deserve; hence I consider this measure only a degree better than starving at Hampton or Yorktown."[48]

The whole scheme was fraught with difficulties. Some of the agents offering their services in the North were clearly exploiting the blacks sent to them. O. P. St. John, whose schemes for black employment in New York had been earlier rejected by Lieutenant Kinsman during the war, tried again with Armstrong. St. John claimed approval from General Howard and wanted primarily young women; he promised jobs for up to 7,000. Armstrong was as suspicious as Kinsman had been; he replied, "Please let me know the kind of employment to be furnished, and every particular detail because these freed people are very inquisitive about distant homes that may be offered them."[50] Even some of the Northern blacks who offered their assistance in placing freedmen were primarily interested in the profits involved. Mrs. L. A. Grimes, a free black of Boston and former teacher at Hampton, had been overseeing the placement of refugees in the Boston area. She charged five dollars a head from each employer, money which she pocketed rather than using it to pay transportation costs as had been intended.[51]

The most basic problem with sending refugees to the North, even if the employment agents could be trusted, was the lack of control over the treatment a black received once placed with an employer. Records show that 522 blacks were sent to the North in 1866 and 1867. Despite efforts to keep track of them, the fate of less than 100 was known with certainty at the end of 1867. For many the notation was "ran away from first place she went to," or "sick, has child with her." Moreover, the efforts involved in Northern placement were not commensurate with the numbers removed. The program was actually doing little to reduce overpopulation. Less than half of the 522 sent north were refugees in Elizabeth City and York Counties; the remainder were from upcountry counties and were only channeled through Hampton on their way north. This was further proof of the freedmen's unwillingness to leave the Peninsula. It also appears that some of those who left Hampton to go north were not refugees but members of the original contraband group who felt they could find greater opportunity in the North.[52]

Clearly, the only effective method of reducing the refugee

population was to remove the freedmen, forcibly if necessary, to their previous homes in the country. How successful the removal program actually was is impossible to determine. The only wartime census of the black population was prepared in early 1864 and does not reflect further increases in the refugee population in the last year and a half of the war. By February 1864, there were 10,449 blacks in the four counties of the lower Peninsula; 9,500 of these were in camps in Elizabeth City and York Counties. This represented at least a doubling of the black populations in those counties from prewar levels.[53]

If the estimates of Bureau and civilian officials of 30,000 to 40,000 refugees on the Peninsula in 1866 are accurate, the policy of removal accomplished its goal. In 1870 the black population of the four lower Peninsula counties was 13,654—only 4,000 more than in 1860. On the other hand, the black population of Elizabeth City and York Counties, the two counties in which conditions were best for freedmen, remained twice their postwar levels while the other two counties, Warwick and James City, suffered declines in their black populations.[54]

It is not certain how much of the population change in the area was due to Bureau policies. Armstrong could force the removal of only those blacks dependent upon the government for support. These tended to be the weakest elements of the black population, i.e., orphans, fatherless families, single women, and the aged. In 1866, of the 248 indigents unable to support themselves reported by Lieutenant Massey in York County, only 2 were adult males. One was blind and the other had no hands. Of the 1,107 indigents in Elizabeth City County reported by Lieutenant Reed, none were adult males. It would appear that adult men, with or without families, were able to support themselves free of government assistance even in that difficult period.[55] By the end of 1866, the last date for which records remain, 2,500 freedmen had been removed from the Peninsula. Of these, 500 left voluntarily at their own expense. Three-quarters of those who left both York and Elizabeth City Counties were women and children.[56]

Armstrong was able to reduce the population of the Peninsula substantially, but where they went and whether they left by force or of their own volition, having found better opportunities elsewhere, cannot be determined. The rapid increase of the black population in Norfolk during this period suggests that some crossed the Roads in search of greater opportunity in that city.[57]

By the end of 1866, Hampton's branch of the Freedmen's Bureau had been brought into line with the objectives of Johnsonian Reconstruction. The first agents of the Bureau had been replaced by those more accepting of government policy. Blacks were being forced back to their home counties and made to pay rent and o- bey contracts. Most had given up hope for free land. The Bureau would remain in Virginia until 1870, though in the last two years its only function was to coordinate educational efforts for freed- men. In 1867 and 1868, the Bureau that blacks had thought to be their own would preside over the dismantling of Reconstruction and further betray the cause of black freedom.

The Emasculated Bureau: Black Hampton and the Freedmen's Bureau, 1867-68

The ex-slaves of the Lower Peninsula were not alone in their disillusionment with the Freedmen's Bureau by the end of 1866. All over the South Andrew Johnson imposed the same pattern on the agency originally intended to make freedmen self-supporting, responsible citizens. Abandoned and confiscated lands were returned to their rebel owners who had been pardoned by the president. Even in the Sea Islands of South Carolina, where the congressional promise of land was buttressed by black occupancy since 1862 and General Sherman's Field Order of January 1865, rebel property was restored and Bureau agent Rufus Saxton maligned for his efforts to prevent it.[1]

Throughout the South, freedmen were required to make labor contracts with their former owners, and local Bureau agents were charged to enforce the terms of these agreements. Black refugees from rural counties were returned to their home plantations despite proof that they would likely be subject to mistreatment. Rather than fostering black independence, the Bureau became an agency to assist Southern whites in perpetuating black subordination. Agents who resisted these perversions of the Bureau's purpose, like Wilder, or Saxton in South Carolina, were dismissed and replaced by officers more amenable to the president and his southern allies.[2]

By 1867 the Bureau had little power to fulfill its original mandate to the freedmen. Congress further hamstrung its operations by the Military Reconstruction Acts of 1867 which permitted Union military commanders to appoint Bureau agents in their districts. Bureau Commissioner Howard thereby lost what little ability he still had to see that agents were sympathetic to freedmen rather than to their former owners.[3] In ad-

dition, Congress provided in the following year that, other than in
education, the Bureau would cease to operate in states readmitted
under the congressional plan for Reconstruction. By 1868 the Bureau had already withdrawn from ten former slave states and
would do the same in Virginia at the end of that year.[4]

The impending demise of the Bureau was clear, but--if any-
thing- demand on it from the freedmen and from Washington increased. Johnsonian leniency toward white Southerners had encouraged them in their ever more harsh treatment of freedmen and
in their cavalier attitudes toward Bureau agents. Clearly the freedmen still needed protection and Bureau officials were charged with
that duty. The Freedmen's Courts, suspended under Johnsonian
Reconstruction, were reactivated in the fall of 1866. Bureau officers were now permitted to represent freedmen in civil court as
well, and, after 1867, Southern civilians could be brought before
military courts for violation of freedmen's rights.[5]

These responsibilities were assigned to the Bureau *after* the
realistic possibility that they could be performed was lost. There
were fewer and fewer Bureau agents in the South after 1866, and
the military power needed to enforce Bureau mandates was usually
unavailable. Moreover, because many Bureau agents were unsym-
pathetic to freedmen, they failed to perform assigned duties even
when the ability to do so existed.

The same facts hold true for the other important duty given
the Bureau in its declining years, that of promoting black suffrage.
The Reconstruction Acts of 1867 gave Southern freedmen the
right to vote. Bureau agents were assigned the job of registration.
Here again the emasculated Bureau was unequal to the task. There
were too few agents remaining to make up an effective corps of
registrars. Actual registration was carried out by local Union military officers, some of whom also seconded as Bureau agents. More
importantly, black suffrage came as a substitute for, rather than in
addition to, basic rights and protection that freedmen required to
be independent citizens. The ballot meant little to a man who
must vote as he was told by his employer or risk the starvation of
his family.[6]

The South-wide decline of the Bureau afflicted the freedmen
of Virginia's lower Peninsula just as it did those in other areas.
Most remained impoverished and grew increasingly demoralized as
they saw the promise of freedom betrayed by the same national
government that had granted it two years earlier. The few remaining Bureau agents were equally discouraged and unable, or unwil-

ling to carry out the duties assigned to them. Yet, as had been true of the war period and first two years of Reconstruction, the freedmen around Hampton were able to achieve some advances in spite of opposition from Virginia whites and growing indifference in the North. Within this context, their worst difficulty was often the harsh paternalism of Bureau Agent Samuel Chapman Armstrong. Armstrong seemed to view black initiatives, especially in politics, as defiance of his own vision for the freedmen's future. In his mind, they were to become a black yeomanry that through education, hard work, *and* fidelity to contracts with white landowners would gradually acquire the competence to participate more fully in American life. The last years of Reconstruction in Virginia pitted Armstrong's vision against the freedmen's just aspirations for equality.

On most of the lower Peninsula and for most of its freedmen, Armstrong's prescription of black passivity and accommodation seemed the wiser course in 1867. This resulted, however, not from black failings, as Armstrong tended to insist, but rather from the assertiveness of local whites.[7]

Among the most serious denials of black freedom was the attempt to reenslave black children. Having lost a generation of black adults to the contamination of freedom, some white Southerners seemed determined that black youth would know its place and proper duties. The impressment of black children by former masters became a major problem on the Peninsula. In some instances, children had been left behind in the escape to freedom during the war and now the masters refused to release them. In others, former masters came to a black man's home and literally kidnapped his children, claiming that they were legally bound to him until adulthood. In many cases, the civil authorities of a county conspired with the former owner to hire out a black child to him without the consent or even knowledge of the parents. Often the terms of these contracts provided no wages or even guarantee of good treatment for the child involved. The number of complaints coming to the Bureau about these practices increased steadily in 1867 and 1868, but records of resolutions satisfactory to black parent and child are few.[8]

Requests for the return of adult freedmen, usually on the grounds that they had deserted wife and family and had broken their contracts, continued to come from upcountry counties, especially Middlesex County where the local Bureau agent had special sympathy for the complaints of landowners. But by 1867 these requests had decreased markedly, masters having apparently discovered the liberating effects that time in Hampton had on former bondsmen. In any case, Armstrong tended to regard such complaints with the same suspicion as C.B. Wilder had and was very hesitant to force the return of such a freedman unless he was on the government dole.[9]

Connivance of the civil courts in the "binding out" of black children was far from the only injustice blacks encountered upon the restoration of local civil authorities. Armstrong complained to Orlando Brown that "the civil courts cannot be relied upon to render justice irrespective of color." He had some confidence in the higher judges and some of the magistrates, but none at all in local juries. As was to be expected, whites charged with crimes against blacks were invariably acquitted; blacks charged with crimes against whites were invariably found guilty. Blacks were ordered to do road work by the local courts while whites were exempted; blacks who refused were arrested.[10] In Elizabeth City County, magistrates refused to act upon cases in which blacks were plaintiffs. "The Commonwealth Attorney for this county," reported Lieutenant Reed, in charge of Elizabeth City, "is an imbecile formerly an inmate of the Lunatic Asylum at Staunton, Va., and utterly unfitted for the position."[11]

In Gloucester County across the York River, the sanity of the prosecuting attorney was not in question but the reality of justice was. There former slaves were being tried for the theft or destruction of property abandoned by its owners during the war. Even when blacks made voluntary restitution by returning the property or paying for its value, they were brought to court and charged court costs. One freedman paid eighteen dollars to the former owner for the doors of a gutted house that he had taken to use as firewood. Although he came to court with the owner's receipt of payment, he was fined costs, and, lacking the money to pay them, was jailed.[12] Blacks could not even be sure of justice from local military officials. Lieutenant Massey complained that a Lieutenant Alcott of the garrison of Williamsburg had arrested some blacks for stealing, imprisoned all of them, and punished one by hanging him up by the thumbs. After Massey's intercession, the prisoners were released to the civil court where one confessed and was found guilty; the others were released.[13]

The worst feature of civil courts, and the provocation for reactivating the Freedmen's Courts, was the former's refusal to take action in cases of white intimidation or violence against blacks. As elsewhere in the South, whites who burned black schoolhouses or punished "uppity" freedmen were well known by local residents, but never charged with crimes. After mid-1866, such crimes became increasingly frequent on the Peninsula. The only hope for redress was from the Union army, but local whites had learned that the military was overextended. If troops arrived to put down a white riot against blacks, the rioters simply disappeared until the troops withdrew. Whites refused to give evidence; blacks were afraid to, knowing full well that the troops would leave again. And when they did, white violence against blacks redoubled, especially against those who had complained to the soldiers. In these cases, too, blacks had reason to be cautious about trusting Union soldiers. The tendency of Northern soldiers to shoot blacks for no reason continued in peacetime; the chance of bringing such soldiers to justice was almost as remote as successfully charging a Southern white in civil court.[14]

Perhaps the best index of the changed relationship between black and white on the Peninsula was the increasing contempt that whites expressed toward the Bureau. One, addressing Armstrong as "Chief Ruler over the Peninsula of James," demanded that the general reverse a judgment against him testified to only by blacks. Others simply refused to appear in Freedmen's Court at all, provoking Lieutenant Massey in Yorktown to request a garrison of Union troops and a jailhouse to hold white criminals. Absentee landowners treated the Bureau as a free alternative to overseers, demanding that it collect rent from their tenants and pronouncing unreasonable rent increases which they wished the Bureau to enforce. John Slaughter of Williamsburg went so far as to demand that the Bureau provide rations for him and his family even though he was one of the more prosperous citizens of the village, owning more than $4,000 worth of property within the city limits.[15]

Disdain for the Bureau was scarcely confined to private citizens. Governor Pierpoint of Virginia requested the restoration of the Elizabeth City Courthouse to civil authorities. The building, which the freedmen and AMA missionaries had rebuilt, was duly returned on condition that the two groups be reimbursed for their expenses. But once the courthouse was again in civilian hands, court officials refused to pay nor would they attend meetings to discuss the matter. Captain Flagg of the Bureau, who had endorsed the restoration, suggested seizure of the courthouse until payment was made. But times had changed in Hampton. The courthouse was not repossessed nor is there any record that the freedmen or missionaries were compensated for their losses.[16]

Growing white resistance and violence against blacks led to changes in Bureau policy after 1866. In 1865, Orlando Brown, following the lead of Commissioner Howard, had argued that the Bureau must be a neutral arbiter between the races. By the end of 1867, he was insisting that the Bureau's primary role was to protect the freedmen and their interests. Blacks were to have their new privilege of suffrage explained to them and be protected in their exercise of it. Bureau agents, once permitted to serve only as observers in court cases involving freedmen, were given the right to act as attorneys for the blacks. Monthly meetings were to be held in each black settlement; the local agent was to hear all complaints from freedmen and try to resolve them. Any reported outrages against blacks were to be investigated and a full report sent to Richmond.[17]

The vigorous new policy of the Bureau, so close to what Wilder had wanted two years before, did not represent a newfound concern for the freedmen on the part of Brown. According to national policy, enfranchisement of the freedmen gave them all the rights of other free men so they would no longer need the special protection of the federal government. The Bureau wanted to withdraw from Virginia with at least some proof that this was in fact the case. Therefore, intimidation and persecution of freedmen had to be suppressed.[18]

But the Bureau's turnabout was too little, too late, and both the freedmen and former rebels knew it. The Bureau had neither the legal authority nor the military muscle really to protect the freedmen. A freedman had to take his grievances through the civil courts and everyone knew he would receive no satisfaction there. A black man fired from his job because he tried to vote knew that the Bureau would not feed him and his family. Asking protection against white violence from federal troops meant only greater persecution when the troops left, as they inevitably would.

Local Bureau officials were equally aware of their impotence. With the Bureau's official tasks on the Peninsula almost over, its agents were becoming increasingly demoralized. As an economy measure, agents who resigned were not replaced. The remaining agents were given ever larger geographic areas as their responsibility. Some were so large that it was physically impossible for an officer to make all of his rounds within a month, and some officers lacked horses with which to make their rounds in any case. Rather

Samuel Chapman Armstrong, founder and first principal of Hampton Institute. Here he is astride a black horse, contrary to the legends that always have him mounted on a white horse. Photograph ca. 1880. (Courtesy of the Hampton Institute Archives)

than attend the scheduled meetings of freedmen, thereby confronting innumerable complaints upon which they were powerless
to act, and facing the contempt of Southern whites everywhere
they went, Bureau agents spent more and more of their time in
their offices doing paper work.[19] Armstrong complained to
Brown, "Your officers are really doing nothing....The work is in
the saddle but low pay makes it impossible for them to spend
many days travelling around their counties."[20]

Armstrong himself was of two minds on the conditions in his
district. On the one hand, he supported the withdrawal of Union
troops. The danger of violent racial outbreaks in his counties, he
argued, was minimal, and the populace "cannot but suffer from
the presence of soldiers (unless their morality is remarkable)."[21]
On the other hand, even the optimistic Armstrong was increasingly
disillusioned. He acknowledged that the Bureau's job in terms of
the freedmen had yet to be accomplished:

> the condition of freedmen in this sub-district is unchanged....
> They are barely getting along, the chief end of life is to subsist;
> there is no progress, no chance of any, as things are now. Fi-
> nancially he receives nothing more than enough to get him
> through the following winter. He never gets ahead. The freed-
> men are precisely, in a pecuniary point of view, where they
> were two years ago.[22]

Intemperance among blacks continued unabated, and despite much
crime, they refused to identify the criminal element among them
for the authorities. There was considerable "public worship," but,
Armstrong complained, "religion here seems to lack the fibre of
morality." Of black workers he said, "one third are eye servants,
and worth little or nothing"; of the remainder, only another third
could really be considered good workmen.[23] But the worst feature of the freedmen was their "supineness." "They have no aspirations or healthy ambitions; everything about them, their clothes,
their houses, their lands, their fences all bear witness to their shiftless propensity." Having a school nearby seemed to give a better
"tone" to black settlements, but the Northern teachers would be
forced to withdraw unless the government provided further assistance.[24]

There was considerable evidence in Armstrong's district to
support his description of the freedmen's conditions but not his
analysis of causation. Most freedmen *were* discouraged and impoverished, but not because of their "shiftless propensity." Rather

they were immobilized by the apostasy of the Bureau that was supposed to be theirs and by the oppression of their former masters. Some became so despondent that they willingly permitted their former masters to take away their children. Other drifted off to die or wander aimlessly in the confusing new world that seemed to possess all the disadvantages of slavery but none of the promised benefits of freedom. Still others, seeing that they could expect no justice from society, showed no respect for it in turn. Many men of this type did much to foster the folklore of the "bad nigger" who wreaked havoc wherever he went, always staying one step ahead of the law and outraged black husbands. One such man, William Scott, caused quite a stir in Hampton before being arrested. He was reported to have beaten and robbed his white employer in Richmond; shortly thereafter he was driven from the city because of "lewdness among the colored women." At his next stop, Yorktown, he broke up a marriage of twenty years' standing by his "lisceviousness [*sic*]." Scott was much engaged in similar activities in Elizabeth City County when apprehended. He was found out only because he talked his way into a job as orderly in the Yorktown Military Dispensary. The Bureau, in checking his suitability for the position, discovered his colorful past—as well as numerous warrants for his arrest.[25]

The behavior of a few black individuals like Scott reinforced Armstrong's preconceptions about the freedmen, but he tended to ignore a greater number of black individuals who found Scott as objectionable as he did. This bias was reflected in Armstrong's final report to the Bureau in 1868. Calling for some sort of permanent agency to assist blacks, he argued:

> The few years that have passed since the slaves were liberated have no more than served to well arrange the forces, mental and moral, that should be steadily applied for generations.... They are children:—but are in the hands of an educated, shrewd, hostile race....The educated white looks with contempt upon the enfranchised colored citizen; the poor white is bitterly jealous of him. Of such men are chosen the judges and juries that administer the laws and decide the destinies of the freedmen....No outrage upon the virtue of colored females or violation of freedmen's rights receives any general condemnation from southern society.[26]

The only hope, Armstrong felt, was the continuation of schools for the freedmen. But these must be run by Northerners; if Sou-

therners were permitted to control them, there would be "no conflict of ideas"; pupils would be "led along a narrow, dreary, almost
meaningless course of study."[27]

Here Armstrong acknowledged the problem: Southern white
repression of blacks. At the same time, and like so many of his
contemporaries, North and South, he placed the responsibility of
improvement on the repressed, not the repressers. Blacks, he
claimed, were "children." The task of responsible and decent men
was not to force the represser to desist; rather it was to provide
more benevolent guides to the abused children. Armstrong himself
had decided to become such a guide as the first principal of Hampton Institute. The education he would offer was not dreary nor
meaningless, but it was narrow. As we shall see, it tried to teach
blacks that they should adopt the forms of behavior deemed "respectable" by Northerners without also demanding the same re-
wards Northerners expected for their respectability.

The Institute did not quite live up to Armstrong's expectations,
and became better than it might have been, because of a group
that the general steadfastly ignored in his reports to Richmond
and Washington. They were the freedmen who did not give up,
who tried to take advantage of the greater opportunities that freedom provided. Many were members of the original contraband
group, but many more were refugees from outlying counties who
had come to Hampton during the war. Both groups were determined to protect their freedom from racism, whether it came in
the guise of Southern white oppression or Northern white paternalism.

Realizing again, as they had at war's end, that progress would
depend primarily upon themselves, the blacks in York and Elizabeth City Counties sought to achieve those goals they had always
identified with freedom: political rights, property rights, education, and religious independence. Progress would be painfully slow,
but even by 1870, blacks could point to accomplishments that
counterbalanced Armstrong's negative appraisal.

These were the freedmen who had been agitating for suffrage
from the moment they were freed. When it came in 1867 they
were already organized to use it. Because so many of them worked
independently of white landowners, they were more immune to
the economic pressures against voting that such property holders
could apply. Freedmen in York and Elizabeth City also knew the
population ratios in their districts. In both counties, blacks outnumbered whites by about two to one.[28] The numerical superiori-

ty did not result in black domination of officeholding in either county once suffrage was received. Freedmen were still novices at political organization and susceptible to manipulation by whites. The majority of officeholders on the Peninsula throughout the postwar era were white; but from 1868 to 1890 most were also Republicans, dependent on the black vote for election. Because of that dependence, blacks, even in this early stage of exercising their franchise, were able to extract important concessions from the white Republicans.

The most effective black political organizations on the Peninsula were formed in York County by Daniel Norton and, in Elizabeth City County, by his brother, Robert Norton. (A third brother, Frederick, was politically active in neighboring James City County.)[29] Daniel Norton, still embittered by the Freedmen's Bureau's rejection of him as a Freedmen's Court judge, distrusted the Bureau and white Republicans. Rather than cooperate with the Republicans, he created the "Lone Star Society," a secret organization which denied membership to all whites and to black members of the "Union League," the local black arm of the Republican Party. General Armstrong and his subordinates saw the society as a dangerously radical aberration on the part of a few blacks and did all in their power to suppress it. But once again, Armstrong misjudged the black community. The Nortons *did* command the support of the black majorities in their counties and white Republicans found it expedient to acknowledge this fact. In 1867-68 Daniel Norton served as a Republican delegate to the State Constitutional Convention representing York County. Both Daniel and Robert Norton later served in the Virginia State Legislature.[30]

In Hampton black political activity continued to be based in the churches. The Reverends William Taylor and William Roscoe Davis, both members of the original black community in the village, were leaders of the movement for political involvement. Though they were not candidates themselves, their positions as heads of large black congregations in Hampton made their endorsements important. Most of the early black candidates for office in Hampton were members of the Reverend Taylor's First Baptist Church. Thomas Peake, for example, was widower of Mary Peake, first teacher of Hampton's freed slaves; he was also a deacon of First Baptist Church. Peake served as a deputy sheriff immediately after the war, as a school trustee, and in 1870 was elected Superintendent of the County Poorhouse, a position he held for seventeen years. Isaiah Lyons, who served in the Virginia Senate from

1869 until his death in 1871, and Thomas Canady, who was elected constable in Elizabeth City, were also members of First Baptist Church.[31]

These black political activities developed despite the opposition of the local Bureau subcommissioner, Samuel Chapman Armstrong. Armstrong, like his most renowned pupil, Booker T. Washington, never cared for black politicians though, again like Washington, he would later find it very useful to cooperate with them. But in 1868 Armstrong was defying Bureau policy and discouraging black involvement in politics. He argued that black politicians were agitators and troublemakers, not legitimate spokesmen of their community. He believed that blacks were unready for suffrage and that given the violent white reaction to black efforts to vote, blacks would be wiser to stay out of politics. In Armstrong's mind, black leaders had to carry out the more important tasks of educating and uplifting their race. Those blacks who dabbled in politics were dissipating their energies on a tangential issue. Convinced that he knew best what was right for the freedmen, Armstrong lashed out at blacks who did not heed his advice. He was particularly incensed by Daniel Norton's and William Taylor's criticisms of the Bureau. In his reports to Richmond on "leading citizens and freedmen," the general refused to mention either man despite the fact that Taylor was head of the largest black church on the Peninsula and that Daniel Norton had been elected as a delegate to the State Constitutional Convention.[32] The freedmen were not swayed by Armstrong's arguments. They understood, as he did not, that political participation was vital to the maintenance of black rights, particularly since federal protection through the Freedmen's Bureau, inadequate though it had been, was coming to an end.

One of those rights which freedmen meant to safeguard through their suffrage was the right to hold property. As in all else, 1870 represented only the modest beginning, but some progress had been made. Here again, Armstrong reported only on widespread deprivation; he did not acknowledge that the process of black land acquisition was already well started.

Many blacks who had owned property before the Civil War suffered losses during the conflict, just as did their white neighbors. When the Confederates burned Hampton in 1861, homes of black men like Thomas Peake and James Bailey had been destroyed. By 1870, many blacks had recouped their wartime losses. Between 1860 and 1870 total property owned by blacks tripled from

$20,900 to $64,351. The number of black landowners increased from 17 to 121. In comparison to white Hampton, of course, black property holdings were minuscule. The wealthiest white man in Elizabeth City County alone owned over $500,000 in real property with a half-dozen other whites as close seconds. Such comparisons, however, obscure a vitally important point of which both black and white Hamptonians were aware. Blacks, having begun with almost no resources in 1865, were actually improving their economic condition while many white Hamptonians were suffering severe reversals.[33]

Wealth among blacks in Hampton was more equitably distributed in 1870 than it had been in 1860. The ten black men with property worth more than $1,000 in 1860 had owned more than 69 percent of the total wealth of the black community; in 1870 the thirteen black men with property worth more than $1,000 owned only 27 percent of the black community's total wealth. Hampton's black men of property did not rise much above their impoverished brethren either before or after the war. The wealthiest black in Hampton in 1860, William (Colton) Taylor, owned only $2,700 in property. Ten years later, Dallas Lee, a butcher, and Charles Dixon, a clerk, were the wealthiest men with only $1,700 worth of property; Cary Nettles, an ante-bellum free black farmer, was close behind with $1,650 in property.[34]

Freedom before the war was not a necessary condition for doing well in the postwar period. Of the more prosperous free blacks reported in 1860, only two definitely reappear in the census of 1870; two others appear to have changed their names but retained the same occupations and property. Most of Hampton's ante-bellum free blacks were poorer than they had been in 1860; others had died or moved away. In one instance, however, the explanation for decline in wealth was a happy one. William Taylor had owned $1,200 of real property and $1,500 of personal property in 1860. Ten years later, he claimed no personal property because that $1,500 had represented his wife and child whom he had purchased but, under Virginia law, had been unable to free before the war.[35]

As Hampton blacks worked to gain political office and property they also strived to create those institutions and values within their community that would enable it to prosper. The community's enthusiasm for education continued unabated in 1870. Though illiteracy remained high among black adults, a larger proportion of black children than white attended schools in the county.[36] The five black churches of the county remained the core a-

round which black community activities centered. There was
much cooperation among the congregations on both temporal and
spiritual matters. Political meetings rotated among the several
churches. When First Baptist erected a new church, members of
the other congregations assisted in the fund raising and construction. Ministers often exchanged pulpits, and the Reverend William
Thorton of Zion Baptist preached the funeral sermon for the Reverend Taylor in the new First Baptist Church when the latter died
in 1873.[37]

Hampton's black community in 1870 included the criminal,
improvident, and incompetent elements that Armstrong described,
but it also contained the majority who were determined to improve their condition and were beginning to do so in very difficult
circumstances. As important, black Hampton had developed men
and women who could provide the leadership needed to guide the
community whether or not it received Northern assistance. Black
leadership in post-bellum Hampton was based on neither wealth
nor status, nor even membership in one of the old ante-bellum families. Members of such families as the Davises, Peakes, Nettles,
and Thortons remained prominent among Hampton's leaders, but
they were joined by newcomers. Some of them, like James and
George Fields, or R. M. Smith, had been refugees who had come
to Hampton aboard Union gunboats; all three would soon play important roles in the county. Other newcomers, like the Norton
brothers and Isaiah Lyons, were black Northerners who came to
seek their fortunes among the newly freed slaves; they, too, would
make important contributions to black Hampton in the post-Reconstruction era. The principal criteria for leadership in black
Hampton appeared to be ability, determination, and skill in working with both blacks and whites. The desire to do well permeated
black Hampton; only those who could foster that process could
command the community's respect.

In 1870 black Hampton confronted the problem of survival in
a hostile environment with only the semblance of federal protection. It seemed to face that prospect with little trepidation. Perhaps the source of that mood of optimism was the sense of pride
and self-respect that had evolved in the community during the difficult years of war and Reconstruction. Symbolic of that mood
was William Roscoe Davis, one of the original Hampton contraband. Davis never surrendered the dignity that had made him independent even as a slave. He threatened to whip any of his children who addressed their former owner as "master." When one

young white woman passed him on the streets of Hampton and greeted him as "Uncle Billy," he drew himself up to the full extent of his more than six feet of height and replied, "Madam, I am not your father's brother! The name is Davis—William Davis!"[39]

In 1861 the black people of Hampton had believed freedom was at hand only to be quickly disabused of that notion by hostile treatment from Union army officials. In 1865 they had believed freedom was securely theirs only to be disillusioned a second time. And once again it was primarily Northern officials who demonstrated how limited black freedom was to be. Northern whites set high goals for the newly freed slaves, conspired with former rebels to see that these goals could not be attained, and then condemned the freedmen for failing to make good use of their freedom.

The blacks of Hampton did not, at first, understand the situation. Cynicism and suspicion about the North did not come naturally to them. They believed Northern promises despite previous disappointments. They needed absolute proof of Northern indifference before they would lose faith. The Northerners whom they encountered did not hesitate long before providing it. In the three short years between 1865 and 1868, the Freedmen's Bureau reneged on its promise of land to provide freedmen with a secure economic base; it denied blacks the right to live where they chose; and it forced blacks into unfair labor contracts with their former owners. When suffrage was finally granted, the North refused to provide blacks the needed protection so they could exercise it freely. Many of the Northern civilians who proclaimed themselves allies of the freedmen proved equally undependable. Some bamboozled and cheated the naive blacks at every turn. And, as will be seen, even the most stalwart friends of the freedmen—the missionaires—began to withdraw from the South after 1868.

The Freedmen's Bureau, conceived by ex-slaves and missionaries as a tool for black uplift, proved instead to be an agency for pacification and economic restoration of the South, often at the freedmen's expense. The Bureau presumed to define the goals of freedmen without attention to whether its goals were in the best interests of—or even desired by—the blacks. The freed people were moved about by the Bureau like so many ciphers, a process inspired more by the desires of ex-rebels than the needs of the freedmen. Nowhere were the barriers to communication between Bureau and freedmen more evident than in the disappearance of blacks as individual people in the Bureau records. C. B. Wilder in 1865 could write "this man is personally known by me to be an honest and hardworking freedman."[39] Samuel Armstrong in 1868 apparently could not; certainly he did not. Quite the contrary, those blacks who showed initiative, who sought to organize their community independently of the Bureau, tended to be singled out for omission from Bureau recognition and assistance.

Blacks in Hampton did not share the general disillusion of their white allies when the Bureau began to wind down its activities in 1868. They had never had a voice in determining the Bureau's goals and methods; they felt less despair at the end of something that had never been theirs in the first place. Instead they began to work quietly, modestly, toward the attainment of their own goals within the context of the postwar Southern community in which they lived. The supreme irony of their situation was that blacks were beginning to accomplish and, certainly aiming for, those very goals that the Bureau and missionaries had advocated but that some now concluded blacks were ill-equipped to attain.

In the years after 1870, Samuel Chapman Armstrong would style his program at Hampton Institute as "Education for Life." The blacks of Hampton village had already received their advanced training in that curriculum under Armstrong, the Freedmen's Bureau assistant subcommissioner. Reconstruction proved to be the difficult, but necessary, culmination of the blacks' wartime education about Northern ambivalence toward them and the limits to the freedom permitted them. Thereafter they knew they would have to depend primarily upon themselves and to do things in their own way. That realization was what made Armstrong's Hampton Institute a success. More importantly, the blacks' determination enabled them to disprove Armstrong's dire predictions about their future—at least until the reality of their success, rather than the mere threat of it, forced white Hampton to react.

Freedom's Fleeting Triumph

The "Old South" passed in Hampton in 1861. What was called the "New South" took decades to arrive in the village. Although Virginia was restored to the Union in 1869, more than twenty years would pass before Hampton whites could securely declare themselves and their community a part of that new post-Reconstruction South. In the interim, black Hampton demonstrated what forms the "New South" might have taken had Northerners been more stalwart in their commitment to freedom and had blacks been less repressed in their efforts to exercise their newly won rights.

In the years between 1870 and 1890, blacks in Hampton took full advantage of their numerical superiority and of the insights they had gained about white power and politics during the war and Reconstruction. Blacks participated fully in the governance of their town and county; they saw to the education of their children; and, to a remarkable extent, they acquired what, to them, was the most precious symbol of freedom—property of their own. They achieved these things through hard work, and, more importantly, sophistication in the skillful forming and reforming of alliances with whites in the county.

Unlike many other areas of the New South, post-bellum Hampton possessed a politically, economically, and socially variegated white community. Each element of that community had differing interests, and each, in turn, often found it expedient to cast its lot with the blacks for the attainment of shared goals. The postwar black community included ex-slaves, those who were formerly "free Negroes," native-born blacks, and refugees from throughout Virginia. So, too, postwar white Hampton included many besides the old natives. There were Northerners who came South to do good and did so well that the capital-starved white natives never called them "carpetbaggers"—at least to their faces. There were also Union soldiers at Fortress Monroe and Union veterans at the integrated Soldiers' Home who discovered, in the post-bellum era, a concern for blacks they had never demonstrated during the war. And there were the missionary teachers who remained even after Reconstruction ended. Blacks found ways of working with all these groups at one time or another. In the process they proved that an interracial community in which all elements participated could succeed. None need necessarily like the other, but even in the face of long-standing antagonisms, cooperation worked better than overt hostility. Indeed, the blacks and whites of Hampton demonstrated that such a community might prosper more than ever before.

Black Hampton and Armstrong's Institute

In post-bellum Hampton, no black-white alliance proved more valuable to the freedmen than that with the missionary teachers who remained after the war. On the other hand, nothing more clearly illustrated the complexities of such alliances than the evolution of Hampton Institute, the school founded by these missionaries. Neither the blacks of the village nor the Northern white creators of the school changed their attitudes toward one another. Blacks continued to be suspicious of white motives and intentions. The Northern white teachers continued their drift toward greater paternalism and acquiescence to a permanently inferior status for blacks in American society. These suspicions and differing visions of the black future provoked continuing tension between blacks and whites associated with the school. But in the early years of the Institute, the two groups needed each other equally. Black Hampton needed a school of quality for its youth; it could not afford to provide one from its own resources. Institute teachers needed students already literate and already committed to at least some of the values that the missionaries held themselves. As a consequence, the whites were forced to operate the Institute in a fashion more responsive to black defined goals than some of its white founders intended.

The founding of Hampton Normal and Agricultural Institute was a direct consequence of the dilemma in which the American Missionary Association found itself in 1865. Final emancipation meant there were four million freedmen in need of education and religion. Even though the Freedmen's Bureau was prepared to help build schools, the demand for teachers alone far exceeded the resources of the AMA and its fellow benevolent societies. Moreover, the violent opposition to freed-men's education from unrepentant rebels made the position of missionary teachers already in the South increasingly untenable. Even in Virginia, schoolhouses were being burned and the "nigger" teachers driven from town by enraged whites.[1] A Norfolk paper, reflecting the prevailing white sentiment, gleefully, though prematurely, proclaimed, "The Negro 'schoolmarms' are gone, going, or to go, and we don't much care which, whereto, or how—whether it be to the more frigid regions of the northern zone; or to a still more torrid climate."[2]

Neither the AMA workers in Virginia nor their leaders in the North intended to abandon the ex-slaves, the Norfolk *Journal* to the contrary notwithstanding. Nevertheless, some accommodation with the new postwar realities of the South had to be found.[3] When the war ended, missionaries, like the blacks, had believed that freedom would be shored up and protected through the granting of land and political rights to freedmen. The land was, of course, never given and, by 1870, it appeared that blacks would be denied effective use of the franchise as well.

The growing Northern disinterest in the "Negro question" that had led to these developments was plaguing the AMA in a crucial fashion. By 1868 Northern white contributions to freedmen's aid organizations had all but ceased. George Whipple, corresponding secretary of the AMA, was forced to confide to agents in the field, "Our treasury is greatly overdrawn, our credit is used already as far as we dare go, and our daily receipts do not meet current expenses."[4] Some new way had to be found to continue the work of education and proselytization among blacks, a way that fit within the severe financial limitations of the Association. Missionaries and their leaders debated alternatives throughout the early years of Reconstruction. The AMA evolved a new negative vision of the freedmen and a method of operation which removed almost all missionaries from direct contact with the black masses. In the process, as the missionaries considered their options, they began to lose sight of the reason that had provoked the need for a new approach. Rather than focusing on the failure of white Americans to provide the needed funds for black uplift and advancement, the missionaries began to emphasize the faults in the victims of society's penuriousness.

The postwar direction of missionary understanding of the freedmen had been foreshadowed in Hampton well before the war's end. AMA workers there had begun to lose sight of the blacks as individuals and had taken to referring to them as one un-differentiated mass. The things they said about them, too, had be-gun to change. It was no longer the positive attributes of blacks, but their weaknesses which were emphasized. In 1865 Samuel Hunt had warned that "many Freedmen are ignorant, vicious and degraded."[5] In the years that followed, this came to be the predo-minant view among AMA workers.

Within this general trend of criticizing the freedmen for their weaknesses, there was an even more ominous change in missionary thinking. Most AMA workers, like Hunt himself, ascribed black in-adequacies to slavery, but increasingly, some missionary spokes-men discussed these failings as inherent to the black race, regard-less of slavery. The Reverend S. R. Dennen, for example, argued that "the warm and sensuous nature of the African race" needed the drill of the school "to steady and poise it,...to make it effec-tive."[6]

Reducing the problems of the freedmen to racial terms led lo-gically to the next serious change in the AMA's views. Black ad-vancement was to be measured by the gradual progress of the en-tire race rather than by the attainments of individual blacks. Sla-very had left the black race at a lower level of civilization than that of white men. With the aid of northern missionaries, blacks would be "released from the disabilities of bondage" and "some-where find and maintain [their] own appropriate social position." The goal was no longer equality but merely an unspecified "social position" appropriate to the black race.[7]

The AMA also came to agree with the prevailing wisdom in the North about the process of black achievement. The path of ad-vancement could not be controlled by government. The imperson-al forces of society would determine black accomplishment. "The irresistable progress of events in our country," the *American Mis-sionary* warned, "...portent for good or ill to this plastic and wait-ing people." It was for blacks themselves, with the help of the missionaries, to determine how far and how fast they could ad-vance.[8]

The romantic racialism of the early missionaries had given way to the more straightforward American racist variety. Fortunately, the missionaries did not act upon their racism in the same fashion as other whites. Indeed, their new view evolved gradually in their debate about how to best serve the freedmen given limited resour-ces. Moreover, the AMA's statements were a call to action, not ac-quiescence to the *status quo*. The future of the black race was "a

problem to be determined...by the measure of our Christian activity," argued the *American Missionary*. "Every day's neglect, or
every day's efforts, will do much to determine this solution."[9]

The American Missionary Association's experience with the
freedmen and its changing view of the nature of their problems
led inevitably to the solution upon which it finally settled. The
freedmen had to be prepared to educate themselves. The AMA
would consolidate its efforts in a small number of schools which
would train blacks to carry on the work of civilizing their race.[10]
To this end, the Association sought to provide the major black population centers with teacher training schools. During 1867 and
1868, it founded eight such schools in the South. Normal schools
were opened in Macon, Savannah, and Atlanta, Georgia; in Charles-
ton, South Carolina; Louisville, Kentucky; Nashville, Tennessee;
Talledega, Alabama; and Hampton, Virginia. At most of these
schools, the missionary teachers worked enthusiastically to make
them first-rate institutions of higher learning, even though they
all began with students and curriculums at the grammar school level. The course of the Normal School at Hampton, however,
proved to be rather different largely because of its principal, Samuel Chapman Armstrong.[11]

The Peninsula of Virginia was a natural choice for the location
of one of the AMA's new normal schools. The Association's work
with freedmen had begun there in 1861; Hampton had a large and,
relatively speaking, well-educated black population. The missionaries and teachers at Hampton proposed the idea of a black college
for the area as soon as the war had ended. C. B. Wilder and H. C.
Percy, superintendent of Freedmen Schools in Norfolk, supported
the idea enthusiastically. Real progress toward the creation of a
school, however, came only after the arrival of Armstrong.[12]

As Armstrong had grown more disillusioned with the prospects
of the Freedmen's Bureau, he had turned to education as the most
likely means of black advancement. What was needed was "a tender, judicious and patient, yet vigorous educational system" for
blacks. Armstrong shared with many of the missionaries the growing belief that the freedman's problems were more the result of his
weaknesses than of white opposition. Writing in the Hampton
catalogue, he argued:

What are [his] vices? They are improvidence, low ideas of
honor and morality, and a general lack of directive energy,

judgment and foresight.... His deficiencies of character are, I believe, worse for him and the world than his ignorance. But with these deficiencies are docility and enthusiasm for improvement and a perseverance in the pursuit of it, which forms a basis of great hope.[13]

When Armstrong heard of the AMA's plans to build a college in his district, he wrote George Whipple promising his full support and cooperation: "only colored men can do the work of penetrating and permeating the country with schools; we must have colored teachers as soon as possible—and a Normal school wherein to prepare them...a sort of manual labor institution. There is now nothing of the sort."[14]

The black man's chief problem, Armstrong argued, was his passivity. He needed a system of "tender violence" to "rouse him." That educational system could not follow the traditional college format; Armstrong was convinced that "more conceptions of a higher plane of life" would not "elevate" the freedmen. The black man needed, above all, to acquire "habits of labor." "The demand for poets and orators is in a fair way of fulfillment," the prospective principal believed, "that for men of tremendous energy is well-nigh hopeless. Improvidence and laziness must be overcome by some propelling force; hence the manual labor feature of this school." The trouble with the black man was not his inability to learn but his unwillingness to work. Armstrong's goal, therefore, was "to make of them not accomplished scholars, but to build up character and manhood."[15]

Armstrong, like the missionaries, was not unappreciative of the unique attributes possessed by the blacks. Returning from a black church service in 1878, he wrote to his wife of the "natural eloquence" of black preachers. "It makes the matter of civilization a puzzle," he commented. "Should we educate them out of all of this...that was needed to carry them through slavery?" But such doubts seldom plagued Armstrong. He had an unshakable faith in the superiority of his own culture; backward peoples had to be taught how to live in that culture. If the black man's "natural eloquence" survived the process of civilization, well and good; if not, it was the acquisition of civilization that was more important.[16]

Armstrong's vision for Hampton Institute was very grand indeed. Unlike other AMA-founded schools, it would not cater merely to the local black population. Armstrong intended, quite literally, to educate the whole black race by creating the people who would be its teachers and leaders. The need, he felt, was urgent. Hampton

> should strive quite as much to be a center of moral as of intellectual light, for the deficiency of moral force and self-respect are the chief misfortunes of the race....The plastic character of the race puts them completely under the control of their leaders....A most unfortunate result of this blind leading the blind is already seen in the belief that political rights are better obtained by political warfare than by advancement in knowledge and in ability to care for themselves. How to withstand these dangers...is one of the problems most urgently pressing on Southern society.[17]

Here was the basic purpose Armstrong saw for Negro education. The black man, in his current state of ignorance, was a danger to white society. The goal of educating the black man was at least as much the preservation of existing society as the edification of the Negro.

It was clear to Armstrong that the "temporal salvation of the colored race, for some time to come, is to be won out of the ground."[18] The need, then, was for a school to prepare self-respecting leaders with the proper "moral force" and with the willingness to concentrate on teaching agriculture rather than politics. "Political warfare," the standard weapon of American democracy, was forbidden to the uncivilized blacks. They could use it only when white men deemed them ready.

To achieve these goals Armstrong proposed the creation of a school which taught agricultural and mechanical skills as well as academic subjects. In this way students could earn money to finance their education, supplement their low teachers' pay in later life, and, most importantly, learn and teach the dignity of labor. Armstrong also insisted upon coeducation. He believed immorality to be a major weakness of the black race; by learning together under the careful supervision of white teachers, the students would learn proper moral conduct and develop mutual respect. "Those on whom equally depends the future of their people," Armstrong stated in defense of the idea of coeducation, "must be given an equal chance." Most important of all would be the "home" aspect of the Institute. Hampton Institute was to be a "little world" in which all the proper attitudes of morality, diligence, thrift and responsibility were to be assiduously cultivated.[19]

At Hampton Institute the classical curriculum of the traditional college would be omitted. Armstrong did not want to educate his students out of sympathy with the people they must teach. Besides, he argued:

> An English course embracing reading and elocution, geography and mathematics, history, the sciences, the study of the mother-tongue and its literature, the leading principles of mental and moral science, and or political economy would, I think ...exhaust the best powers of nineteen-twentieths of those who would for years come to the Institute.[20]

Armstrong's ideas for the new school at Hampton merely carried the new AMA approach on freedmen's problems to its logical conclusion. But seeing the potential consequences of their approach boldly stated caused many missionaries to blanch. The Association workers had initially welcomed Armstrong as one of their own, but his plans for the new normal school forced a reconsideration of that attitude. Though circumstances of Reconstruction had caused the AMA to stray rather far from its original commitment to Christian egalitarianism, it was not prepared to acknowledge its apostasy as openly as Armstrong proposed. In the minds of most Hampton missionaries and teachers, Armstrong might be right as to what blacks could do immediately, but he was wrong in constructing a predetermined barrier beyond which a black student could not pass. A good "English course" was adequate for the moment, but times and students would change; no upper limit should be placed upon the curriculum. The missionaries might not swear to the equality of the black man, but they believed he should be encouraged to achieve as much as he could.[21]

The disagreement over the kind of school that Hampton Institute should become was intensified by evidence that Armstrong wished to control it. He besieged the AMA offices in New York with messages of advice and encouragement. As a site for the school, the general proposed the purchase of "Little Scotland," a 125-acre farm on which the Butler Freedmen's School and the Chesapeake Female Seminary were located. In a long letter to George Whipple, Armstrong also carefully outlined the details of what the new school's curriculum should be. When Whipple hesi-

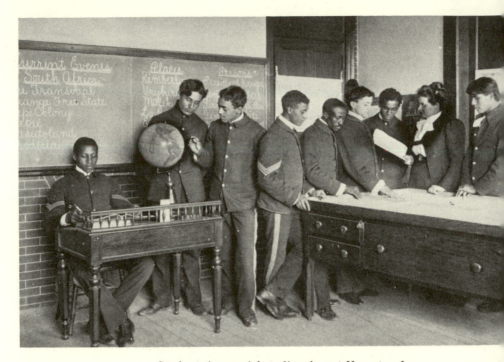

*Students in a social studies class at Hampton In-
stitute, ca. 1890. Note the uniforms, required of
all male students, and the Indian students in the
picture. Many Indian students at Hampton were
of mixed black-Indian parentage. Also note the
lesson on South Africa being taught. (Courtesy
of the Hampton Institute Archives)*

tated and some of the village's missionaries objected to the voca-
tional rather than academic orientation in Armstrong's design, the
young general announced that he would go north to raise money
to purchase the land on his own. Faced with such determination,
Whipple acceded and creation of the new school was announced.[22]

There was widespread support for the creation of Hampton Institute; the same could not be said for the idea of making Armstrong its principal. Though Armstrong clearly desired the position,
it was first offered to another Williams College graduate whose
philosophy on Negro education was apparently more in keeping
with that of the Association. This candidate, E. B. Parsons, turned
down the job, and George Whipple could not ignore the obvious
second choice. Armstrong himself had been confident that he

would gain the post all along. In the interim while Parsons considered the job, Armstrong had rejected an offer to become president of Howard University because he believed its emphasis on academic education to be inappropriate for most blacks. Whipple offered the principalship to Armstrong; the latter accepted with alacrity and set out to make Hampton Institute an expression of his understanding of Negro education.[23]

There had been much debate between Armstrong and the missionaries over what kind of school Hampton Institute would be, but, ironically, on at least one count the veteran missionaries were not as different from Samuel Armstrong as they flattered themselves to believe. They implicitly agreed that the Institute would be a *white* school for *black* students. Those to receive education were to be freedmen, but what they would learn and how they would learn it was for their white teachers to decide. Despite the missionaries' confession of fiscal bankruptcy and acknowledgement that the work of black uplift must be carried out primarily by blacks themselves, Hampton's blacks were never consulted on how best to proceed. The Peninsula's black communities had within them a few men of considerable formal education such as physician Daniel Norton and lawyer Robert Norton, both active and increasingly successful politicians.[24] These communities also included many men of great intelligence and much influence within their black constituencies such as ministers William Taylor, William Davis, William Thorton, and landowners Thomas Peake and Cary Nettles. The advice of these men was never solicited as discussions over the normal school evolved. Both Armstrong and the veteran missionaries presumed that only they were competent to determine the structure of the new Institute.

The few freedmen who learned of Hampton Institute's circumscribed curriculum and peculiar vision of black needs were acrid in their denunciations. William Roscoe Davis viewed the idea of teaching a people, who had been slaves all their lives, how to work as "the height of foolishness." "If Negroes don't get any better education than Armstrong is giving them," he is reported to have said, "[then] they may as well have stayed in slavery!"[25]

Such criticisms of the new normal school did not deter Principal Armstrong. In April of 1868, Hampton Agricultural and Normal Institute opened its doors. It had five teachers and fifteen students, most of whom were from families of the village's black elite, including the family of William Roscoe Davis.[26] Students were to be of "good character," be able to read and write at the fifth-grade level, and be between the ages of fifteen and twenty-five. Admissions procedures were lax; students usually appeared at the school, were briefly interviewed by a teacher, and accepted "on trial." Those who had a trade were admonished to "bring your tools along."[27]

Once the Institute was opened, Armstrong did not forgive those who had initially objected to his design for the school. Missionaries who insisted that blacks should have the opportunity to receive the same education as whites were considered by Armstrong to be softheaded. Such people, he thought, were ignoring the realities of the black future in the post-Reconstruction South. His solution was to make Hampton Institute independent from AMA control, and he moved quickly.[28] Never one to brook much dissent from either whites or blacks, Armstrong first set out to rid himself and the Institute of those who had differed with him. Shortly after the school opened, he dismissed the three veteran missionary teachers in his faculty of five. The key to independence was financial security, so for four years Armstrong directed most of his efforts to giving Hampton an independent financial base. In 1872, with the unheralded help of black legislators like Daniel Norton, Armstrong secured one-third of Virginia's Morrill Act Land Grant funds and his goal was assured. From that date, the Institute was virtually independent of the American Missionary Association.[29]

In independence, Hampton Institute prospered; academic standards rose and, by 1887, the curriculum was roughly equivalent to that of a high school. Students received degrees after three years. Seniors were required to do practice teaching in the Butler School on the Institute campus. Three new programs—agriculture, mechanics, and commerce—were incorporated into the curriculum. Each of these was combined with some courses in the academic or "Normal" program.[30]

As the curriculum evolved, so did the role of manual training in the Institute. Students had, at first, spent each morning on the school farm or in the kitchens and laundry; afternoons were devoted to classes and the evenings to study.[31] Such a program quickly proved inadequate both in terms of mastery of academic skills and of proficiency at mechanical or agricultural techniques. Armstrong encountered the problem experienced by all earlier manual labor schools. At Oneida, Oberlin, Lane, and at contemporaneously founded Cornell, manual labor foundered on the shoals of ineffective student labor. School farms did not require the masses of students available to work at particular times, but did need constant supervision and care which part-time workers could not give.[32] At the colleges in which manual labor was merely the means for students to finance their educations or to get physical exercise, the system was gradually abandoned. But at Hampton, experience in manual labor was an end in itself. To Armstrong, the cost of manual labor training for blacks was irrelevant. "Of course it cannot pay in a *money* way," he argued, "but it will pay in a *moral* way. It will make them men and women as nothing else will. It is the only way to make them Christians."[33]

The fact remained, however, that Hampton was an unendowed school for impoverished students. It could not operate its manual training program at a loss. Armstrong's compromise was the expedient and practical one. With his usual deftness at combining educational ideas with practical necessity, he created a "Night School." Students of the Night School could not enter the regular Normal program for lack of money or academic preparation. They worked a full day for the school and took classes at night. Thus, they were able to save money and get the academic background necessary for enrollment in the Normal School. The Institute profited equally from the system. It now had the full-time labor required to make its various shops and farms financially tenable.

Under the system, regular Hampton students worked one to two full days a week and devoted the rest of their time to study. Regular students worked mostly in the laundry, kitchens, and dining halls. Night students operated the more complex shops such as the school printing office, blacksmith and wheelwright shops, the sawmill, and the farm. It was a neat plan; by 1884 Hampton's manual labor system was working efficiently. Of a total of 654 students, 228, or over one-third, were night students doing the full-time labor of the industrial departments and farms. Most of these night students, it appears, never actually completed the regular Normal program.[34]

The manual labor program was just one method in Armstrong's system to make his students Christians. Among the factors which made Hampton unique was the school's intensive program to indoctrinate its students in the proper way of life. The teachers at Hampton were educated, middle-class Northerners; naturally their concept of the "proper way of life" was the way that they lived themselves. Thus, they stressed to their pupils the need to acquire middle-class styles of behavior, perhaps more intently than they emphasized middle-class goals and aspirations.

This process, when put into practice, meant the Hampton student's life was programmed from "rising bell" at 5:15 A.M. to "lights out" at 9:30 P.M. They attended chapel twice daily. Male students were organized into a cadet corps. Uniforms were required of all male students, which was a boon to most of them as they could not afford other decent clothing. The corps marched to classes and meals; inspection of each student and his room was performed daily. Women students were not as regimented, but were as closely supervised by their teachers and dormitory matrons. The girls were taught to cook and sew, to set a proper table, to acquire all the graces that would make a good housewife—or housekeeper. Habits of neatness and cleanliness, never required of many slaves, were insisted upon for both sexes.[35] To keep the little world of Hampton Institute free from contamination, students were permitted to leave campus only one day a week, a day carefully selected so that it did not coincide with village market day when the forces of corruption were about.[36]

Hampton Institute student teaching freedpeople, ca. 1880. (Courtesy of the Hampton Institute Archives)

There were enough problems at Hampton to justify this rigid scheduling and close supervision of students. Many black students of the Institute arrived with standards of behavior that contrasted sharply with those of the Northern teachers. Despite all precautions, there were constant disciplinary problems in the formative years of Hampton. Though few records survive of the number of expulsions, Armstrong's letters mention them frequently, and they were usually for causes of "immorality." Two students were expelled in 1878 after being "corrupted by outside girls" at the "very gate" of the Institute. Two others followed shortly for peeking into the bathrooms of the girls' dormitory. Some students proved so incorrigible that the local civil authorities had to intervene. In November 1885, for example, two Institute students were incarcerated in the local jail, one for "cutting with a knife," the other for "pure, unadulterated badness." "The darky," Armstrong wrote, despairingly, "is an ugly thing to manage."[37]

In explaining his work at Hampton, Armstrong argued that, "the interest in schools like this is that the teacher has a far more decisive formative work to do than among more advanced races."[38] Such a philosophy gave Hampton teachers the right to intrude much more intimately into the lives of their students than was acceptable even in the paternalistic Northern white colleges. They did so with considerable intensity, paticularly in the area of goals formation. Their students, on the other hand, whose options had long been limited to being a good slave or a bad slave, were more receptive to the advice of their well-meaning teachers than Northern white students would have been.

There is no better example of what this "formative work" meant in practice than Samuel Armstrong's own role at Hampton. He taught a course of moral philosophy, concentrating on advice as to the "practical conduct of life." At Sunday evening chapel he would deliver his "Talks." On one such occasion he advised his students: "Spend your life doing what you can do well. If you can teach, teach. If you can't teach, but can cook well, do that. If a man can black boots better than anything else, what had he better do? Black boots."[39] Do what you can do well. Sound general advice, but, like the purposes of Hampton itself, seemingly circumscribed to fit the needs of a "less advanced" race.

In his educational practices, Armstrong was a skillful borrower, using, for example, his mentor Mark Hopkins of Williams as the model for some of his own roles at Hampton. But in the vital area of public support and finances, Armstrong showed signs of original

Samuel Chapman Armstrong. This is his official portrait as principal of Hampton Institute, probably made after his stroke ca. 1890. (Courtesy of the Hampton Institute Archives)

Early Hampton Institute with Virginia Hall, its earliest permanent brick structure, on the left. The principal's house is in the middle, and the original chapel is on the right. (Courtesy of the Hampton Institute Archives)

genius. When Hampton opened in 1868, there was still considerable Southern opposition to Negro education. With consummate skill, the general charmed important members of Virginia's political hierarchy, thereby winning one-third of its Land Grant funds.[40]

The general employed similar tactics of charm and persuasiveness in fund-raising among Northerners. He assiduously cultivated his friendships with wartime colleagues like O. O. Howard and James Garfield, both of whom became Hampton trustees. He won the support of Mark Hopkins at Williams, and of prominent Northern families like the Bacons and Woolseys. Rebecca Bacon, daughter of Leonard Bacon, minister of First Church in New Haven, and Jane Stuart Woolsey, of New York, were among Armstrong's first faculty appointments at Hampton.[41] Armstrong used all of these contacts to raise money for the school, occasionally to the irritation of the victim. Rebecca Bacon, for example, grew increasingly irritated at the use of her name for fund-raising purposes and finally resigned in protest.[42] Such setbacks did not phase the energetic young Armstrong. He was ever on the look out for new ways to finance his venture at Hampton. Following the example of Fisk University's Jubilee Choir, he organized the Hampton Singers who, through concerts in Northern cities, "sang up" Virginia Hall, the girls' dormitory.[43]

Perhaps Armstrong's most notable achievement in public relations was winning Southern white approbation for his Institute. The general assured Southerners that his graduates would teach Negroes to become better workers, not political activists. He rejected the thought of potential conflict between the races, stressing instead signs of progress and cooperation, and criticizing blacks who failed to work hard and quietly. He agreed that the white Southerner understood and could handle the Negro better than Northerners, thus disarming Southerners angered by the meddling of egalitarian-minded Yankees. He would never say that the black was *innately* inferior; Negroes were inferior at present, but, he stressed, they were "improvable." Whether they could ever be improved to the level of equality with white men, Armstrong never said publicly; indeed, he seems never to have been certain about the idea himself.[44]

Armstrong's combination of charm and sympathy for the white Southerner's problem worked superbly. The Norfolk *Journal* which, in 1867, had so caustically heralded the departure of "Yankee schoolmarms" found Hampton Institute much more to its liking. In 1871 it wrote, "the place indicates the most perfect system and the proficiency of the scholars demonstrates a higher capacity for knowledge than is generally accorded the negro [*sic*]." Of Armstrong, it said he "is an active, energetic man, polite, gentlemanly and dignified in his manner,...admirably fitted for the duties of his office."[45]

Thus by 1872, the importance and success of Armstrong's work at Hampton was apparent. The school was financially secure, its work was heralded by Northerners and Southerners alike. Hampton graduates were anxiously sought by school systems all over the South. By 1880, Hampton graduates were teaching nearly 10,000 Southern black children.[46]

That Hampton Institute was a success is undeniable, but it is well that Southern papers like the Norfolk *Journal* did not probe too deeply for the causes of that success. The reality of what went on at the Institute contrasted sharply with the public image that Armstrong carefully created. Hampton Institute was not, in fact, a school of which white Southerners would have approved for two reasons: Samuel Armstrong was less than candid in his portrayal of the school's mission, and blacks, especially those from the town, used their educations at Hampton to pursue goals greatly at variance with the Institute's public philosophy.

Armstrong was not entirely disingenuous in what he told his Northern white benefactors and Southern white supporters. He was serious when he argued that the freedmen, in their present state, represented a danger to Southern society. He was equally serious when he criticized blacks for their "improvidence, low ideas of honor and morality," and when he cited "passivity" as the freedmen's chief problem. On the other hand, Armstrong's supporters overlooked—and the general chose not to emphasize—the other half of his message, i.e., Hampton Institute was designed to correct these weaknesses in the black race. It was intended to make black people self-respecting men and women. That it also tended to encourage them to strive toward professional careers and political involvement was a consequence of which Armstrong was clearly aware and about which he said very little.

Though Armstrong never gave up his habit of referring to blacks as "darkies" in his private correspondence, he did much at Hampton Institute to guarantee that his students never thought of themselves as such. In 1874, Armstrong established a Senior Cottage for male students, complete with its own student court to oversee disciplinary problems. When one student, Dennis F. Douglas, was expelled without the case coming before the student court, its members took umbrage and wrote a letter of protest to Armstrong:

> Sir:
> We as members of the Senior Cottage and its court feel that the case of D. F. Douglas was not carried to you in its proper form and that it was not by consent of the court but rather by a great abridgement of our rights, we therefore petition for said case for a legal trial. We feel that our rights should be respected as long as we are recognized as a court but we cannot think that our court has any authority where cases are wrestled from us as at present.[47]

Twenty-two members of the student court, including the nineteen-year-old Booker T. Washington, signed the letter. Armstrong, always one to insist that rules be obeyed, admitted his error; Dennis Douglas was reinstated, graduated with his class, and was one of the commencement speakers.[48] Of equal note is that Armstrong so respected the students who had reminded him of the rules that within five years, he hired five of them as staff members of the Institute. Two of the five, Booker T. Washington and Warren Logan, also became principal and treasurer, respectively, of Tuskegee Institute. A sixth, W. M. Reid, became one of three curators of Hampton Institute, appointed by the governor of Virginia to oversee the schools' use of Land Grant funds.[49]

The women students at Hampton Institute showed no more inclination towards docility than their male colleagues. When Armstrong proposed that women also do farm work to help finance their educations, the protest from the women students was so spirited that the general beat a hasty retreat. The idea, he explained, had been to permit women to *volunteer* for farm work. Moreover, they would work in a garden plot behind Virginia Hall, the girls' dormitory, not in the fields with male students. The purpose, Armstrong assured his indignant female students, was "to give them an experience in raising flowers and vegetables, which will be of value...in after life [*sic*]."[50]

Armstrong not only tolerated assertiveness by students on campus, he encouraged advanced education for his best graduates. Again, Armstrong's actions were not entirely contrary to his public statements. He had claimed that the education he offered at Hampton would "exhaust the best powers of nineteen-twentieths of those who would for years come to the Institute."[51] The actual figures were closer to nine-tenths. Of the 723 graduates between 1871 and 1890 for whom records exist, 67 went directly from the Institute to Northern colleges and universities. Seventeen others went first to Northern prep schools and then on to Northern colleges. Several others "read law" with Northern attorneys and became lawyers themselves.[52]

These students did not pursue advanced education in defiance of their mentor at Hampton Institute but rather with his enthusiastic encouragement. Most of them received their admission and scholarships at places like Oberlin, University of Pennsylvania, Boston University, Harvard, and Yale through the mediation of Samuel Armstrong. Some, like George Washington Fields, became professionals more from Armstrong's insistence than their own initiative. After graduating from Hampton, Fields obtained several jobs as a manservant in prominent Northern white families, all of which were arranged for him by Armstrong. His last position was with Governor Cornell of New York who encouraged him to enter the law school at the University named for the governor. Though at first timid, Fields finally submitted to the persuasion of Cornell

Booker T. Washington as a young man at Hampton Institute, ca. 1879-81. (Courtesy of the Hampton Institute Archives)

and Armstrong. He went on to become Cornell University's first black law graduate.[53]

Armstrong did not limit his efforts to aid black people to the boundaries of his Institute. Nothing better illustrates the contrast between the general's public statements for white consumption and private acts for black advancement than the affection with which he is still regarded by black Hampton residents who knew him. Their affection grew from the valuable services Armstrong and his Institute provided to the community. The first hospital in Hampton, Dixie Hospital, named after Institute teacher Alice Bacon's horse rather than the South's Lost Cause, was founded as part of the Institute's nursing school.[54] For many years it was the Institute's student fire department that helped save the village from the conflagrations that continually plagued the business district.[55]

Most important, however, was the role that Armstrong himself played. The general had begun his career in Hampton by presiding over the eviction of freedmen from rebel-owned land, but he never gave up his belief that black progress was inextricably linked to the ownership of property. Since blacks would not receive land from the government, Armstrong set out to aid them in acquiring it through purchase. Until crippled by a stroke, it was Armstrong's habit to ride through the black sections of the village each day, stopping at each house if its occupants were out-of-doors. He justified his stop by asking to water his horse. Once dismounted, he asked the residents two questions: did they own the house in which they lived, and were their children in school? If they replied negatively to the first inquiry, he instructed them on procedures for buying property, on where property might be for sale, and on how to save money for the purchase. If they replied negatively to his second question, he offered a more immediate solution. Taking any of the youngsters who were of school age up on his horse, he delivered them to the Butler Freedmen's School on the Institute campus. Many a black Hampton youngster's first memory of school was arriving there aboard Armstrong's white stallion.[56]

Armstrong's solicitude for black well-being and his encouragement of black initiative appear to have been entirely sincere; but, as was always the case with Armstrong, his actions were practical and expedient as well. The Institute needed black support as badly as blacks needed the education it offered. In large part, needed black support was political in nature, and it was available to the school primarily because Hampton graduates did exactly what

Armstrong professed to believe—among white Southerners—blacks should not do, that is, enter politics.

Though the vast majority of Hampton Institute graduates did pursue careers in education, those graduates from the village of Hampton showed a marked inclination to follow other pursuits or to combine teaching with such pursuits. The preferred professions were the ministry and the law, both of which usually led to political involvement as well. By 1890, all of the black ministers in Hampton with advanced training were graduates of Hampton Institute. Of these, the Reverend Young Jackson also served on the County Board of Supervisors, and the Reverend Richard Spiller was a dominant figure in the county Republican organization.[57]

Black officeholders in Hampton and the adjacent counties were usually graduates of the Institute, if they had college degrees at all. In addition to Jackson and Spiller, there were M. D. Wright, lawyer and commissioner of revenue for Warwick County, Edward Canady, merchant and commissioner of revenue for James City County, Luke B. Phillips, merchant and city councilman in Hampton, James Fields, lawyer, commonwealth attorney for Warwick County, and member of the Virginia House of Delegates, and John Robinson, lawyer and member of the Virginia House of delegates—all of them graduates of Hampton Institute. Two other graduates, William Ash and Peter Carter, served in the Virginia legislature, representing counties outside the Peninsula.[58]

Graduates of the Institute who remained in the village and did not enter politics prospered as well. Several became merchants. Some, like A. W. E. Bassette, a lawyer, acquired several pieces of property in Hampton and Newport News. Another, John Mallory Phillips, founded his own seafood company. In 1887, when the directors of the black-owned People's Building and Loan Association first met, the gathering was very much a Hampton Institute reunion; eight of the fifteen directors were graduates of the Institute.[59]

These graduates of Hampton Institute maintained close alliances with other black political and economic leaders on the Peninsula, and through their efforts the Institute received many benefits. It was black legislator James Bland who, in 1870, introduced the bill which ultimately led to the Institute's receipt of Land Grant funds. R. M. Smith of Hampton led the continuing and unsuccessful fight to win yearly state appropriations for the Institute. It was the black delegates in the legislature and black merchants in Hampton village who led the defense in refuting charges in 1886 and 1887 that the Institute's various shops constituted an illegal restraint on local trade. In keeping with his pragmatic strategy, General Armstrong never publicly acknowledged the assistance he received from black politicians, both graduates and nongraduates. On the other hand, it was undoubtedly the general himself who did much of the orchestrating of these efforts.

Hampton Institute was more than a white school for black students. It was a partnership between well-meaning, if paternalistic, whites and able, assertive blacks. The Institute was also very much a part of the black Hampton community. It was black Hampton's window to the world, and that community showed itself disposed to look out long and carefully. There is perhaps no better illustration of the differing directions in which black and white Hampton were moving, nor of the Institute's role in that process, than a strange juxtaposition of events in the spring and summer of 1886. During that period, black Hampton enjoyed the visits to the Institute of a German navy training vessel; of General Fisk, founder of Fisk University and commissioner of Indian Affairs; and, most impressively, the visit of ten United States senators and representatives who came for Anniversary Day. Seated on the platform with these luminaries was Hampton village's own William Thorton, former slave and contraband, who delivered an address on "The Old and New Virginia." During that same period, white Hampton enjoyed the highlight of its summer social season: the annual jousting contest between the younger white men of the village, complete with armor, lances, and "fair maidens cheering on their heroes."[60]

The partnership between the Institute and the black community would remain equal only so long as the community could contribute as much to the school as it received in benefits, and so long as the Institute was led by a man who had the wisdom to make the subtle distinctions between what he *said* and what he *did*.[61] Both of these conditions would pass as part of the general reduction of black rights in Virginia after 1890. But for two decades, between 1870 and 1890, the partnership prospered, as did the partners. Together they provided a model for what could be done between blacks and whites in the South.

Black Hampton: A Propertied Community

During the two decades after 1870, blacks in Hampton pursued other major goals as well as education. Two of the most important were finding acceptable employment and acquiring property. Blacks made much progress toward these goals, in large part because of the ways in which war and Reconstruction had altered life on the lower Peninsula in general, and in Elizabeth City County in particular.

Hampton village in the 1870s had more the appearance of a new settlement on the western frontier than that of a two hundred-year-old Southern town. It had been burned to the ground during the war and even as late as 1886 was described as "a straggling collection of small wooden houses and shanties." Its unlighted streets were impassable mud bogs in winter and spring, changing into choking alleys of dust in the drier months. Merchants were forced to keep their goods behind closed doors to protect them from the filth of the streets, but they usually found even this measure inadequate against the dust and mud. Only the restored courthouse and St. John's Episcopal Church gave hints of the elegance that had once typified the village center.[1] In the new settlement of Phoebus near Fortress Monroe, conditions were somewhat better. Phoebus had become the center for tourism in the county; located there were the new resort hotels, including the splendid Hygeia Hotel which catered to Northern visitors seeking Hampton's mild winter climate.[2]

Many other characteristics of Hampton also recalled life further to the west. Hampton was a garrison town, deriving much of its business from the presence of military people at Fortress Monroe and the Soldiers' Home. It was also a boom town; much

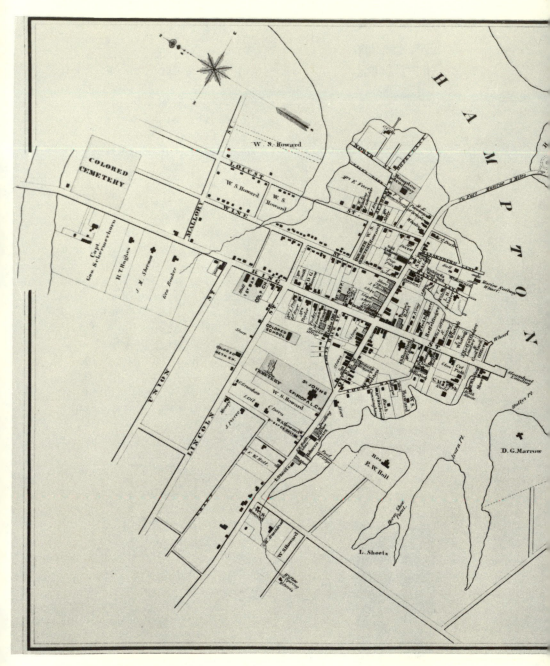

Hampton City, 1877

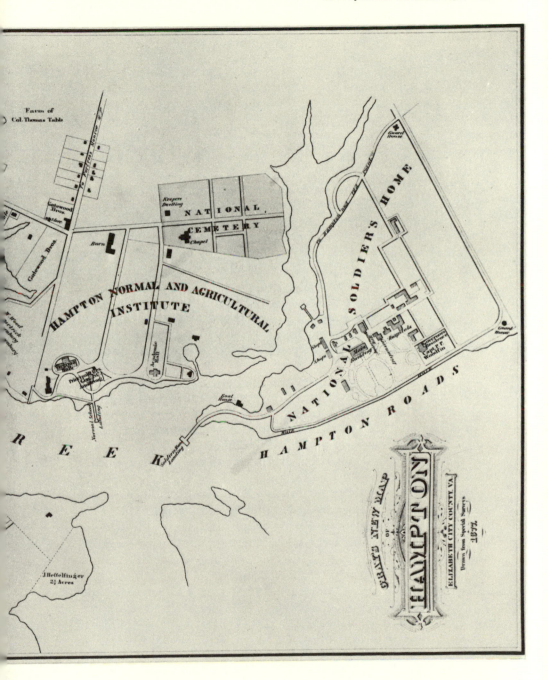

new investment was coming in, new buildings, churches, and schools were springing up. Town merchants, black and white, were unashamed boosters of their village. When the two main streets, King and Queen, were finally paved, these businessmen were reminded of the building of Rome's aqueducts; and when the railway and electric lights came to Hampton in the late 1880's, these merchants pronounced their village to be one of the "the leading cities in the South."[3]

Rapid growth tends to foster social disorder, and here again, Hampton shared much with the West. It was a wide open town catering to the wants of soldiers and tourists. A black minister's daughter, obeying her father's injunction that she keep her eyes to the ground whenever she passed a saloon or bawdyhouse, recalled that these establishments were so numerous that she never saw Hampton's skyline until she was a grown woman![4] Gambling, drunkenness, and violence kept black sheriff Andrew Williams and his deputies constantly occupied. "Floating crap games" were especially popular among town blacks; "shootouts" between deputies and players frequently occurred when one of these games was located. Violence was both interracial and intraracial; the preferred weapons were fists or knives, and the preferred occasions were village market days. A particularly cruel but popular sport among young men of the village was mugging the disabled veterans of the Soldiers' Home. These unfortunate survivors of the Civil War patronized the village eating places in search of supplements to their tasteless diet of boiled meat, boiled potatoes, and boiled fruit (usually prunes) served at the Home. They also stopped at the saloons, and once intoxicated, they became prime victims for the town rowdies.[5]

One final characteristic of post-bellum Hampton also recalled the frontier: the village was a community of newcomers. In 1860 the county had contained 5,597 people, 2,417 of whom were black, 3,180 of whom were white. In 1870 it contained 8,308 people, 5,471 of whom were black, 2,837 of whom were white. Of the more than 3,000 additional blacks in 1870, most were refugees who had arrived during the Civil War. The white population had actually declined between 1860 and 1870; its composition had changed as well. Of the 2,837 whites in the county in 1870, 376 were foreign born, 672 were from states other than Virginia. In short, more than one-third of the white population, more than one-half of the black population, and more than one-half of the total population had not lived in the county in 1860.

Because Hampton was a military town, hundreds of other new-comers came and left again without appearing in the decennial population count.[6]

This trend toward an increasing proportion of outsiders dwell-ing in the county continued in 1880 when the population was 10,687, 6,531 black, 4,156 white; and in 1890 when the popula-tion was 16,168, 7,890 black and 8,278 white. Most important for black life in the county was that the white population grew by 65 percent between 1870 and 1890; the black population grew by only 40 percent. By 1890, whites outnumbered blacks for the first time since the Civil War.[7]

As important as the new numbers of people that came to Hampton were the new resources that they brought with them. Most of the whites came to seek their fortunes and many suc-ceeded. While newcomers were not always welcomed by the na-tive white Hamptonians, their money certainly was. The capital of these Northern "carpetbaggers" financed the revitalization of Hampton's economy.[8]

One aspect of this economic resurgence was in agriculture. Agricultural goods, especially fresh fruits and vegetables, were shipped across the Roads to Norfolk. From there they were ex-ported daily to New York aboard Old Dominion Line steamships which made the run to New York in twenty-four hours. In the late spring of each year, ships sailed daily loaded with nothing but fresh strawberries bound for the New York and Philadelphia mar-kets.[9]

Northerners, on their arrival in Hampton, had invested heavily in land. Native whites, ruined by the war and faced with over-whelming tax bills, were happy to sell. By 1870, Northern and foreign immigrants owned $208,725 worth of real property, $175,650 worth of personal property. Fully one-third of the com-munity's wealth and 85 percent of its personal property was owned by these white newcomers. As a result, agricultural goods being exported were grown primarily on land owned by these Northern newcomers. The Old Dominion Steamship Line upon which these goods were exported was also largely owned by Nor-therners.[10]

One of the reasons Northerners stayed in Hampton was its pleasant climate, and they encouraged their friends back home to come and sample the fine weather. The result was a booming tourist business in the county. Friends and relatives of the new-comers, families of soldiers stationed at the Fortress or Veterans'

Home, came to stay in the new hotels and boarding houses of the county. Foremost among these was the refurbished Hygeia Hotel adjacent to the Fortress, managed by Harrison Phoebus, a Marylander and Union army veteran.[11] Negroes were not welcomed at the Hygeia (other than as servants), so many enterprising blacks opened boardinghouses and restaurants which catered to blacks visiting relatives at the Soldiers' Home and to the seasonal workers who came during the strawberry and oyster harvesting seasons.[12]

The most important business in post-Reconstruction Hampton was seafood processing. Fishing and oystering were not new to the area, but under the direction of the Northern immigrants, they became major industries with fleets of ships, canning factories, and wholesale outlets as far away as England and Oregon. J. S. Darling, a New Yorker, was a pioneer in Hampton's fishing industry. He began in 1870 with a fish oil factory and a fleet of ten schooners to catch the fish. The oil was exported to the North and Europe; the solid refuse was sold locally for fertilizer.[13]

In 1884, Darling established the firm Darling and Sons which soon became the largest oyster business in the world. Shuckers opened and cleaned as many as 200,000 bushels of oysters a year. These were placed in wooden casks or pails and were known to reach ports as far away as Liverpool still in fresh condition. Darling employed 160 workers in his plants (more in the fall when oysters were harvested and opened) and 100 more on his fleet of thirty oystering canoes.[14] Another Northern innovator, James McMenamin developed the process for canning crabmeat. His factory employed several score workers and his product, shipped via the newly opened C & O railroad from Hampton, was available throughout the United States and Europe.[15]

Hampton's many businesses and ability to attract income from throughout the world made it prosperous. But that prosperity came at a price. Streets were barely passable; buildings were crude firetraps. Life was invigorating, but also potentially dangerous. Worst of all was a necessary consequence of the burgeoning seafood business: when the wind blew from the direction of the seafood factories, the stench was unbearable; residents and tourists alike took to the closest conveyance and fled the city.[16]

None of these drawbacks were particularly distressing to Hampton's black community. The prosperity and openness of the town permitted opportunities for black people that they could enjoy in few other places in the South. Most important of these was the opportunity to select from a variety of jobs open to them. Blacks were not confined to farm labor and sharecropping as were so many of their fellows elsewhere in the South. In Hampton there were a number of relatively well-paying jobs and many opportunities to pursue independent livelihoods. Few blacks became wealthy, but most prospered more than they could have outside of Hampton.

By 1880 blacks in Hampton represented an increasingly urban and variegated work force. Occupational lists from the 1880 census for Hampton show that only 83 (9.8 percent) of the 848 blacks with occupations were involved in farming; 339 (40 percent) pursued what were considered skilled crafts in the area. Forty blacks (4.7 percent) had professions or owned businesses. The remaining workers, 386 (45.5 percent), were unskilled laborers.[17] (See table 1.)

The trend toward an urbanized work force continued throughout the 1880s. In 1896 Chataigne's City and Business Directories for Hampton listed 864 blacks with occupations. (See table 2.) In that year, only 11 blacks (1.4 percent) were listed as farmers, 273 (35.7 percent) were in skilled crafts, 90 (12.8 percent) had

Coston crab pickers. (Cheyne Collection, courtesy of the Syms-Eaton Museum)

Table 1		
Black Occupations	**Skilled Crafts**	
in Hampton, Virginia, 1880	**339**	**40%**
n = 848		
	107	oystermen
	56	fishermen
	22	carpenters
	18	seamstresses
	14	hackmen
	11	clerks
	10	watermen
	13	boatmen
	8	woodcutters
	8	bakers
	8	brickmasons
	7	blacksmiths
	8	shoemakers
	5	butchers
	5	sailors
	5	confectionaries
	6	teamsters
	28	other (less than 5%)

SOURCE: Tenth United States Census, 1880. Manuscript Returns for Elizabeth City County, National Archives, Washington, D.C.

Table 2		
Black Occupations	**Skilled Crafts**	
in Hampton, Virginia, 1896	**273**	**35.7%**
n = 764*		
	94	oystermen
	39	teamsters
	31	waiters
	23	carpenters
	12	cooks
	9	shoemakers
	6	firemen
	5	seamstresses
	7	U.S. Army
	4	plasterers
	4	draymen
	4	elevatormen
	4	painters
	4	butchers
	3	blacksmiths
	3	brickmasons
	2	moulders
	2	shipyard workers
	2	bartenders
	2	boatmen
	2	watchmen
	2	dyers
	9	other (less than 2%)

SOURCE: Chataigne's *Hampton Directory* (Hampton, 1896)

*The sample from Chataigne's *Directory* is considerably less complete than the 1880 census. Not only are divisions not made among unskilled labor, but several professionals and skilled craftsmen known to be in Hampton from other sources are missing. These figures are used as the best available, the 1890 manuscript census having been destroyed.

Professional/Business	Farm	Unskilled Labor
40 4.7%	**83 9.8%**	**386 45.5%**
8 school teachers	24 farmers	125 servants
7 saloonkeepers	59 farm laborers	107 washerwomen
3 ministers		73 factory workers
3 undertakers		76 day laborers
2 brothelkeepers		5 prostitutes
3 barbers		
1 constable		
1 nurse		
1 matron		
1 miller		
1 engineer		
1 justice of peace		
1 midwife		
1 jailer		
1 boatbuilder		
1 livery stable		
1 boardinghouse		
1 dry goods		
1 sailmaker		
1 booking agent		

Professional/Business	Farm	Unskilled Labor
98 12.8%	**11 1.4%**	**382 50%**
18 barbers	11 farm owners	382 laborers
18 teachers		
10 restaurateurs		
8 grocers		
6 school principals		
4 bakers		
4 butchershop owners		
4 ministers		
3 saloonkeepers		
2 coal & wood dealers		
2 insurance agents		
2 printers		
2 lawyers		
2 undertakers		
2 bank clerks		
2 dry goods		
2 doctors		
1 editor/publisher		
1 boatbuilder		
1 confectionary		
1 constable		
1 lighthouse keeper		
1 junk dealer		
1 engineer		

professions or owned businesses. Three hundred and eighty-two blacks (50 percent) were unskilled laborers.[18] These figures for 1896 are less useful than those from 1880 for a number of reasons. Washerwomen and servants, over half the unskilled laborers in 1880, are omitted in the Directory. If they existed in approximately the same numbers in 1896, the number of unskilled laborers would be greatly increased. Washerwomen, female servants (half the total), and other women workers were an important part of black employment in Hampton in 1880. Most of them, especially the washerwomen, were married; their wages represented an important element in the capital accumulation that allowed blacks to buy property in the 1880s.[19]

The category "laborer" is not broken down in the 1896 Directories as it is in the 1880 census. Many of the 370 laborers in 1896 were undoubtedly farm workers and servants. The decline in the number of black skilled craftsmen from 1880 to 1896 reflects a general downtrend in the town's economy in the 1890s. It may also reflect the beginnings of the onslaught against black craftsmen in the South during the '90s. Black craftsmen in Hampton, however, were not complaining of increased job discrimination in those years although the town's black politicians were vocal in protesting their declining fortunes during that same period.[20]

Black job distribution between 1880 and 1896 illustrates the special opportunities that Hampton's variegated economy and proximity to water provided for black employment. In 1880, 298 workers (35.1 percent) were in water-related trades as oystermen, fishermen, boatmen, and sailors. Most of the 73 factory workers in 1880 were employees of Darling or McMenamin seafood plants. Labor in these factories, though unpleasant, paid relatively well. Oyster shuckers earned $1.50 a day. If they completed their quota of thirty quarts they could leave early, which most did, not because they were too lazy to work long, as whites suggested, but rather to escape the stench, which sometimes adhered to the body even after the oyster season was over.[21]

Factory work offered an advantage common to most of the more popular occupations in black Hampton, that is, a degree of freedom from close white supervision. The trade that epitomized this sort of independence, and the largest single occupation pursued by blacks between 1880 and 1896, was oystering. The category of oystermen may be inflated in both 1880 and 1896 by seafood factory workers who sought additional status by defining themselves as such. Real oystermen were jealous of their occupation, however, and considered those who merely worked on land as distinctly inferior. Oystering was a favorite occupation among blacks for a number of reasons. One was that oystering was seasonal work. Large amounts of money could be made during the two-month oyster season, often enough to sustain a person for the remainder of the year. The real attraction of the oystering trade, however, was the independence it allowed the men who practiced it. Black oystermen, many of whom owned their own boats, harvested the oyster crop at their own pace and sold their catch to one of the seafood factories. A few, like John Mallory Phillips and Henry Armstead, owned oyster grounds—designated beds in Hampton Roads which only they could harvest. Phillips had a fleet of seven boats and organized his own seafood company through which he exported his catch to the North.[22]

There was another advantage of the oyster trade for those who owned their boats. These vessels could continue to be used for

McMenamin crab fleet of log canoes in Hampton Creek, 1907. The built-up log canoe is believed to have been imported from Africa; see John Michael Vlach, The Afro-American Tradition in Decorative Arts *(Cleveland, 1978), p. 102. (Cheyne Collection, courtesy of the Syms-Eaton Museum)*

profit even after the oyster season ended. Hampton Roads and the coastal waters of the Atlantic were rich in other sea products; most black oystermen were fishermen in the off season. The area around Hampton Roads remained heavily dependent on water routes for transportation, so black boat owners found ready opportunities for hauling cargo and passengers. John Phillips, for example, used his largest boat, a sloop, to carry black excursion groups around the Roads during the summer month.[23]

Another occupation which was attractive to blacks because of the independence it provided was that of driver or teamster. Those listed as drivers in the census and directories were everything from prosperous teamsters with sturdy wagons and fine strings of horses to ne'er-do-wells with only a broken down cart and equally decrepit ox. Some of the second group of drivers had regular routes for carrying passengers between the village and the Fortress or Soldiers' Home, but customers traveled at their own risk given the probable insobriety of the driver and the equally probable poor condition of the roads. Other black drivers, with more elegant conveyances and greater personal decorum, made a good living carrying tourists from the hotels near Old Point Comfort. The major demand for drivers, however, was in hauling cargo. Hampton was a rapidly growing town with goods to be hauled from farm to wharves, from wharves to factory, and from town to town. There was plenty of work for those who wanted it; even those disinclined to work hard could make an adequate living.[24]

Among those blacks who were craftsmen and those who were businessmen, there was much overlap. The craftsmen in the building trades, many of whom had acquired their skills in the shops of Hampton Institute, usually worked from job to job for different contractors. A few of them, like carpenters Robert and Henry Thorton of the Phoebus district, had small companies of their own which contracted directly with builders. In a city simultaneously rebuilding and rapidly expanding, there was much work in the construction trades. Certainly there was enough work to support the forty-four black men who were listed in the building trades, some of whom became substantial landowners in the county.[25]

Overlap between business and crafts was greater for those in trades which required heavy equipment and shops. All of the county's Negro blacksmiths in 1896 appear to have owned their own shops and were businessmen in their own right. Richard Palmer, for example, owned a dry goods store on one side of Queen Street near Armistead Avenue; across the street he also owned a large blacksmith shop. Another enterprising black man in Phoebus owned an entire block front near the main intersection of that settlement. He provided a blacksmith shop, a livery stable, grocery, dry goods store, restaurant, and—it was rumored—a bawdyhouse, all right next to the other.[26]

The business community of black Hampton was so varied that any product or service desired could be obtained from a black merchant. Some of these men had large businesses which catered to blacks and whites alike, others had only tiny family stores located on the side streets well away from the center of town. Most important to note about the former group of merchants is that many of them owned the largest businesses, black or white, in the village, and that most of them were located on the main business streets of the town. From the beginning of Queen Street at Hamp-

An ox-cart with father and daughter, the typical mode of black transportation in post-Reconstruction Hampton. (Courtesy of the Hampton Institute Archives.)

ton bridge westward to the end of the then settled area just west of Armistead Avenue, as many as half of all businesses were owned by blacks. A similar pattern existed along King Street northward to the edge of town.[27]

It was a ramshackle business district of black-owned boarding-houses, barbershops, eating places, and saloons intermixed with a few imposing structures and homes such as St. John's Church, the Courthouse, and the residences of black Sheriff Andrew Williams and black Commissioner of Revenue R. M. Smith, both of which were adjacent to St. John's. The most imposing store along Queen Street was the emporium of Thomas Harmon, a black merchant who sold groceries and dry goods. Moving westward along Queen Street, there were located the dry cleaning store of Kate Williams, the butcher shop of Walter Hickman, and the furniture store of David Pratt. Toward the end of Queen, located appropriately enough on Hope Street was the black undertaking establishment of Andrew and Warren Smith. Along King Street could be found additional grocers, barbers, butchers, the wood and coal companies of William Nelson and P. J. Taliferro, and the law offices of George Fields. At the corner of Lincoln and King Streets were the offices of Dr. Thomas Addison, physician; just off King was the office of Sara Banks, editor and publisher of the weekly *County Journal*.[28]

Between 1880 and 1896, the major portion of the black business community was very nearly synonymous with the *Hampton* business community. While some merchants—barbers, a few dressmakers—would accept only white clients, and the boardinghouses and many restaurants had only black customers, most merchants had customers of both races. Old residents remember black and white women seated together in Tom Harmon's dry goods store on market day, nursing their babies and comparing notes on child care while their husbands attended to the weekly errands. Unfortunately, some of these husbands were also likely to be drinking together in black-owned saloons nearby, and market day seldom ended without one or two drunken brawls. Sheriff William's home adjacent to the main business streets enabled him to be readily available to break up such confrontations.[29]

There were close relationships and much interaction among the craftsmen, merchants, and professional classes of the black community. But unlike the merchants and craftsmen, the black professionals of Hampton—the teachers, principals, doctors, lawyers, ministers, and undertakers—served an almost exclusively black clientele. The teachers taught in black city schools or at

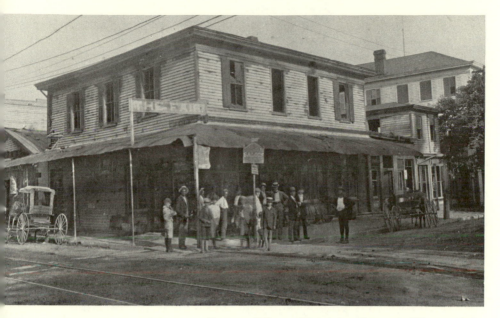

Corner of Queen Street, looking east. (Cheyne Collection, courtesy of the Syms-Eaton Museum)

Hampton Institute; the doctors and lawyers served only black clients, the ministers preached only in black churches, and the undertakers buried only black bodies. By and large this group was well-educated. Most of the teachers were graduates of Hampton Institute, as were the ministers. Lawyers George W. Fields and A. W. E. Bassette were Hampton graduates; Fields was also a graduate of Cornell Law School.[30]

The black professional group, although small in number, was of vital importance to the black community of Hampton. Members of this group were the acknowledged leaders of the community. They played a large role in shaping the goals and directions of its inhabitants. Anyone who sought respectability within the community had to belong to a church, and it was the ministers who spelled out the norms of acceptable social and religious behavior. Teachers, accepting the Hampton Institute belief in "formative work" among their pupils, did far more than teach reading, writing, and arithmetic. They helped reinforce the norms taught on Sunday in church, and passed on to their students the belief in the importance of education that had typified blacks of Hampton since

1861. Black lawyers played a crucial role in helping blacks acquire property and in protecting them from being cheated out of it once they had it. Black professionals also played another vital, if less concrete, role in shaping the community. They symbolized to the young of the town the heights to which black people might aspire. Despite the prejudice of whites, these professionals were living proof that there were few limits to what a black person might become.[31]

As a tangible demonstration of the progress they had made, and to help promote black ownership of property, blacks created their own savings institution, the People's Building and Loan Association, in 1886. The composition of the board of directors of the new Association reflected the diversity of occupations in black Hampton and the willingness of different groups to work together. The board included two oystermen, three black teachers from Hampton Institute, a merchant, a waiter, a fireman, a boatman, an insurance agent, and a laborer. Capital for the Association was accumulated by selling small shares to black residents of the town. The Association was soon a cause for considerable pride in the black community. It prospered and made possible the purchase of homes by hundreds of blacks. Equally important, the Association was proof that blacks could succeed in the world of finance just as they could in other areas. The People's Building and Loan exists today as one of only two large black business that have survived since the 1880's.[32]

The prosperity and expansion of Hampton enabled blacks to enter all levels of occupation during the post-Reconstruction period. Blacks were everything from common laborers to doctors, lawyers, and businessmen. They almost entirely escaped the onerous condition of peonage; instead, they were overwhelmingly an urban work force. The majority of their jobs provided them with considerable independence from white supervision and the chance to work at their own pace. There were many opportunities for upward mobility; men like Tom Harmon, Richard Palmer, and George W. Fields had started with nothing after the war and became prosperous. Whatever jobs blacks held, they enjoyed the right to use their incomes as they saw fit. For great numbers of them, the best possible use of their money was the realization of a dream that had been old even on Emancipation Day: "buying a little piece of land of their own."[33]

The success of Hampton blacks in acquiring property during the two and a half decades after 1870 is impressive. It is all the more notable because the blacks were forced to acquire it entirely through their own resources, without any aid from the government. In 1870, 121 blacks in Elizabeth City County had owned property totaling about 240 acres and assessed at $52,000.[34] In 1896, 1,619 blacks in the county owned property. Eight hundred and eighty-four owned city lots in Hampton and the adjoining townships of Chesapeake City (Phoebus) and Wythe assessed at $319,710; 735 owned county tracts totaling 2,957 acres assessed at $149,217. Approximately 300 of those with county tracts and 380 of those with city lots had owned these properties for ten years or more. Whites, of course, still owned the bulk of the land. They held 1,323 city lots and 26,401 county acres assessed at a total of $1,658,037. Nonetheless, the numbers of black landowners and the amount of property they owned had multiplied ten times over twenty-five years. The value of their property had increased by 900 percent.[35]

This record of black achievement must be qualified, however, by a closer look at the kind of property blacks were acquiring. Blacks had spoken longingly of "a little piece of land," and that is exactly what most of them got. The average size of county tracts owned by blacks was only four acres compared to an average size of forty-seven acres for county tracts owned by whites. Ironically, there were more black than white owners of county tracts and black-owned land was assessed at more per acre than white land: $50.46 as compared to $21.77. These anomalies disappear, however, when it is remembered how small black land tracts were and that the higher value of black land resulted from dwellings built upon it. Most blacks lived on the few acres they owned; whites used most of their acreage in farming or idle fields. A more revealing comparison is that unimproved black land was valued at only four cents an acre and unimproved white land was valued at seven cents an acre.[36]

Most black property holders owned the average four acres or less. Only sixty-seven blacks in the county owned more than ten acres, only six owned more than forty acres, the amount once promised by the government, and only two owned substantial farms of more than one hundred acres. These two men, Cary Nettles and Thomas Peake, were local free blacks who had begun to acquire property before the Civil War.[37] In short, black landowners in the county got only land no one else wanted and in small plots adequate only for subsistence farming.

A similar situation existed among black owners of city lots.

Black-owned plots tended to be located in areas whites did not want and were worth less than half the value per lot of white-owned lots. Black lots were worth an average of only $362 as compared to an average of $819 for white-owned city lots. Of the 273 blacks who owned lots in the town of Hampton, 113 owned property worth more than the average value, but only 25 owned property worth more than $1,000. These were the families of wealth in black Hampton; they owned several lots and often owned county acreage as well.[38]

A clearly posed, but nonetheless revealing picture of "Freedom's First Generation" and their descendants at home in Hampton, ca. 1880. (Courtesy of the Hampton Institute Archives)

Black businessmen, politicians, and lawyers—in that order—seemed to have had a particular facility for acquiring property. The wealthiest black landowner in Hampton, with over $5,000 worth of property, was Thomas Harmon, the Queen Street merchant and city councilman, who owned properties in both Hampton and Phoebus. In the same category were R. M. Smith, Elizabeth City County Commissioner of Revenue, and James Fields, Warwick County Commonwealth Attorney. Both of these men had holdings throughout Elizabeth City County and in adjoining counties. The combined holdings of the Fields family, including George, the Hampton attorney, may have made it one of the wealthiest black families on the Peninsula. Not quite as well-off but still prosperous were Andrew Williams, the county sheriff, A. W. E. Bassette, the lawyer, and Simon Bryant, a grocer.[39]

The process by which blacks acquired most of their property in the county helps explain the small size and lower value of their holdings. As was often the case in postwar Hampton, blacks turned white misfortune to their own advantage. In this instance, two of ante-bellum Hampton's wealthiest white men found themselves in dire financial straits in the aftermath of the war. Jefferson Sinclair, a diehard rebel who owned a majority of what is now downtown Hampton, and Joseph Segar, owner of the Hygeia Hotel and much of the land between Fortress Monroe and Hampton Institute, had frequently signed each others' notes as security on loans. Losses during the war forced both men into bankruptcy. Moreover, the destruction of their records when Hampton was burned left them with little idea who owed them money and to whom they were in debt. To settle their debts, Sinclair and Segar placed their property in the hands of the court and asked it to advertise for all those with claims against them. Their land was to be sold to satisfy such claims.[40] When these cases first came to court in 1868, the land market in Elizabeth City County was glutted. Northern speculators had already snapped up the choicest pieces of property and showed little interest in the Sinclair tract. In search of a solution, the court-appointed administrators of the estate struck upon the idea of laying out streets and dividing the estates into city lots. The lots were extremely narrow, sometimes only thirty to fifty feet along the street front, and very deep, usually half a block. One group would be most interested in such property, the blacks, and the administrators clearly had them in mind. Prices were very low, sometimes as little as eighty-five dollars; the administrators themselves carried the mortgages for many who could not pay the full amount upon purchase.[41]

In this manner, a new subdivision of Hampton village, stretching from the intersection of King and Queen Streets, north along King and west along Queen, came into being. The names of its streets—Grant, Lincoln, Union, Liberty—had a peculiar ring for a Southern town, but were clearly indicative of the black population which dwelled on them. A similar process was applied to much of the Segar properties, with similar results though without such evocative street names. By 1888, when the last of the Segar estate was subdivided, a new, predominantly black, settlement called Phoebus had grown up between the Institute and the Fortress.[42]

It is ironic that Jefferson Sinclair, who had so little sympathy for the black man's cause, was instrumental in enabling blacks to acquire property. It is more ironic that the blacks of Hampton, through their hunger for property, voluntarily created the first racially distinct neighborhoods in Hampton. Until the breakup of the Sinclair and Segar estates, the black and white populations of Hampton had been thoroughly intermixed. Even the breakup did not create racially exclusive neighborhoods; there were whites living on almost every block along the new streets of the Sinclair tract. Nevertheless, a distinctly black district in which a third of all black families lived and in which most black churches, businesses, and schools were located, had come into being. In this peculiar instance, blacks created black neighborhoods in pursuit of home ownership rather than being forced into such neighborhoods by discriminatory whites.[43]

The blacks of Hampton had fulfilled many of their dreams in the years between 1870 and 1896. They had obtained jobs that gave them freedom from plantation life. They had produced a middle class of craftsmen, businessmen, and professionals who served the community and provided leadership for it. They had acquired the property which they had so long desired. There were, however, many trials along the way. Jobs and property did not end the social disorders which periodically plagued the community. In fact, the kinds of jobs that many blacks held, that is, well-paid seasonal work which left them idle for months at a time, gave rise to problems of drunkenness and violence. The new, predominantly black-owned Sinclair section of the town was already taking on characteristics later identified with black ghettos. There was overcrowding because of the small size of lots. This condition was aggravated by the tendency of some landowners to build a second house on the rear of their long, narrow lots which they rented out as a source of additional income. There were the accompanying problems of unsanitary conditions which were further intensified because the inhabitants of the Sinclair estate numbered hundreds of dogs, cats, chickens, horses, and oxen as well as people.[44]

The new black neighborhood also faced problems of social control. There were too few churches, schools, and lodges, but too many saloons, eating places, and bawdyhouses. Most important of the problems facing black Hamptonians, however, was the question of whether they would have the power in government to protect what they had achieved and to build upon it. They made admirable strides in putting their own community in order, but, at the very height of their success in the early 1890s, their ability to protect that success at the ballot box and in political office was snatched from them.

Black Hampton: A Social and Political Community

The leaders of black Hampton did not acquire their middle-class values from the white teachers of Hampton Institute; rather, most of them had held those values even prior to Emancipation. To them, as to Samuel Armstrong, sobriety, ambition, education, hard work, stable family life, and church membership were the ingredients that made up respectability. Respectability was of great importance to these people who had been so demeaned during the years of slavery. They believed the prosperity of their community depended upon the acceptance of the ingredients of responsibility by community members. As a consequence—and like so many other middle-class people of different races and in different places—the black leaders of Hampton tried to impose their values on less "enlightened" community members, many of whom had not the least desire to change their ways.

Because their standards of respectability were the same as those of whites, Hampton's middle-class blacks tended to accept white evaluations of how "respectable" their community was becoming. The judgments were not encouraging, and, unfortunately, many of the criticisms had substance. There was much fighting and cutting in the black community; bawdyhouses and saloons created many disturbances. The summer months, when the heat seemingly aggravated tempers, were especially troublesome.[1]

In response to these conditions, black leaders attempted to provide alternative activities for their young people, especially on Saturday nights, and to bring the collective weight of community disapprobation down upon the most blatant transgressors of community standards. The Vanguard of Freedom and Temperance Society, for example, held regular meetings for its young men on Saturday evenings to discourage visits to local "watering holes." In another instance, the ladies of Queen Street Baptist Church decided to begin their Saturday night prayer meeting with a candlelight march and hymn sing past the notorious "Lee's Corner" on Grant Street where so many drunkards and rowdies congregated. Neither of these tactics was particularly effective. Men likely to come to a temperance meeting were unlikely to be out drinking in any case. Likewise, the ladies of Queen Street Baptist made no converts, but they had many more souls to pray for, given the expletives with which they were showered during their march.[2]

In these two instances, the efforts by the black middle class to discipline—or at least to shame—their errant fellows were failures. These examples, nevertheless, were indicative of the strategy employed by blacks in the attempt to refine their community. The heart of the strategy was the church. There were eight black churches in Hampton by the 1880s; six Baptist, one African Methodist Episcopal, and one Protestant Episcopal. To be a "respectable" member of the black community, one had to belong to one of these churches and to obey the moral and social strictures laid down by their congregations and ministers. A distinct hierarchy developed in each church; those parishioners most esteemed within their church were also the people most respected in the community as a whole. Thus as one moved up the ladder from junior deacon to deacon to head deacon, or moved along a parallel ladder among the many "ladies' auxiliary" groups within the churches, one also acquired greater status in the community at large. This system of status granting seemingly operated independent of one's economic or educational position within the community. But because there was a pecking order among the churches themselves, one might attain more status by being, for example, a junior deacon at First Baptist than by being a senior deacon at another church. Under such a system, Luke Phillips and his brother William, neither of whom were particularly wealthy men even by the standards of the black community, acquired considerable standing in the community as superintendents of the Third Baptist and First Baptist Sunday Schools, respectively.[3]

There were minor rivalries among the black churches. The Baptists sometimes accused the African Methodist Episcopals of thinking themselves to be better than Baptists, and both groups suspected the Episcopalians of being snobbish, an attitude which the Episcopalians apparently encouraged. In general, however, there was great cooperation among the churches, particularly the Baptist churches. There was, in addition, unanimity among all of the churches in terms of the social goals they pursued. Indicative of this cooperation was the county-wide Deacons' Union among the Baptists. The Union met every few months for prayers, hymns, and discussions of members' duties. The meetings rotated among the several Baptist churches. Each meeting, and the chief participants, were reported in the local newspaper, the *Home Bulletin*, published at the Union Soldiers' Home. Cooperation also extended to the exchange of pulpits among Baptist ministers and the sharing of the time of distinguished preachers who visited from other towns. These close relationships among the churches left the "sinner" little room for transgression. He could not hope to be accepted into another congregation if he was expelled from his own; the whole churchgoing community knew the exact nature of his "sin."[4]

At the same time that the churches attempted to prohibit certain forms of behavior, they attempted to encourage activities thought to have positive value. Toward this end, the ministers and deacons of the several churches joined with teachers from Hampton Institute to organize a Young Men's Christian Association for black young people. The Association and its inevitable "ladies' auxiliary" sponsored prayer meetings, talks by visiting ministers and politicians, a debating society, and a literary society. Probably the activities that the young people enjoyed most were the periodic socials sponsored by the Association. On these occasions they could gather for music, refreshments, and a bit of courting, all of this, however, under the watchful eyes of their elders. The leaders of the YMCA were the same prominent churchmen who led other black social organizations in the town. Luke Phillips, of the Third Baptist, was one of its first presidents; James A. Fields, Warwick County Commonwealth Attorney and member of First Baptist, was its treasurer. Fields was succeeded by George Davis, Hampton Institute teacher and son of the Reverend William Roscoe Davis. R.M. Smith, Elizabeth City County Commissioner of Revenue and deacon of First Baptist, provided the space for the organization's meetings. The Reverend Shorts of Queen Street Baptist, the Reverend Weeden of Third Baptist, and the Reverend Jackson of the First Baptist, among others, delivered talks at the weekly meetings.[5]

The adults of black Hampton also had their myriad of fraternal orders, societies and organizations which sponsored activities for the betterment of their members and of the community. The Odd Fellows had two lodges in town; the ubiquitous Vanguards of Freedom and Temperance had three chapters for adults and a special junior branch for young people. In addition, there were lodges of True Reformers, Good Samaritans, and the James A. Garfield post of the Grand Army of the Republic. The ladies of the town originated the United Order of Tents, a society dedicated to aiding the sick and elderly. All of these organizations also had close ties with the churches. It was almost impossible that a person could be a member of one of them without also being a member in good standing in one of the churches. The churches also were the usual meeting places for most of these societies.[6]

The black churches and organizations of Hampton put much emphasis on proper—even decorous—behavior, but it should not be assumed that black Hampton was a somber, joyless community. Churches and lodges were the primary sponsors of community social events, and almost any excuse was used for holding some sort of celebration. Churches held innumerable dinners, picnics, and bazaars. Members of the lodges would don their uniforms and march in parades at every opportunity. Founders' Day, Anniversary Day, and Commencement Day at Hampton Institute always brought out the entire community, as did Emancipation Day and anniversary celebrations at the various churches. Nor were these affairs as gentile as many of Hampton's black elite might have wished. There were always a few injuries following the Emancipation Day Parade due to guns being fired indiscriminately and to marchers being overcome by "John Barleycorn." Even the members of the very proper First Baptist Church suffered occasional embarrassment when their annual excursions ended in general free-for-alls. In such instances, Deacon Andrew Williams was forced to put on his other hat as county sheriff and arrest the errant members of his congregation.[7]

Most black social occasions were at once opportunities to have a good time and to reinforce the prevailing values of the community. Thus the graduations at Lincoln School in town and at Butler School on the Institute campus were two of the most widely attended events of the year. They were followed, of course, by parties sponsored by proud parents of the graduating children. As standards for admission at the Institute rose, private academies were created to supplement the public school curriculum. The Reverend Spiller of First Baptist was principal of his own academy which annually sponsored plays and musicales by students and adult members of the community. These occasions, too, were inevitably followed by social gatherings, the decorum of which was usually determined by whether the Reverend Spiller or one of his fellow pastors chose to grace them with their presence.[8]

The social life of black Hampton was never quite as proper as some might have wanted, nor was it entirely segregated. The close relationships that had evolved between masters and slaves, and sometimes between blood relatives across the color line, continued in post-bellum Hampton. These relationships were especially apparent on occasions such as weddings. Weddings were always grand events in black Hampton; the guests, attire of the bride, and the presents received were given prominent mention in the local paper.[9]

One such wedding is illustrative of the complex interrelationships among blacks and white of Hampton village. In January of 1889, Shepard Mallory married Miss Ann Bailey. Both bride and groom were members of respectable black families. Mallory was one of the first three contraband who had escaped across Hamp-

Children of the Whittier School (ca. 1885) learning agriculture with their teachers from Hampton Institute's faculty. The Whittier School replaced the Butler School, its name being less offensive to Southern white sensibilities. The school building is in the background. (Courtesy of the Hampton Institute Archives)

ton bridge to Fortress Monroe in May of 1861. Ann Bailey was a descendant of the late James Bailey, son-in-law of Cesar Tarrant, the black revolutionary war hero, and a major black landowner in the county. The executor of Bailey's estate was Charles Mallory, white, owner of Shepard Mallory in 1861, and the man with whom Bailey had dined on numerous occasions in his declining years. (It is not recorded whether the two ate in the same room.) In attendance at the wedding, along with Mr. and Mrs. Charles Mallory, were the white mayor of Hampton and his wife. Also present was black sheriff Andrew Williams who, two years earlier, had required that the bridegroom, Shepard Mallory, give a fifty dollar "good behavior" bond as a result of a knifing incident with John Phillips—who also attended the wedding. "Numerous presents were received from friends of both colors."[10]

Although the aspirations of Hampton's black elite caused it to share many of the values and behavior styles of local whites and

One of the early classes at Butler School on Hampton Institute's campus. (Courtesy of the Hampton Institute Archives)

Northern missionaries, these blacks did not forget either their color nor the hostile environment in which they lived. Indeed, their efforts to make their own community orderly and secure appear to be a direct consequence of their awareness that its survival was constantly in danger. They were particularly conscious of the struggle of former Afro-Americans in Liberia. That nation was, to black Hampton, a symbol of what blacks might achieve on their own resources, and they were intolerant of any white criticism about it. When Frank Ruffin, descendant of Edmund Jr., the suicidally unreconcilable rebel, published a pamphlet condemning blacks in general and Liberian blacks in particular, black Hampton launched a spirited defense. Ruffin's sources were discredited and comparisons uncomplimentary to Ruffin's ancestors were made between what Americo-Liberians and Virginia cavaliers had accomplished in the same length of time. An ostentatious display of welcome was arranged for the arrival of the wife of former Liberian President Roberts in 1890. She and her entourage were feted at Hampton Institute and at the finest black homes of the town. Mrs. R. M. Smith became the most exalted hostess of the black community by having Mrs. Roberts and her party as house guests.[11]

Black Hampton was equally sensitive to the sufferings of black people closer to home. Meetings of protest were held because of white injustices against black people elsewhere in the South and in the local area. The black community was furious when the case of Charlie Crandall (white) was thrown out of court because a black member of the jury was ruled ineligible to serve. Crandall had cold-bloodedly murdered one black man and wounded another in an argument at a country store. The blacks were even more enraged when a second trial jury acquitted Crandall of all wrongdoing.[12]

Spokesmen for the black community of Hampton were neither apologetic nor compromising when proclaiming black rights. In their condemnation of racist tracts, they reminded white Southerners of whose sweat had made the ante-bellum South prosperous. To the comment by a white man in Williamsburg that "Almighty God only intended the people he made with straight hair and blue eyes to rule," young W. H. Bonaparte, a rising black politician responded:

> there are so many straight-haired and blue-eyed citizens here who do not belong to the white race [that] we are indebted to the "aged fossil," the moss-covered statesman of Williamsburg for the choice bit of comfort he gave to his brothers whose

very features wear the impress of the white man's degradation and [of] the worst system of concubinage the world ever witnessed. Men should tread softly when they talk about "straight hair and blue eyes," least [sic] nearly a quarter of a million blue eyes should be staring at them from Negro cradles and the arms of Negro mothers.[13]

Bonaparte knew that of which he spoke when he talked of "straight hair and blue eyes." As a light-skinned mulatto, Bonaparte, himself, would shortly discover the dangers attendant to his appearance.[14]

In their annual Emancipation Day speeches, black spokesmen were no less compromising than Bonaparte had been. They heralded their country and the prominent role that blacks had played in its major wars, but they also celebrated those men who were anathema to the white South: Denmark Vesey, Nat Turner, the blacks who had fought with John Brown at Harper's Ferry.[15]

Awareness of past trials and of continuing abuse made black Hamptonians especially sensitive to the need for political power through which their economic and social gains could be protected. Commissioner of Revenue R. M. Smith, in his speech commemorating black revolutionists like Vesey and Turner also argued that, "I do not believe our white brethren would do this [persecute] to us again, had they the power."[16] Smith was wrong; two years later, whites once again had the power, and he was driven from his position along with most black officeholders. Other Hampton blacks were never as optimistic about white people as Smith in any case. They had fought to gain political power, held it tenaciously during the brief decade in which they exercised it, and struggled unsuccessfully to keep it in the years of defeat after 1887.

The black struggle for political rights on the Virginia Peninsula had begun as soon as the war ended. Their efforts to place one of their own, Daniel Norton, on the Freedmen's Bureau Court, had ended with the abrogation of their vote by the determined paternalists of the Bureau. They were more successful thereafter, sending Daniel Norton to the State Constitutional Convention in 1868, and electing him to the State Senate in 1871. His brother, Robert, was elected to the House of Delegates in 1869. From 1869 to 1890, Elizabeth City County was represented in the legislature by at least one black and, for some periods, by two or three. These black members of the legislature were unable to have much impact on state government except during the brief years of Readjuster domination (1879-83) when the black state delegation numbered fifteen and their votes were sought after by conflicting white factions.[17]

The real focus of black political activity in post-Reconstruction Virginia was on the local level and there, too, blacks did not fare well until 1879. Blacks did begin to serve in appointive offices in Elizabeth City soon after the war. Thomas Peake, for example, briefly held the office of deputy sheriff in 1865. In 1870 Peake was elected overseer of the poor; Thomas Canady was elected as a constable; and Rufus Jones elected clerk of the county court. Whites of the county were not yet reconciled to black possession of any office with real power. Since they could not defeat Jones at the polls, they challenged the sureties of the $5,000 bond required to hold the clerkship. A local white judge found one signer of the bond guilty of perjury and declared the clerkship vacant. A white man was appointed in Jones' place. In the next election (1872), Jones was elected to the House of Delegates and the clerkship was won by a white man. Blacks were never again able to win that position.[18]

After 1879, Elizabeth City blacks were finally able to convert their numerical superiority into political clout. In those years there were nine county elective offices, not including the county board of supervisors. They were: clerk, treasurer, commonwealth attorney, sheriff, constable, surveyor, justice of the peace, commissioner of revenue, and overseer of the poor. During the 1880s, blacks controlled five of these offices as well as placing several members on the county board of supervisors. Andrew Williams was sheriff; Thomas Canady continued as constable; Rufus Jones served periodically as justice of the peace; R. M. Smith, after a term in the House of Delegates, was elected commissioner of revenue; and Thomas Peake remained overseer of the poor. Possession of these offices did not amount to "black domination" of local government, but it did assure blacks of a powerful voice in the government of their county. Black men determined who would be arrested and held over for trial; a black man supervised the care of the indigent, most of whom were black; and, perhaps most important of all, a black man determined who would pay taxes and how much.[19]

Political leadership coincided almost exactly with social and economic leadership in black Hampton. The black elite did not share its power readily. Sheriff Williams was also a major landowner and deacon of his church, as was R. M. Smith. Thomas Peake was prominent in his church, one of the original "free coloreds" of the village, and owner of the most valuable black farm in the county.

Rufus Jones was owner of several properties in town, a deacon, and head of the local chapter of the Grand Army of the Republic. Other blacks who held political office were of the same class: Young Jackson, pastor of First Baptist Church, and Sandy Parker, businessman and landowner, both served on the county board of supervisors. Thomas Harmon and Luke Phillips; who served on the Hampton city council in the late 1880s, were prominent business-men and social leaders. William Roscoe Davis, who also briefly served on city council, was a minister and sire of one of the most respected black families in the community. John H. Robinson and James A. Fields, black Hampton's last two delegates to the state legislature, were both graduates of Hampton Institute, lawyers, and large property holders.[20]

Blacks in Hampton exercised their political power with mod-eration and competence. Black officials joined with white ones in striving for all manner of civic improvements, including the incor-poration of the village. Visitors to the community were invariably impressed by how well blacks and whites were able to work together in local government. For most of the 1880s, black officeholders in the country also proved immune to the standard white Southern charge of corruption. When these charges were made in 1889, they were motivated as much by desire for political advantage as by any evidence of wrongdoing.[21]

The surface appearance of harmony in Hampton merely ob-scured the deep and continuing hostility to black political partici-pation among local whites. Two basic changes were occurring that would soon force blacks from most of their political offices. The first was the collapse of the Readjuster Movement and the restora-tion of white conservative rule in Virginia politics. The second change was the result of the impersonal forces of demography. For the first time since the Civil War, blacks were beginning to lose their numerical superiority in the county.[22]

Local whites were quick to seize upon the opportunities that these changes provided. Their first ploy was the seemingly reason-able proposition that the village of Hampton be incorporated as a city. The justification was that incorporation would permit badly needed civic improvements and more responsive local government. These arguments were sound, and even prominent black business-men were initially in support of the idea. Closer inspection, how-ever, revealed certain drawbacks to blacks if incorporation should occur. First, the new city would request exemption from, or re-duction of, certain taxes paid to the county. This meant that the predominately black county government would be deprived of the wealthiest portion of its tax base. Secondly, incorporation was to be limited to the central village of Hampton. Adjacent townships, which were predominantly black, were excluded from the city. Thirdly, and most important, the proposed city charter was clearly designed to minimize black political power. The new city, extending east from Hampton bridge to north Armistead Avenue, and north from Hampton River to Union Street, would be divided into three wards. The first ward would include all the area south of Queen Street; the second ward would include all the area north of Queen Street and east of King Street; and the third ward would include all the area north of Queen Street and west of King Street. Each ward would have two councilmen.[23]

The incorporation plan proved to be a neat example of racial gerrymandering. Although the three wards were nearly equal in size, they differed sharply in population. The boundaries of the third ward were almost exactly coterminous with the old Sinclair Estate. That ward was at once predominantly black and more heavily populated than the other two. Blacks, although they were still almost a majority of the town's population, would be able to elect only two of the six councilmen. The committee advocating incorporation acknowledged as much. In its proposal for interim councilmen until the first city elections, it submitted J. S. Darling and J. W. Richardson (whites) as councilmen for the first ward, A. D. Wallace and James McMenamin (whites) for the second ward and R. M. Smith and Richard Bolling (blacks) for the third ward. Despite reservations expressed by politicians like R. M. Smith, the plan of incorporation was approved by the state legislature, and in 1887 the new, white-controlled city of Hampton was born.[24]

The alliance made among white businessmen and politicians during the incorporation debates should have been warnings to blacks of the trials yet to come. J. S. Darling and James McMenamin, both Northern immigrants, had cast their lots with the old natives in this instance, and they continued to do so thereafter. Black politicians, however, were too involved in internecine squabbles to heed the signals.

The breakup of the Readjuster coalition among white voters in the county was reflected among black voters as well. Beginning in 1886, black politicians split between those who supported the "regular" Republican party of the state, which was dominated by whites, and those who sought to maintain black control of the local Republican party. The disputes were as much jockeying for personal advantage as they were debates about race or principle. Andrew Williams and Thomas Peake remained committed to the regulars throughout, but Sandy Parker, A. W. E. Bassette, John Robinson, and others jumped from faction to faction in search of the best chance to win office. Especially notable in this regard was R. M. Smith who desperately wanted the Republican nomination for the district's congressional seat. Failing that, he momentarily flirted with the black Republican group; but when it was clear that a nomination from that group would be an empty honor, he hastily repaired his alliances with the "regulars" and accepted renomination as commissioner of revenue. The 1886 campaign for Republican nominations was marred throughout by riotous meetings among the different factions. The preelection turmoil was climaxed by the ambush murder of a black opponent of R. M. Smith; the guilty parties were never apprehended.[25] Both black and white voters were apparently disgusted by these spectacles; though the Republicans won, voter turnout dropped by 30 percent with most of the decline on the Republican side.[26]

The whites of the county, observing that the blacks and Republicans were in disarray, were quick to press their advantage. They mounted a full-scale assault on black politicians, sparing few innuendoes and demonstrating complete disregard for the truth. Council candidate T. N. Brown, for example, was denounced as "a mulatto who has been conspicuous on several occasions in his efforts to stir up strife between the white and black races."[27] Brown's defense that, "I have on no occasion sought to 'stir up strife.' I have simply tried to do my duty as a citizen and a man on all occasions," was ignored or cited as proof of the original accusation.[28]

Likewise, the Reverend Spiller of First Baptist Church was denounced in the Democratic press for a letter signed by most of the county's black ministers. The letter read in part:

> A ticket has been presented which the past demonstrates is not unfriendly to our race. The only cry left the Democratic Party is the stale one of "Negro domination." The Negro cannot be truthfully charged with any desire for supremacy in the administration of public affairs: all we want and ask are our rights before the law and a fair chance unhindered by political malevolence in the race of life. We continue in the belief that this can best be done through the medium of the Republican Party.[29]

This endorsement of the Republican party was condemed as a vicious effort of the clergy to intervene in the affairs of state and an attempt to convert black churches into centers for Republican politics. As with the Brown case, Spiller's defense that clergy had the right to political opinion, that several white clergy served in the Democratic state government, and that the letter was not presented from the pulpit, was ignored.[30] White Democrats were out to discredit blacks and Republicans, especially when they were one and the same; no distortion of the truth would be spared in pursuit of that goal. Then suddenly, in the winter of 1889, whites of Elizabeth City County were presented with a scandal, the sordidness of which was unparalleled in the recent history of the county. It served better than all of the white distortions and half-truths to discredit black politicians.

One of black Hampton's most promising young men was W.H. Bonaparte. Bonaparte, a native of Hampton, had graduated from the Institute in 1874 and had gone north where he had been associate editor of the Boston *Advocate*, a black newspaper. In 1888 he had returned to Hampton and married Miss Emma Lee, daughter of one of Hampton's most respected black businessmen. Young Bonaparte's political star rose rapidly; the leaders of the community honored him by designating him "orator of the day" at the 1889 Emancipation Day celebration. His speech was widely acclaimed and black leaders began to speculate on what office Bonaparte should seek in the next elections. Less than three weeks later, and barely three months after his marriage, Bonaparte was in jail, accused of raping a thirteen-year-old white girl.[31]

The trial of W. H. Bonaparte brought to light much of the seamy side of Hampton life, embarrassing both blacks and whites. It also revealed the depths of viciousness to which infighting among black politicians had descended. The trial was convened with unseemly haste—less than a week after Bonaparte's arrest. During the interim the town had been close to riot with white newspapers throughout the state calling for the "God ordained" punishment that black violators of white women were to suffer. Black supporters of Bonaparte kept a nightly armed vigil outside the Hampton jail to prevent just such an event.[32]

From the beginning, it was clear that Bonaparte was guilty of something—of monumental indiscretion if nothing more. As the case evolved, however, what he was being tried for and why became more and more evident. The first startling development was the decision of the commonwealth attorney to change the charge from rape to "abduction and seduction." It had developed that the young lady involved (Ruth Tennelle) had gone to her liaisons with Bonaparte voluntarily, and that she believed him to be white. It was further revealed that she, rather than Bonaparte, may have initiated the affair. Young Miss Tennelle had written letters to at least two other light-skinned youths of the village. They, having better sense than Bonaparte, had burned the notes or ignored the invitation proffered therein.[33]

Another factor, upon which the judge refused to permit elaboration but about which defense attorneys made continuing reference, was Bonaparte's political standing. His political views were apparently so radical as to offend many other black politicians. Certainly the *Home Bulletin*, departing from its usual custom, had omitted a synopsis of his speech as "orator of the day" at the most recent Emancipation celebration. Bonaparte was described in court as a "black Republican" and an "anti-Williams [Sheriff Andrew] man."[34]

Bonaparte's white defense attorneys acknowledged that he was guilty of adultery, a crime they abhorred, but not of "abduction or seduction" as he was charged. The age of consent in Virginia was thirteen; the relevant statute required that Bonaparte be involving his victim in prostitution, and that her involvement be involuntary. Since none of this was true, his attorneys argued that Bonaparte must be found not guilty. The state's case, throughout, centered around the reputed "libidiousness of mulattoes" like Bonaparte and the lost purity of poor Miss Tennelle. Commonwealth Attorney Segar concluded his case with allusions to the "lost blossom" in the young girl's cheeks and with the claim: "Upon the action of this jury depends the future welfare and security of this town." Bonaparte was found guilty and sentenced to five years at hard labor—a surprisingly mild sentence given the passions aroused by the case.[35]

The scandal caused by Bonaparte did not end with his conviction. Bonaparte broke out of the Hampton jail in October 1889 and fled to Delaware. When making his escape he broke his leg; during his flight to Delaware he contracted pneumonia. Bonaparte died in 1891 without ever being returned to Hampton. Ruth Tennelle and her father moved to Norfolk, but Mrs. Tennelle remained in Hampton where she is said to have never appeared in public without a veil over her face.[36]

All of the issues involved in black Hampton's advancement after the war—and all of the fears that advancement inspired in whites—

came together in the Bonaparte case. Interracial sex was not new to Hampton, as Bonaparte's own light coloration demonstrated. But in the past it had been chiefly white males and black females. In this instance the opposite had been true. Bonaparte was better educated and more prosperous than his white lover. He was a rising politician; she was only the daughter of a poor storekeeper. The Bonaparte affair seemed to justify the basic fear that had always inspired white opposition to black progress: black economic and political equality would lead to black sexual equality.

Black leaders in Hampton were well aware of the potential for their own destruction in the anger released by the scandal. The Bonaparte case had electrified white opinion in Virginia and had put all black politicians on the defense. Whites in Elizabeth City County pursued their advantage and began attacks on Bonaparte's allies, particularly R. M. Smith, the commissioner of revenue. Smith, in the first several months of 1889, was once again on the "outs" with the regular Republican faction in the county and therefore an "anti-Williams" man as was Bonaparte. As commissioner of revenue, Smith was also one of the most powerful men in the county since he determined who would pay how much taxes. In late August of 1889, Smith was accused of malfeasance in office by the county clerk (white and Democratic). With the same speed manifested in the Bonaparte case, the county empaneled a grand jury which reviewed Smith's books, and, by 7 September 1889, charged him with failing to follow the tax laws, "gross neglect of official duty, and gross carelessness." Rather than face prosecution, Smith resigned. In December, J. M. Peek, the same magistrate who had presided at the Bonaparte trial, appointed V. P. Hold (white) as interim commissioner. The new commissioner proved no more efficient than Smith, but he did reestablish, for the first time since 1870, the division of black and white taxpayers into separate lists.[37]

Smith's removal marked the effective end of black political power in the county. If Sheriff Williams had helped to orchestrate either the Bonaparte or Smith cases, and there is no evidence that he did, he had chosen unwisely. Williams too was marked for removal. He was made all the more vulnerable by Bonaparte's escape from his jail in October 1889. Sheriff Williams made the requisite trip to Richmond for extradition papers to bring Bonaparte back from Delaware, but he was defeated for reelection in 1891, and he too left office.[38]

The downfalls of Bonaparte, Smith, and Williams after 1889

did not bring an end to black officeholding in Hampton, nor in the surrounding county. What was ended was black political *power* in the town and county. The new white majority of the county tolerated black officeholders in city council, the county board of supervisors, and even in the legislature for yet a few more years.[39] But the ability of blacks to protect their rights through their own officials in government was at an end. White Virginians were once more in control.

Epilogue

It took Hampton blacks more than twenty years to achieve the success they enjoyed by the mid-1880s. Their decline, symbolized by their removal from powerful political offices after 1890, was also gradual, but it was inexorably downward. A few blacks continued to hold lesser elective office in Hampton until Virginia effectively disfranchised blacks in 1902, but meaningful black political participation ended with the political debacles of 1889 and 1890.

In the same manner, many black businesses in Hampton continued to operate into the early twentieth century, but even in the 1890s there were ominous hints of the impending economic decline. The numbers of blacks in skilled crafts had fallen; the percentage of blacks in unskilled labor had increased. (See table 1 and 2.) Some of the skilled trades in which blacks were prominent— such as oysterman, teamster, seamstress, blacksmith—were becoming obsolete. Others, like the building crafts, were the very ones from which white trade unions most successfully excluded blacks in the years after 1900.

Even the more than twofold increase in black businessmen and professionals between 1880 and 1896 was of ambiguous significance. The increase came primarily in professions that catered exclusively to a black clientele—teachers, principals, doctors, lawyers, and insurance agents. They provided services to blacks that they could not get from white professionals in the increasingly segregated town. During this same period, there was little increase in major black businesses such as retail merchandising or banking. After 1900, the black-owned businesses along King and Queen Streets began to fall into white hands either through sale by the original proprietor's heirs or their neglect to pay taxes on the property. Although many of these children of the first freed generation had taken advantage of the exceptional social and educational opportunities Hampton offered, they had moved elsewhere. Few of them had any desire to return to the increasingly circumscribed life post-disfranchisement Hampton offered.

The factors which defeated black Hampton after 1890 had always been there: Southern white racism, Northern white indifference or hostility, unstable economic conditions, and corrupt political ones. But between 1861 and the late 1880s, Hampton blacks were able to manipulate these forces so that the full power of white repression did not weigh as heavily on their town as it did on less fortunate areas of the South.

In fact, black success in Hampton partially resulted from an irony that casts considerable light on Northern misunderstanding of blacks and indifference toward them. Black progress in Hampton was possible because much of the Northern plan for Southern reconstruction worked there. In the South as a whole, the North gradually abandoned its designs for reshaping Southern society. Citing black incompetence rather than lack of will on the part of most white Northerners, the federal government abandoned ex-slaves to the control of their former masters.

In Hampton, however, events took a different course. There the North unwittingly permitted its Reconstruction plan to be tested. Northern investment brought about the diversification of the area's economy. This enabled blacks to pursue nonagricultural jobs, freed them from the tyranny of white landowners, and gave them a cash income that allowed accumulation of savings. Northern political strategies also worked, although not quite as many Republicans had intended. Virginia whites were kept divided politically, particularly during the Readjuster period. (In fact, many business-minded Republicans felt closer kinship to the conservatives who wanted to pay off state railroad bonds than to the blacks' allies, the Readjustors, who wanted to renege on them.)

Enfranchisement of blacks and Northern immigration helped create a workable Republican party in Virginia through which many blacks, like those in Hampton, were able to gain elective office. Northern maintenance of a military presence through the troops of Fortress Monroe helped prevent excesses of violence by whites upon blacks, especially during Reconstruction. Northern military presence, not only at the Fort but at the integrated Soldier's Home, also brought additional money into the town economy.

Most importantly, Northerners provided Hampton blacks with continuing educational assistance that most had argued all blacks would need. The missionary schools, during the war and Reconstruction, and Hampton Institute thereafter, offered to blacks the best education available to either race in the county. These Northern-run schools also expended considerable energy in attempting to shape black people along lines deemed best for them in terms of values and behavior. Hampton's blacks did strive to acquire education, property, and other attributes of "respectability" (as defined by Northerners), but not because they had internalized the Northern vision for their future. They had decided upon most of those goals before they met the first Northern missionary.

Northern involvement in Hampton made black success possible, but it was the blacks' own efforts that made success a reality. The ante-bellum experiences of both the original contraband and the black refugees to Hampton had provided a foundation upon which they could build. They were the black men, women, and children who had learned enough about freedom to know that their masters would go to war rather than grant it to them, and who had fled when the war began in order to gain it. Once these blacks had achieved freedom they sought to put it to good use. They pursued the same rights and privileges enjoyed by other free Americans. In Hampton blacks gradually learned that not even their Northern allies had intended full black equality in the emancipation of slaves. Nevertheless, they remained determined that something at least approximating equality would be their goal.

Black Hamptonians nearly achieved their goal through skillful interaction and cooperation with whites and through their own solidarity, courage, tenacity, and ambition. They learned how to work together across class lines; they acquired the skill to defend themselves even against whites who claimed to be friends. They overcame disappointment at the failure of the government's land redistribution program and bought land on their own. Most importantly, Hampton blacks convinced themselves, and then demonstrated, that there was little a white man could do that a black man could not do equally well.

By 1890, when resurgent Southern racism overpowered even successful black communities like Hampton, that town's blacks had learned to participate and to succeed in Southern society by following the rules established and by seizing the available opportunities. Faced with this reality whites took the only course open to them once they had the chance: they changed the rules and removed the opportunities. When whites achieved a voting majority in Hampton they denied blacks elective office and later supported black disfranchisement. They began to segregate the town and to exclude blacks from the skilled crafts. They took advantage of black disenchantment and began to buy up black-owned property and businesses.

Black appeals for Northern assistance were of no avail; indeed most such assistance had long since been withdrawn. Northerners claimed that the failure of blacks to make good use of advantages granted them in Reconstruction was proof of their backwardness; blacks were to make peace with their former owners and advance as best they could. In reality, except in a few communities like Hampton, the promised advantages had never been provided. Northern abandonment of blacks in Reconstruction was better a measure of Northern racism and indifference about black equality than it was proof of black incompetence, as the blacks' successes in Hampton clearly demonstrate.

There is an additional tragedy in the relationship between Hampton's blacks and their Northern allies. Hampton Institute, long an important resource for the black community, cooperated in the black defeats of the 1890s and helped formulate the justification for it. The history of Hampton's black community has always been subsumed within that of Hampton Institute. Faults found with the Institute have also been ascribed to black Hampton, the town. Such portrayals are distortions of the facts. For the first twenty years of its existence, the Institute was heavily dependent upon the town's black community because of its educated young people, ambitious and hardworking adults, its successful businessmen, and its skillful politicians. A community with these attributes offered a model for black progress very different from the accommodationism being advocated by Armstrong and his foremost pupil—Booker T. Washington.

In the face of twenty years' evidence that full black participation in Southern society was beneficial to both blacks and whites, evidence provided by a black community with which Armstrong and Washington were intimately associated over those twenty years, both insisted upon an alternate and demeaning vision for the black man's future. Armstrong never swayed from his public insistence upon black incompetence, upon the need for blacks to devote themselves to agriculture and education, upon the requirement that blacks refrain from involvement in politics. With the exception of obtaining an education, Armstrong's program denied blacks pursuit of the very ingredients that had made black Hampton, the town, a demonstrable success.

Armstrong died in 1893 at the age of fifty-four. His legacies to America were Hampton Institute, Tuskegee Institute, black accommodation, and Booker T. Washington. All were heralded in the last decade of the nineteenth century as models for the black future in America. But none were true products of the black man's struggle and success in Hampton; that was ignored. Rather all four legacies were evidence of the white man's victory over black advancement and of Armstrong's complicity in the process.

Washington and accommodation were momentarily triumphant in the climate of rampant racism at the turn of the century. After 1910 the real model for black advancement offered by black Hampton was once more ascendant in organizations like the NAACP.

Surviving members of the first generation did not give up. Attorney George W. Fields, for example, despite being blinded in a fishing accident, continued to fight for black voting throughout his

Hampton Institute viewed from the town of Hampton, ca. 1890. Note the wharf and the new bell tower on the chapel (cf. photo p. 153).(Courtesy of the Hampton Institute Archives)

life. His daughter, also an attorney, has carried on that tradition. The children and grandchildren of William Roscoe Davis continued in his footsteps as activists in the cause of black rights, particularly in education. But most of them, like so many others in the succeeding generations, had to leave Hampton to exercise their talents fully. The town's surrender to racism forced them elsewhere; it was Hampton's loss. Scores of descendants of that first generation— a disproportionate number from so small a town— have made important contributions to their communities and the nation in education, business, and the professions. They are the proudest product of "Freedom's First Generation." That their origins, and the special people and events that created them, have been nearly forgotten illustrates how little we yet know or understand about black life in the post-bellum South.

Chapter 1

1. Lyon G. Tyler, *The History of Hampton and Elizabeth City County, Virginia* (Hampton, 1922), pp. 46-47.

2. Ibid., p. 50; E. K. Graham, "To Teach and to Lead." Manuscript for centennial history of Hampton Institute. Chapter 1, "As It Was in the Beginning," p. 30.

3. Ibid.; Tyler, *History of Hampton*, pp. 46-47, 50.

4. Ibid.

5. Graham, "To Teach," pp. 24-28.

6. Tyler, *History of Hampton*, pp. 42-46.

7. Ibid.

8. Eighth U. S. Census, 1860. Manuscript Returns for Elizabeth City County, National Archives, Washington, D. C.; Tyler, *History of Hampton*, p. 39.

9. Eighth U.S. Census, 1860; Graham, "To Teach," pp. 13,26.

10. Frederick Douglass, *Narrative of the Life of Frederick Douglass.* Edited by Benjamin Quarles (Cambridge, MA, 1960), p. 133.

11. Graham, "To Teach," pp. 13,26.

12. "List of Land Tax, 1860;" "Taxable Property Book, 1860," Elizabeth City County Court Records (hereinafter ECCR).

13. *American Missionary Magazine* 15(1871): 196 (hereinafter *AMM*); Graham, "To Teach," pp. 9-10; Mrs. Dottie Peake Anderson, interview, Hampton, Va., 31 July 1973.

14. Ibid.; "Tax List, 1860," ECCR.

15. *AMM* 15(1871): 196; Anderson, interview. The missionaries later claimed that Mrs. Peake's ante-bellum teaching had been done in secret, but this belief appears mistaken. The missionaries were never able to fathom the complexities of race relations in Hampton.

16. Audrey Jackson Walker, *Centennial Celebration of First Baptist Church*, "The History of First Baptist Church" (Hampton, 1963); Anderson, interview; Graham, "To Teach," pp. 10, 12; William N. Armstrong, "Vignettes of Slavery Days: Uncle Billy Taylor," *Southern Workman* 30 (1902): 604-5.

17. "Persons, Property and other Subjects of Taxation, 1860," ECCR.

18. Eighth U.S. Census, 1860; Tyler, *History of Hampton*, pp. 13,26.

19. Eighth U.S. Census, 1860.

20. Ibid.; these figures tend to confirm

Gutman's findings in Herbert Gutman, *The Black Family in Slavery and Free-dom* (New York, 1976).

21. Walker, "History of First Baptist."

22. Edward L. Pierce, *Enfranchisement and Citizenship: Addresses and Papers* (Boston, 1896), p. 49; Armstrong, "Vignettes of Slavery Days," pp. 604-7.

23. Lewis C. Lockwood to American Missionary Association (hereinafter AMA), 20 March 1862, 17 April 1862, American Missionary Association (AMA), Archives, Dillard University; *AMM* 15(1871): 196; Graham, "To Teach," pp. 18-19.

24. Lockwood to AMA, 17 April 1862, AMA Archives.

25. Graham, "To Teach," p. 21.

26. Ibid., p. 9, Lockwood to AMA, 6 January, 17 April 1862, AMA Archives.

27. Interview with Mrs. Louise Davis Stone, Philadelphia, Pa., 27 September 1977; Arthur P. Davis, "William Roscoe Davis and his Descendants," *The Negro History Bulletin* 13(1950): 75-80.

28. Ibid.; Graham, "To Teach," pp. 9,20; *AMM* 5(1861): 248.

29. Walker, "History of First Baptist;" Lockwood to AMA, 17 April, 20 March 1862, AMA Archives.

30. Howard P. Nash, Jr., *Stormy Petrel: The Life and Times of General Benjamin F. Butler, 1818-1893* (Rutherford, N.J., 1969) p. 102; *Official Records of the Union and Confederate Armies, The War of the Rebellion*, 1st series, 2: 649, 797-98.

31. Ibid., p. 862.

32. Ibid., pp. 797-98; Edward H. Bonekemper, "Negro Ownership of Property in Hampton and Elizabeth City County, Va., 1860-1870," *Journal of Negro History* 55(1970): 169.

33. Nash, *Stormy Petrel*, pp. 95-101.

34. Ibid.

35. For a brief summary of the problems presented to the North by escaping slaves in 1861, see J. G. Randall and David Donald, *The Civil War and Reconstruction* (Lexington, Mass, 1969), pp. 370-73.

36. *Official Records* 2: 649. Butler's suspicions about rebel use of slaves were well-founded. General Benjamin Ewell called for the use of slaves for the building of defenses in his "Proclamation to the Citizens of James City, York, and Warwick Counties," n.d. (but obviously 1861), Ewell Papers, William and Mary College Archives.

37. *Official Records* 2: 650.

38. Ibid., pp. 862-63, 886-87.

39. Yorktown *Cavalier*, (25 June 1862); Benjamin Ewell to Lizza Ewell, 31 December 1862, Ewell Papers.

40. Pierce, *Enfranchisement*, pp. 24-29; *Official Records* 2: 53. Most of the early refugees were drawn from the 2,400 slaves in Elizabeth City County. The location of Confederate lines made it difficult for fugitives from neighboring counties to reach Hampton.

Chapter 2

1. *AMM* 5(1861): 249; Richard Drake, "The American Missionary Association and the Southern Negro, 1861-1888," Ph.D. Dissertation, Emory

University, 1951, p. 10; Charles Demon to Sarah (Demon?), 30 January 1862, Demon Papers, Southern Collection, University of North Carolina; Arthur P. Davis, "William Roscoe Davis and his Descendants," p. 77; Lewis Lockwood to AMA, 3 January 1862, AMA Archives; *Official Records*, 2: 765.

2. Edward L. Pierce, *Enfranchisement and Citizenship*, pp. 35-40.

3. *Official Records*, 2: 1004.

4. George P. Erwin to Mrs. Erwin, 28 July 1861, George Phifer Papers, Southern Collection, Yorktown *Cavalier*, 25 June 1862.

5. Howard P. Nash, Jr., *Stormy Petrel*, p. 73.

6. Lewis Tappan to Benjamin Butler, 3 August 1861; Butler to Tappan, 10 August 1861, AMA Archives.

7. *AMM* 12(1868): 97-99; James McPherson, *The Struggle for Equality: Abolitionists and the Negro in the Civil War and Reconstruction* (Princeton, 1964), pp. 5-6.

8. It is difficult to determine the exact number of AMA missionaries and teachers who served in the South during the Civil War and Reconstruction because of the frequent turnover of workers and poor record keeping. The author's estimates are based upon reports published in the *AMM* for the years 1862-68.

9. *AMM* 5(1861): 260.

10. 37th Congress, 2nd Session, House of Representatives, *Executive Document No. 85*, "Africans in Fort Monroe Military District: A Letter from the Secretary of War" (Washington, 1863), p. 2.

11. Lockwood to AMA, 4 January 1862, AMA Archives.

12. "Africans in Fort Monroe," pp. 5, 7-8; Lockwood to AMA, 3 January 1862, C. B. Wilder to George Whipple, 20 March 1862, AMA Archives.

13. Lockwood to AMA, 3 January 1862, ibid., *AMM* 5(1861); 287.

14. Lockwood to AMA, 27 January 1862, AMA Archives.

15. C. P. Day to Whipple, 8 April 1862, AMA Archives.

16. Lockwood to AMA, 4, 5, 14 February, 4 March 1862, AMA Archives; George Whipple to John A. Wilder, 31 March 1862, Wilder Papers, Yale University.

17. Lockwood to AMA, 4 March 1862, John Linson to Whipple, 22 March 1862, AMA Archives.

18. C. B. Wilder to E. M. Stanton, n.d. (but from context between March and October 1862), Wilder Papers; *AMM* 6(1862): 232.

19. Ibid., 2(1862): 108; Lockwood to AMA, 11, 15 March 1862, J. J. Simson to S. S. Jocelyn, 10 April 1862, AMA Archives.

20. Lockwood to AMA, 3 April, 7 April 1862, ibid.

21. Wilder to AMA, 3 June 1862, Oliver to AMA, 27 July 1862, ibid.

22. C. B. Wilder to Whipple, 9 June 1862, Whipple to Jocelyn, 8, 12, 15, 16, 18 July 1862, ibid.; "Statement of Facts submitted to General John A. Dix, 1 July 1862," Wilder Papers.

23. *AMM* 6(1862), 208, 209; Oliver to AMA, 5 August 1862, Wilder to AMA, 3 June 1862, AMA Archives.

24. C. P. Day to Whiting, 31 August, 30 September 1862, ibid.

25. Lockwood to AMA, 7, 11, April, 2 June 1862, ibid.

26. W. L. Coan to AMA, 5 September 1863, ibid.

27. C. B. Wilder to Whipple, 28 December 1862, ibid.

28. For a thorough discussion of the Proclamation and its provisions,

see J. G. Randall and David Donald, *The Civil War and Reconstruction*, pp. 379-91.

29. *AMM* 7(1863): 202-212.

30. Ibid.; Butler to Lieutenant J. B. Kinsman, 11 December 1863. Bureau of Refugees, Freedmen, and Abandoned Lands, National Archives, Washington, D. C. (hereinafter BRFAL, Va.).

31. Virginia Bureau of Negro Affairs, "Negro Census Report, February, 1864," ibid.

32. C. P. Day to Whipple, 29 April 1865, AMA Archives.

33. General Order, 14 November 1863, "Rations Issued, December, 1863," BRFAL, Va.; *AMM* 7(1863): 136, (1863): 232; Helen W. Ludlow, ed., "Personal Memories and Letters of General S. C. Armstrong; Hawaii, Williams, War, Hampton," (unpublished manuscript), p. 530, Hampton Institute Archives. The Union army began to enlist black soldiers in 1863. For a study of these troops see Dudley Cornish, *The Sable Arm* (New York, 1966).

34. Orlando Brown to J. B. Kinsman, 20 June, 24 June 1864, BRFAL, Va.

35. Oliver P. St. John to Kinsman, 31 August 1864, ibid.

36. Orlando Brown to Kinsman, 15 June, 14 July 1864, ibid.

37. Kinsman to Butler, 14 July 1864, Butler to Kinsman, 18 July 1864, ibid.

38. John L. Truman to Kinsman, 31 August 1864; Oliver P. St. John to Kinsman, 19 November 1864, ibid.

39. Ibid.

40. Kinsman to Butler, 14 July 1864, ibid.

41. Special Order 15, 163, 144, ibid.; *AMM* 8(1864): 37.

42. General J. J. Wister to Butler, 18 March 1864, Lieutenant R. Churchill to Kinsman, 5 April 1864, Wister to Kinsman, April 1864, BRFAL, Va.; George L. Neville to his father, 23 August 1863, George Neville Papers, University of Virginia.

43. Brown to Captain Lyon, 14 February 1864, Beals to Butler, n.d., 1863, Kinsman to Butler, 12 December 1863, Lieutenant Darlington to C. B. Wilder, 9 January 1863, Mrs. Jane Wallis to The Reverend Woodbury, 10 December 1863, BRFAL, Va.

44. Butler to Kinsman, 11 December 1863, Kinsman to Butler, 12 December 1863, ibid.

45. P. Litts to Whiting, 24 March 1863, Thomas Peake to Whipple, 26 March 1863, C. P. Day to Jocelyn, 8 July 1863, C. B. Wilder to AMA, 1 April 1865, C. P. Day to Whipple, 4 April 1865, AMA Archives; *AMM* 8 (1864): 233.

Chapter 3

1. For a history of the Port Royal Experiment, see Willie Lee Rose, *Rehearsal for Reconstruction*, (New York, 1964).

2. Lewis Lockwood to L. Tappan, G. Whipple and S. S. Jocelyn, 4 September, 1861, AMA Archives.

3. Ibid.

4. *AMM* 5(1861): 159, 15(1871): 196, 5(1861): 289; Bell Irvin Wiley, *Southern Negroes, 1861-1865*, (New Haven, 1938) p. 206.

5. Lockwood to Tappan and Whipple, 3 September 1861, Lockwood to AMA, 23 December 1861, AMA Archives.

6. Lockwood to Tappan, 10 September 1861, 28 May 1862, ibid.

7. Lockwood to Tappan, Whipple, Jocelyn, 4 September 1861, ibid.

8. Lockwood to AMA, 10 September 1861, 12, 21, 23 May 1862, John Oliver to AMA, 2 June 1862, ibid.

9. Lockwood to AMA, 23 December 1861, ibid.; *AMM* 5(1861): 257.

10. Lockwood to AMA, 23 December 1861, 4 January 1862, Mary Peake to Jocelyn, January 1862, AMA Archives.

11. Lockwood to AMA, 6 March 1862, ibid.

12. C. P. Day to Whipple, 8 April 1862, John Linson to Whipple, 22 March 1862; Lockwood to AMA, 23 May 1862, T. D. Tucker to AMA, 27 November 1862, Wilder to AMA, 27 November 1862, ibid.; *AMM* 6(1862): 183.

13. Lockwood to AMA, 25 January 1862, AMA Archives; *AMM* 6 (1862): 83.

14. Ibid., (1862): 108.

15. C. P. Day to Whipple, 8 April 1862, AMA Archives.

16. John Oliver to AMA, 2 June 1862, ibid.; *AMM* 6(1862): 184.

17. Ibid., p. 183; T. D. Tucker to AMA, 27 November 1862, C. B. Wilder to AMA, 27 November 1862, AMA Archives. Two other missionaries, John Bancroft and a Mr. Hardcastle, also came to Hampton in this period, but were forced to leave after a short stay due to ill health. Lockwood to AMA, 4, 19 February 1862, ibid.

18. *AMM* 6(1862): 34.

19. Ibid., 5(1861): 256; C. P. Day to AMA, 30 September 1862, George Hyde to Whiting, 21 February 1862, AMA Archives.

20. Ibid.

21. Lockwood to AMA, 13 May 1862, ibid.

22. Many letters from missionaries in these early years were reprinted in the *AMM*. The manuscript letters still bear the editor's red pencil which deleted, not only extraneous detail, but also any negative comments about the blacks.

23. Hyde to Jocelyn, 18 January 1862, AMA Archives.

24. *AMM* 6(1862): 60.

25. Lockwood to AMA 27 January, 23 April, 7 May 1862, AMA Archives; *AMM* 6(1862): 83. Davis liked the North so much he considered staying there. His long absence caused his wife Nancy to grow suspicious so she packed up her family, went north and brought William back to Hampton. Arthur P. Davis, "William Roscoe Davis and his Descendants," p. 80.

26. Lockwood to AMA, 24 May 1862, AMA Archives. At this time there were three black churches in Norfolk, two Baptist, one Methodist; all had white ministers. These churches were the focal point of the black community in Norfolk. Each black man could be identified by his church. When Lockwood landed in Norfolk, he asked the first black man he saw for "Brother Jonas Brown of the First Colored Baptist Church." He was immediately introduced to a member of that congregation who, in turn, took him to meet "Brother Brown." Ibid.

27. *AMM* 7(1862): 202-12, 8(1864): 284, 15(1871): 197-98.

28. Ibid. 7(1863): 137, 8(1864): 172.

29. Lockwood to AMA, 24 May, 15 September 1862, AMA Archives; *AMM* 15(1871): 197; 7(1863): 137, 202-12, 8(1864): 284.

30. Ibid. 7(1863): 108 201-4, 8(1864): 98; W. S. Bell to AMA, 7 December 1863, AMA Archives.

31. T. D. Tucker to AMA, 24 December 1862, H. S. Beals to AMA, 27 October 1863, ibid.; *AMM* 7(1863): 203-4, 8(1864): 37, 293.

32. Day to Jocelyn, 11 August 1862, Mary Green to Whiting, 13 August 1862, AMA Archives.

33. *AMM* 6(1862): 159, 254; C. P. Day to Jocelyn, 11 August 1862, Litts to AMA 10 December 1862, Tucker to AMA, 24 December 1862, Lockwood to AMA, 29 January, 5 May 1862, Whipple to Jocelyn and Whiting, 9 August 1862, AMA Archives.

34. Day to Whipple, 8 May 1863, AMA Archives; *AMM* 7(1863): 135, 7 (1864): 35, 96, 125, 138.

35. Stone to Jocelyn, 9, 10 February 1864, Tucker to Whipple, 24 December 1864, AMA Archives; *AMM* 8(1864): 96.

36. *Centennial Memorial Book, Zion Baptist Church, 1863-1963*; Audrey Jackson Walker, "The History of First Baptist Church."

37. Bernard A. Weisberger, *They Gathered at the River: The Story of the Great Revivalists and Their Impact upon Religion in America* (Boston 1958), pp. 29, 43.

38. Eugene Genovese, *Roll, Jordan, Roll* (New York, 1972), pp. 159-68, 183-284. Genovese's masterful interpretation of slave religion is supported by the evidence this author found for blacks in wartime Hampton.

39. Lucy Peck to Samuel Hunt, 8 January 1866, AMA Archives; *AMM* 7 (1863): 203, 8(1864): 96, 126.

40. Ibid., 10(1866): 147-50.

41. Mrs. J. S. Talcott to Whipple, 12 April 1865, AMA Archives; Charles Young to Kinsman, 15 March 1864, BRFAL, Va.

42. *AMM* 10(1866): 52. (Italics in text.)

43. Alexander Kinmount, *Twelve Lectures on the Natural History of Man* (Cincinnati, 1839) as quoted in George Frederickson, *The Black Image in the White Mind: The Debate on Afro-American Character and Destiny, 1817-1914* (New York, 1971), p. 105. For a full discussion of the school of romantic racialism as developed by Frederickson, see ibid., pp. 97-129.

44. Beals to AMA, 27 October 1863, George Hyde to Jocelyn, 18 January 1862, AMA Archives; *AMM* 7(1863): 160.

45. Ibid. 8(1864): 126-27; Lucy Peck to Hunt, 8 January 1866, AMA Archives.

46. *AMM* 10(1866): 52.

47. Mrs. J. S. Talcott to Whipple, 12 April 1865, Lockwood to AMA, 11 April 1862, AMA Archives.

48. J. B. Lowrey to AMA, 19 May 1863, ibid.

49. J. B. Bebout to Jocelyn, 10 March 1863, ibid.

50. Beals to Whipple, 29 April 1865, ibid.

51. Abbie Guile to Hunt, 21 January 1866, C. B. Wilder to Whipple, 12 December 1864, ibid.; *AMM* 7(1863): 137.

52. Ibid. (1863): 159, 9(1865): 3.

53. C. B. Wilder to Whipple, 22 April, 2 September 1862, Lockwood to AMA, 16 September 1862, C. B. Wilder to Whipple and Jocelyn, 14 November 1862, AMA Archives.

54. Day to Whipple, 27 April 1863, Porter Green to Jocelyn, 28 April 1863, ibid.

55. Day to Whipple, 9 January 1864, Stone to Whipple, 9 February 1864, ibid.

56. *AMM* 8(1864): 172; C. B. Wilder to Jocelyn, 26 March 1863, C. B. Wilder to Whipple, 2 September 1863, Day to Whiting, 14 April 1863, Mrs. J. W. Coan to Whipple, 8 April 1863, AMA Archives.

57. *AMM* 10(1866): 152. (Italics in text.)

Chapter 4

1. Dabney Cosby to Sue Cosby, 8 October 1863, Cosby Papers, Southern Collection, University of North Carolina.

2. Mary T. Hunley Diary, entries for 12, 18 May 1862, ibid. Mrs. Hunley lists the first entry as 12 May 1861, but the text of the diary and other evidence suggest that this was a writing error.

3. Ibid., entries for 4, 5 June 1862.

4. Edwin Ruffin, Jr., Plantation Book, entry for 24 May 1862, ibid.

5. Ibid., entries for 9, 18, 21, 22, 23, 24, 25 June 1862.

6. C. B. Wilder to Orlando Brown, 9 September 1865, BRFAL, Va.

7. George Washington Fields, "Come on, Children: The Autobiography of George Washington Fields, Born a Slave in Hanover County, Virginia," unpublished manuscript, Hampton Association for the Arts and Humanities, Hampton, Va.

8. Ibid., Fields recalled that the escaping slaves also sang the well-known song, "Oh Freedom."

> Oh Freedom, Oh Freedom
> Oh Freedom, Oh Freedom
> And before I'll be a slave
> I'll be buried in my grave
> And go home to my Lord and be Free.

9. C. P. Day to AMA, 11 August 1862, AMA Archives; "Fortress Monroe Memo Book," September, October 1865, BRFAL, Va.; *True Southerner*, 7, 14 December 1865, 12 April 1866.

10. C. Young to J. P. Kinsman, 15 March 1864, BRFAL, Va.; Mrs. J. S. Talcott to Whipple, 12 April 1865, H. L. Beals to Whipple, 29 April 1865, AMA Archives.

11. Beals to Whipple, 29 April 1865, C. B. Wilder to AMA, 17 May 1866, ibid.; *AMM* 9(1865): 212.

12. *True Southerner*, 14 December 1865.

13. Helen W. Ludlow, "Personal Memories and Letters of General S. C. Armstrong," p. 531.

14. Mrs. J. S. Talcott to Whipple, 12 April 1865, Lucy Peck to Hunt, 8 January 1866, AMA Archives; C. Young to Kinsman, 15 March 1865, "Fortress Monroe Journal," entries for 19 September, 13, 20 October 1865, BRFAL, Va.

15. C. B. Wilder to Whipple, 12 December 1864, Abbie Fuile to Hunt, 21 January 1866, AMA Archives.

16. I. F. Massey to Gen. Samuel Chapman Armstrong (hereinafter, SCA), 11 September 1866, M. S. Reed to SCA, 11 September 1866, BRFAL, Va.

17. C. B. Wilder to Brown, 3 January 1866, "Fortress Monroe Memo

Book," entry for 22 September 1865, "Rations Issued," reports from December 1863 to May 1866, ibid.

18. Beals to Whipple, 29 April 1865, J. B. Bebout to Jocelyn, 10 March 1863, AMA Archives.

19. Brown to Captain Lyons, 17 February 1864, BRFAL, Va.; Beals to Whipple, 29 April 1865, AMA Archives. See chapter 2 above concerning Union army raids on black settlements.

20. "Endorsement Book, Fort Monroe," "Land and Property in Elizabeth City County, 1865," BRFAL, Va.

21. Eugene Genovese, *Roll, Jordan, Roll*, pp. 161-68.

22. Lockwood to AMA, 4 January 1962, Tucker to Whipple, 24 December 1864, AMA Archives; *AMM* 10(1866): 147-50. Also see Joseph R. Washington, *Black Religion: The Negro and Christianity in the United States* (Boston, 1964) and Genovese, *Roll, Jordan, Roll*, whose descriptions of the antebellum black church correspond closely to the fragmentary evidence reported by the Hampton missionaries.

23. *AMM* 10(1866): 52, 147-50; Wilder to Whipple, 12 December 1864, AMA Archives.

24. *Centennial Memorial Book, Zion Baptist Church, 1863-1963;* Audrey J. Walker, "History of First Baptist Church;" Charles Whipple to C. B. Wilder, 17 March 1865, BRFAL, Va.

25. Blacks seldom stated directly how they saw the whites supervising them. Their attitudes toward the military are reflected in Bebout's complaints about their unwillingness to labor (Bebout to Whipple, 10 March 1863, AMA Archives) and their growing distrust of all whites noted by C. P. Day (Day to Jocelyn, 8 July 1863, ibid.). The blacks identified C. B. Wilder as the white man whose sympathies they could trust and increasingly took their complaints to him. (See "Fortress Monroe Memo Book, 1865," BRFAL, Va.)

26. Beals to Whipple, 29 April 1865, Abbie Guile to Hunt, 21 January 1866, AMA Archives.

27. Jacob West to C. B. Wilder, 26 July 1864, BRFAL, Va.; *AMM* 8(1864): 188; *Yorktown Cavalier*, 12 October 1863.

28. *AMM* 9(1865): 3.

Chapter 5

1. Rodney Churchill to C. B. Wilder, 14 June 1864, BRFAL, Va.; Helen W. Ludlow, ed., "Personal Memories and Letters of General S. C. Armstrong," pp. 533, 539.

2. C. B. Wilder to Orlando Brown, 18 January 1866, BRFAL, Va.; *True Southerner*, 21 December 1865.

3. Ibid., 25 January 1866; C. B. Wilder to Brown, 18 January 1866, BRFAL, Va.; C. G. Paine to AMA, 2 January 1866, Ellen Benton to S. Hunt, 16 January 1866, AMA Archives.

4. Circular Order, 16 March 1866, SCA to Lieutenant Massey, 20 March 1866, C. B. Wilder to Brown, 18 October 1865, Captain C. H. Warren to SCA, 10 October 1866, "Fortress Monroe Memo Book," September, October 1865, BRFAL, Va.

5. Richmond *Whig*, 15 November 1865; see also the Richmond *Dispatch*, 25 February 1865.

6. C. B. Wilder to Brown, 18 January 1866, BRFAL, Va.; *True Southerner*, 18 January 1866.

7. Massey to SCA, 24 July 1866, Lieutenant H. K. Ayres to Massey, 30 September 1866, BRFAL, Va.; *True Southerner*, 21 December 1865, 15 February 1866.

8. Massey to SCA, 23 May 1866, BRFAL, Va.; *True Southerner*, 18 January 1866, 25 January 1866, 30 November 1866.

9. Isabella G. Sourstan to Manuel Thoustan, 16 July 1865, Manuel Thoustan Papers, Southern Collection, University of North Carolina.

10. C. B. Wilder to Brown, 18 January 1866, BRFAL, Va.

11. Entry for 2 November 1865, "Fortress Monroe Journal," ibid.; *True Southerner*, 18 January 1866.

12. Norfolk *Post* as quoted in ibid., 28 December 1865; ibid., 19 April 1866.

13. Lieutenant M. S. Reed to R. L. Burnett, 24 April 1866, Warren to SCA, 11 May 1866, Massey to SCA, 10, 13 November 1866, Lieutenant C. H. Goodyear to Reed, 28 November 1866, Massey to SCA, 30 June 1866, BRFAL, Va.

14. Massey to SCA, 13 November 1866, SCA to Massey, 22 May 1866, Massey to SCA, 23 May 1866, Massey to R. H. Powers, 1 June 1866, R. H. Powers to Massey, 27 June 1866, ibid.

15. *True Southerner*, 24 November 1865, 1, 14 February, 19 April 1866; *Souvenir Programme of Bethel A.M.E. Church, Hampton, Virginia, November 7-23, 1865*, Naomi W. Boykin, "The History of Bethel A.M.E. Church."

16. Massey to SCA, 15 May 1866, BRFAL, Va.

17. "Fortress Monroe Journal," entries for 13, 20 October 1865, SCA to Brown, 30 September 1866, BRFAL, Va.

18. *True Southerner*, 7, 14 December 1865, 12 February, 15 April 1866, Circular Order Eight, 1865, BRFAL, Va.

19. *True Southerner*, 24, 30 November 1865.

20. Ludlow, "General S. C. Armstrong," p. 32; *True Southerner*, 24 November 1865; SCA to O. Brown, n.d., 1866, William Thorton to SCA, 16, 22, 23, 28 August 1866, BRFAL, Va.

21. *True Southerner*, 7, 21 December 1865, 4 January, 1, 8 February 1866.

22. Ibid., 14 December 1865, 4 January, 8, 15 February 1866.

23. Ibid., 7 December 1865.

24. *American Palladium and Eastern Virginia Gazette*, 30 August 1865.

25. *True Southerner*, 19 April 1866; "Prospectus," ibid., 14 November 1865.

26. Ibid., 30 November 1865, 14 December 1865, 25 January 1866.

27. Ibid., 24 November 1865, 8 February 1866.

28. Ibid., 15 February 1866, 19 April 1866; Gladys Blair, "Northerners in the Reconstruction of Hampton, Virginia, 1865-1870," M. A. Thesis, Old Dominion University, 1975, p. 72.

29. "Fortress Monroe Journal," entries for 22 October, 16, 17, 21 November 1865; Wilder to Brown, 17 November 1866; BRFAL, Va.

30. *True Southerner*, 24 November 1865, 7, 14 December 1865, 1 February 1865.

31. Reed to William Austin, 6 July 1866, Massey to SCA, 10 July 1866, William Austin to Brown, 17 July 1866, Circular Order 9, 19 August 1866, BRFAL, Va.

32. *True Southerner*, 8 March 1866.
33. SCA to Brown, 16 April 1866, BRFAL, Va.; *True Southerner*, 19 April 1866.

Chapter 6
1. William S. McFeely, *Yankee Stepfather*, pp. 3-9.
2. *AMM* 9(1865): 147.
3. Special Orders One, Four, Six, Eight, Twelve, Twenty-two (1865), Circular Order, 2 February 1864, BRFAL, Va.
4. "Fortress Monroe Memo Book," entries for 9, 22, 23, September, 7 October 1865.
5. *True Southerner*, 18 January 1866; C. B. Wilder to Brown, 8 November 1865, Wilder to Captain McEwan, 1, 12 December 1865, Wilder to Lieutenant L. Kilbrith, 20 November 1865, BRFAL, Va.
6. For a full discussion of Circular Order Thirteen, the failure to enforce it, and its ultimate rescission see McFeely, *Yankee Stepfather*, pp. 103-34.
7. C. B. Wilder to Brown, 17 November 1865, BRFAL, Va.
8. Lieutenant R. Churchill to C. B. Wilder, 7 March 1866, Circular Order Four, 25 March 1866, Lieutenant Massey to SCA, 18 March 1866, BRFAL, Va.
9. *True Southerner*, 14 December 1865.
10. Ibid., 21 December 1865, Massey to SCA, 15 May 1866, BRFAL. Va.
11. SCA to Massey, 16 May 1866, ibid.
12. C. B. Wilder to AMA, 15 January 1866, AMA Archives.
13. C. B. Wilder to Brown, 19, 30 December 1865, 18 January 1866, BRFAL, Va.
14. *True Southerner*, 11, 25 January 1866; C. B. Wilder to Churchill, 19 February 1866, BRFAL, Va.
15. Minnie Drew to Austin Drew, 24 December 1865, as quoted in *True Southerner*, 11 January 1866.
16. Ibid., 21 December 1865.
17. Ibid., 1 February 1866; R. M. Manly to D. B. White, as quoted in ibid.
18. Ibid., 25 January 1866; Circular Order, 22 December 1865, BRFAL, Va.
19. C. B. Wilder to Brown, 3 January 1866, E. W. Coffin to C. B. Wilder, 17 August 1865, C. B. Wilder to Churchill, 19 February 1866, ibid.
20. *AMM* 9(1865): 241; *True Southerner*, 11 January 1866.
21. Special Order Thirteen, 19 October 1865, Massey to Robert Powers, 13 February 1866, Churchill to C. B. Wilder, 7 March 1866, BRFAL, Va. One of the specific pleas made by the York County freedmen to O. O. Howard was the return of Churchill and dismissal of Lieutenant Massey whom they considered hostile to them. Peter Corcy and Phillip Tabb to O. O. Howard, 7 December 1866, ibid.
22. Churchill to C. B. Wilder, 26 January 1866, Special Order Three, 22 January 1866, Special Order Twelve, 9 March 1866, C. B. Wilder to Brown, 7 February 1866, J. H. Barlow to Major Stanhope, 29 January 1866, ibid.
23. Circular Order, 4 November 1865, ibid.
24. Ibid.

25. *AMM* 9(1865): 183-84; H. B. Scott to C. B. Wilder, 1 November 1865; C. B. Wilder to Brown, 27 September 1865, 16 November 1865, 5 January 1866, BRFAL, Va.

26. *AMM* 9(1865): 183-84.

27. C. B. Wilder to AMA, 15 January 1866, AMA Archives.

28. *True Southerner,* 15 March 1866.

29. Mary F. Armstrong and Helen Ludlow, *Hampton and Its Students, by Two of its Teachers* (New York, 1865), pp. 21-23; SCA to Mrs. C. C. Armstrong, 17 November 1863, 4 March 1864, quoted in Helen W. Ludlow, "Personal Memories and Letters of General S. C. Armstrong," pp. 351, 366.

30. *True Southerner,* 15 March 1866.

31. Ludlow, "General S. C. Armstrong," pp. 517, 526; SCA to Richard Baxter Armstrong, 3 March 1866, SCA to Mrs. C. C. Armstrong, 14 November 1866, in ibid., pp. 537, 547.

32. SCA to Mrs. C. C. Armstrong, 15 March 1857, in ibid.

33. SCA to Brown, 6 June 1866, SCA to Massey, 16 May 1866, SCA to Brown, 9 September 1866, BRFAL, Va.

34. Ludlow, "General S. C. Armstrong," p. 523; SCA to Brown, 28 March 1866, SCA to Yardley Warner, 1 March 1867, Hampton Institute Archives; SCA to Brown, "Semi-Annual Report," 30 June 1866, BRFAL, Va.

35. Ludlow, "General S. C. Armstrong," p. 523.

36. SCA to Brown, "Semi-Annual Report," 30 June 1866, SCA to Massey, 9 November 1866, Massey to SCA, 17 November 1866, 10 December 1866, Major F. A. Butts to SCA, 12 November 1866, BRFAL, Va.

37. SCA to Brown, "Semi-Annual Report," 30 June 1866, ibid.

38. SCA to Yardley Warner, 1 March 1867, Hampton Institute Archives.

39. SCA to Brown, "Semi-Annual Report," 30 June 1866, BRFAL, Va.

40. Ibid., SCA to Brown, 2 September 1866, ibid.

41. R. H. Powers to Massey, 12 September 1866, I. H. Barlow to Massey, 13 September 1866, Massey to SCA, 24 December 1866, ibid.

42. Circular Order Twenty-Five, 8 June 1866, ibid.

43. Lieutenant Chandler to SCA, 4 October 1866, Lieutenant E. Murphy to SCA, 26 November 1866, ibid.; SCA to Mrs. C. C. Armstrong, 30 April 1867, in Ludlow, "General S. C. Armstrong," p. 585.

44. SCA to Brown, "Semi-Annual Report," 30 June 1866, BRFAL, Va.

45. O. O. Howard to SCA, 15 February 1867, SCA to Asst. Superintendents, Circular Order Twenty-One, 23 November 1866, Lieutenant G. P. Goodyear to SCA, 28 March 1866, SCA to Brown, 28 March 1866, SCA to Asst. Superintendents, Circular Order Ten, 24 May 1866, SCA to Brown, 28 April 1866, ibid.

46. SCA to Lieutenant Colonel Donnell, 9th Regiment, USCT, 12 September 1866, Hampton Institute Archives.

47. Massey to SCA, 17 July 1866, James Bates to SCA, 23 August 1866, Massey to SCA, 8 September 1866, SCA to Brown, 9 September 1866, BRFAL, Va.

48. SCA to Brown, "Semi-Annual Report," 30 June 1866, BRFAL, Va.

49. Massey to SCA, 11, 17 April, 9 May 1867, "List of Colored Persons Sent North, 1866-67," ibid.; SCA to B. L. Stearns, 13 July 1866, Hampton Institute Archives.

50. O. P. St. John to SCA, 27 June 1866, SCA to St. John, 5 July 1866, BRFAL, Va.

51. Mrs. L. A. Grimes to SCA, 5 July 1866, SCA to Mrs. Grimes, 9 July 1866, SCA to B. L. Stearns, 13 July 1866, Hampton Institute Archives.

52. "List of Colored Persons Sent North, 1866-67," BRFAL, Va.

53. Virginia Bureau of Negro Affairs, "Negro Census Report, February 1864," BRFAL, Va.; Eighth U.S. Census, 1860.

54. Ibid.; Ninth U.S. Census, 1870.

55. Massey to SCA, 11 September 1866, Reed to SCA, 11 September 1866, BRFAL, Va.

56. Reed to SCA, 31 December 1866, Massey to SCA, 5 January 1867, SCA to Brown, 12 January 1867, ibid.

57. Ninth U.S. Census, 1870.

Chapter 7

1. William S. McFeely, *Yankee Stepfather*, pp. 220-23.

2. Ibid., pp. 223-28, 245-46, Richmond *Whig*, 15 November 1865, *True Southerner*, 15 March 1866.

3. McFeely, *Yankee Stepfather*, pp. 291-96.

4. Ibid., p. 302. Three of these ten were Maryland, Kentucky and West Virginia which had sided with the Union during the war (West Virginia seceded from Virginia after the latter joined the Confederacy). The others were Tennessee, Alabama, Arkansas, Florida, Louisiana, North Carolina and South Carolina, ibid.

5. Ibid., pp. 270-73.

6. Ibid., pp. 290-91.

7. R. G. Patten to SCA, 23 March 1867, Lieutenant Henry Ayres to Thomas Crocker, Overseer of the Poor, York County, 11 September 1868, SCA to Asst. Superintendents, Circular Order Nine, 18 May 1866, Lieutenant Massey to SCA, 7 June 1866, SCA to O. Brown, "Quarterly Report," 31 December 1867, BRFAL, Va.

8. Massey to SCA, 3 February 1866, Lieutenant Reed to SCA, 6 October 1866, Brown to SCA, 11 January 1867, E. B. Montague to SCA, 20 December 1866 (in this case the commonwealth attorney for King and Queen County, which was outside Armstrong's district, refused to return the children of a Hampton freedman because the local Bureau agent had already investigated the case and approved the indenture.) Massey to SCA, 22 February 1867, George Sherwood to SCA, 20 March 1867, Massey to SCA, 19 March 1867, J. C. Strawbridge to SCA, 22 March 1867, Ayres to SCA, 20 August 1868, ibid. This practice was not confined to Hampton; for other instances, see McFeely, *Yankee Stepfather*, pp. 269-70.

9. Captain William Tidballs to Captain Frank Crandon, 5 April 1866, Crandon to Tidballs, 16 April 1866, SCA to Brown, "Semi-Annual Report," 30 June 1866, ibid. In very few of these cases did a former master ever ask for the return of female or elderly freedmen, only for children and young men.

10. SCA to Brown, "Quarterly Report," 31 December 1867, Ayres to Lewis Ellison, 30 August 1868, ibid.

11. Reed to SCA, 25 March 1867, ibid.

12. Captain John McDonald to SCA, 23 May 1866, ibid.

13. Massey to SCA, 28 June 1867, ibid.

14. SCA to Brown; "Quarterly Report," 31 December 1867, T. Lilliston to General Terry, 9 August 1866, Massey to SCA, 4 April 1867, ibid.

15. Croxton Loomis to SCA, 1 August 1866, Massey to C. B. Wilder, 26 January 1866, SCA to Brown, "Quarterly Report," 31 December 1867, SCA to Massey, 10 February 1867, Massey to SCA 27 April 1867, ibid.

16. SCA to Massey, Circular Order Two, 16 February 1866, Circular Order Three, 21 February 1866, Massey to SCA, 21 January 1866, ibid.

17. Brown to Subcommissioners, Circular Order Nine, 1 May 1867, Circular Order Eight, 2 May 1868, Lieutenant Sherwood to W. Coulter, 5 May 1868, SCA to Brown, 30 May 1868, Ayres to "Colored People of James City County," 16 September 1868, SCA to Asst. Subcommissioners, Circular Order One, 8 September 1868, ibid.

18. Brown to Subcommissioners, Circular Letter Twenty-Five, 2 December 1867, ibid.

19. Garrick Mallery, asst. inspector general, to Brown, 1 June 1868, ibid.

20. SCA to Brown, 26 March 1868, ibid.

21. SCA to Brown, "Quarterly Report," 26 March 1868, ibid.

22. SCA to Brown, "Quarterly Report," 30 June 1868, ibid. The Bureau office in Hampton did a poor job of recording labor contracts; a few are scattered through the records from 1865-67, in the "Letters Sent" and "Letters Retain" files, BRFAL, Va. Also see Contract between F. G. Twyman and Cornelia Brooks, 9 January 1867, for the employment of Mrs. Brooks and her son Frank. The terms were room and board and three dollars a month for Mrs. Brooks in return for "housework, cooking, washing, etc., and to do what she can to promote the general interest of said Twyman." The terms for Frank were room, board, one summer suit, one winter suit, and one pair of winter shoes, but no wages. Mrs. Brooks could quit at any time without loss of accumulated wages; there was no such escape clause for Frank. Also see Contract between Wisley Nash and his employees Fields Overly, Edward Hardy, and Walden Scott, 1 January 1870. In exchange for use of Nash's land, they paid one-half of all crops produced, food and clothing. Each black promised to supply "one woman hand" (apparently their wives) who would be paid at the rate of "two-thirds of a hand." And also see Contract between Fulwar Skipwith and his eighteen employees, 1 January 1870, Skipwith Papers, William and Mary College Library.

23. SCA to Brown, "Quarterly Report," 26 March 1868, BRFAL, Va. "Eye servant," a popular expression among missionaries and Bureau men, refers to those who only work when being watched by supervisors.

24. SCA to Brown, "Quarterly Report," 30 June 1868, ibid.

25. W. Coulter to SCA, 11, 13 April 1868, SCA to Brown, "Quarterly Report," 1 November 1868, Ayres to SCA, 19 September 1867, ibid.

26. SCA to Brown, "Quarterly Report," 1 November 1868, ibid.

27. SCA to Mrs. C. C. Armstrong, 27 December 1868, Helen W. Ludlow, "Personal Memories and Letters of General S. C. Armstrong," p. 697.

28. Ninth U. S. Census, 1870, Figures for Elizabeth City County were: 5,471 blacks, 2,832 whites; York County: 4,691 blacks, 2,507 whites.

29. Luther P. Jackson, *Negro Officeholders in Virginia*, (Norfolk, VA, 1945) p. 30.

30. Ibid., Massey to SCA, 15 May 1866, SCA to Massey, 16 May 1866, Ayres to Brown, 31 August 1868, Ayres to SCA, 11, 30 September 1868, BRFAL, Va.

31. *Southern Workman* 1(1873): 403; 26(1897): 116; Arthur P. Davis "William Roscoe Davis and his Descendants," p. 82, Jackson, *Negro Officeholders*, pp. 26, 62; Audrey J. Walker, "A History of First Baptist Church."

32. Ibid.; *Southern Workman* 1(April 1873): 403; Davis, "William Roscoe Davis," pp. 82–83; *Centennial Memorial Book, Zion Baptist Church.*

33. Eighth U. S. Census, 1860; Ninth U. S. Census, 1870; Edward Bonekemper, "Negro Ownership of Real Property in Elizabeth City County, Va., 1860-1870," *Journal of Negro History* 55(1970): 177. Bonekemper's figures on black wealth, which include only real property, are slightly lower than those presented here.

34. Eighth U. S. Census, 1860; Ninth U. S. Census, 1870.

35. Ibid.

36. Ninth U. S. Census, 1870.

37. Walker, "A History of First Baptist Church," *Centennial Memorial Book, Zion Baptist Church.*

38. Davis, "William Roscoe Davis" pp. 82–83.

39. C. B. Wilder to Brown, 8 November 1865, Wilder to Captain McEwan, 1, 12 December 1865, Wilder to Lieutenant L. Kilbrith, 20 November 1865. BRFAL, Va.

Chapter 8

1. John W. Alvord, *Reports on Schools and Finances of Freedmen*, Bureau of Refugees, Freedmen, and Abandoned Lands, *Seventh Semi-Annual Report* (Washington, 1868), p. 14; *AMM* 9(1865): 197.

2. Norfolk *Journal* as quoted in ibid., 9(1867): 151.

3. Ibid., (1867): 10.

4. George Whipple to SCA, 10 April 1868, Hampton Institute Archives.

5. *AMM* 9(1865): 3.

6. Ibid., 14(1870): 266.

7. Ibid., 12(1868): 223.

8. Ibid., 11(1867): 108.

9. Ibid.

10. Ibid., 11, 10(1866): 190.

11. Ibid., 11(1867): 243, 12(1868): 122, 145, 147-48, 200; Alvord, *Sixth Semi-Annual Report*, 1868, p. 61; *Ninth Semi-Annual Report*, 1870, p. 61.

12. *AMM* 9(1865): 212, 11(1867): 58; Ellen Benton to S. Hunt, 16 January 1866, C. B. Wilder to AMA, 17 May 1866, AMA Archives.

13. *AMM* 13(1869): 123; *Catalogue of the Hampton Normal and Agricultural Institute, Hampton, Virginia, 1870-71* (Hampton, 1870) (hereinafter *Catalogue of HNAI*), pp. 19-20.

14. SCA to Whipple, 6 July 1866, AMA Archives.

15. *Catalogue of HNAI*, 1870-71, p. 19.

16. SCA to Emma Armstrong, n.d., 1878, Armstrong Papers, Williams College Library. I am indebted to Professor E. K. Graham of Hampton Institute for permitting me to use his transcripts of the Armstrong Papers.

17. *Catalogue of HNAI*, 1871-72, p. 21.

18. Ibid., p. 22.

19. Alvord, *Tenth Semi-Annual Report, 1870*, p. 50; *Annual Reports for Academic and Fiscal Year Ending June, 1880* (Hampton, 1880), pp. 5-6.

20. Francis Peabody, *Education for Life* (New York, 1918), pp. 8, 118-19.

21. C. B. Wilder to AMA, 17 May 1866, Augustus Weeks to Whipple, 7 July 1866, AMA Archives.

22. SCA to Whipple, 15 May, 6, 18 July 1866, Augustus Weeks to Whipple, 7 July 1866, AMA Archives; Peabody, *Education for Life*, p. 93.

23. SCA to Whipple, 18 September 1866, SCA to E. P. Smith, 9 October 1867, AMA Archives; Peabody, *Education for Life*, pp. 93, 97.

24. Luther P. Jackson, *Negro Officeholders in Virginia*, p. 30.

25. Arthur P. Davis, "William Roscoe Davis and his Descendants," pp. 80-81.

26. "List of Hampton Students," Ninth U. S. Census, 1870.

27. *Catalogue of HNAI*, 1871-72, pp. 7, 12; SCA to prospective student, 28 May 1868, Hampton Institute Archives.

28. E. K. Graham, "To Teach and to Lead," chapter 1, p. 12. Earlier histories of Hampton Institute have noted only two teachers on opening day. This was to obscure the fact that Armstrong dismissed the other three who were veteran missionary ladies not in sympathy with his plans for the school. Ibid., pp. 12-24.

29. Ibid., pp. 7-32; Peabody, *Education for Life*, p. 113; Helen W. Ludlow, "Personal Memories and Letters of General S. C. Armstrong," p. 645.

30. *Annual Report of the Principal and Officers of Hampton Normal and Agricultural Institute, 1887* (Hampton, 1887), pp. 14, 15.

31. SCA to Whipple, 13 April 1868, AMA Archives.

32. L. F. Anderson, "Manual Labor School Movement," *Educational Review* 47(1913), p. 377; Charles A. Bennett, *A History of Manual and Industrial Education up to 1870* (Peoria, 1926), pp. 187-88, 191-92; Robert S. Fletcher, *A History of Oberlin College* (Oberlin, 1943), (2 vols), v. I pp. 42, 147; Morris Bishop, *A History of Cornell* (Ithaca, 1962), pp. 56-57.

33. Peabody, *Education for Life*, p. 60.

34. *Catalogue of HNAI*, 1884, pp. 9, 17-18.

35. Ibid., pp. 10, 16, 19; *Hampton Annual Report*, 1887: 7.

36. Peabody, *Education for Life*, pp. 8, 119, 135.

37. SCA to Emma Armstrong, 8 January 1878, 17 January 1878, SCA to Emma Armstrong, n.d. (probably 1872 by context), Armstrong Papers, Williams College; *Hampton Home Bulletin*, 28 November 1885 (hereinafter cited as *HHB*).

38. *Catalogue of HNAI*, 1884, p. 12.

39. Peabody, *Education for Life*, pp. 136-37.

40. Alrutheus A. Taylor, *The Negro in the Reconstruction of Virginia*, (Washington, 1926) pp. 168-70.

41. *Annual Reports of Hampton Agricultural and Normal Institute, 1868-1878* (Hampton, 1878), p. 3; Peabody, *Education for Life*, pp. 102-4; Graham, "To Teach," pp. 19-20.

42. Rebecca Bacon to Leonard Bacon, 17 March 1869, 4 January 1870, 4 October 1870, 13 June 1871, Bacon Papers, Yale University.

43. Peabody, *Education for Life*, pp. 132-34.

44. *AMM* 14(1870): 183; 15(1871): 102; Alvord, *Sixth Semi-Annual Report, 1868*, p. 59; *Hampton Annual Report, 1887*, pp. 8-9; SCA to Emma Armstrong, n.d., 1872, Armstrong Papers, Williams College.

45. Norfolk *Journal*, 9 June 1871, in the Bacon Papers, Yale University.

46. Taylor, *Virginia Negro*, p. 169. No other AMA founded school, with its traditional college curriculum and equality advocating faculty could claim such accomplishments.

47. E. A. White, E. A. Byrd, R. Kelser, A. W. Calvin, R. B. Jackson, W. T.

Williams, C. Voorhees, W. Logan, W. M. Ivy, W. R. Unthank, W. M. Reid, R. H. Matthews, E. Harrison, A. Moore, W. A. Forsythe, B. Bradley, R. Smoat, F. D. Banks, P. W. Oliver, B. T. Washington, J. C. Robbins, T. S. D. Berger to SCA (n.d. but probably winter) 1875, Hampton Institute Archives.

48. *Hampton Annual Report, 1878*, p. 5; Graham, "To Teach," chapter 5, pp. 19-21. I am indebted to Professor Graham for bringing this letter to my attention and for tracing the careers of several of the letter's signers.

49. Ibid.

50. *HHB*, 2 April 1886.

51. Peabody, *Education for Life*, p. 118.

52. Graham, "To Teach," chapter 5, p. 45; Rebecca Bacon to Leonard Bacon, 15 January, 1 August 1870, Bacon Papers.

53. Graham, "To Teach," chapter 5, p. 45.

54. Mrs. Lillian Weaden Kemp, interview, Hampton, Va., 9 August 1974; Mrs. Hattie McGrew, interview, Hampton, Va., 31 July 1973; Mrs. Phoencie Armstead Tull, interview, Hampton, Va., 7 August 1973.

55. Ibid.

56. Kemp, interview.

57. Jackson, *Negro Officeholders*, p. 62; Kemp, interview.

58. Jackson, *Negro Officeholders*, pp. 1, 7, 17, 36, 63, 67.

59. Records, *Hampton Institute Students, 1868-1880*, Hampton Institute Archives; ECC Will Book 9, p. 137, ECCR; Hampton *Monitor*, August 1907; Kemp, interview.

60. Jackson, *Negro Officeholders*, p. 73; *HHB*, 10 July 1886, 26 March, 30 April 1887.

61. Ibid., 1, 8, 22 May, 28 August 1886.

Chapter 9

1. *HHB*, 20 November 1866, 7 February 1885; Mr. Alfonso Lively, interview, Hampton, Va., 16 August 1974.

2. *HHB*, 20 November 1886.

3. Ibid., 28 May 1887, 12 April 1890.

4. Tull, interview.

5. *HHB*, 14 November 1885, 28 May 1887, 22 September 1888.

6. Ninth U. S. Census, 1870; Tenth U. S. Census 1880. I am indebted to Ms. Gladys Blair for her tabulations of white newcomers in Hampton. Gladys Blair, "Northerners in the Reconstruction of Hampton, Virginia, 1865-1870," M. A. Thesis, Old Dominion University, 1975.

7. Tenth U. S. Census, 1880; Eleventh U. S. Census, 1890.

8. Blair, "Northerners," p. 25.

9. Ibid., p. 34.

10. Ibid., pp. 34, 63.

11. Ibid., p. 6, 57.

12. Kemp, interview; *HHB*, 20 November 1886.

13. Blair, "Northerners," p. 48.

14. Ibid., pp. 48, 53; *HHB*, 20 November 1886.

15. Ibid., Blair, "Northerners," pp. 53-55.

16. Ibid., p. 56.

17. Tenth U. S. Census, 1880. Manuscript Returns for Elizabeth City County, National Archives, Washington, D. C. The occupational categories lis-

ted here roughly follow those outlined in the Occupational Index proposed by my colleague, Theodore Hershberg, and Richard Dockhorn in *Historical Methods Newsletter* 9(1976): 59-98. Departures are made in identifying skilled versus unskilled labor because of the status which certain jobs such as oysterman and teamster enjoyed in Hampton. A more significant departure from accepted practice is made in the inclusion in these tables of women workers. The primary purpose of the tables and accompanying discussion is to give an approximate picture of black labor in Hampton between 1880 and 1896. It is clear that women played a vital role in black employment, that they filled all levels of occupations from unskilled to teacher and editor. Because they participated so fully in the black community's economic life, it seemed appropriate to include them as I have done.

18. *Chataigne's Hampton City Directory*, *Hampton Business Directory* (Hampton, 1896). Of available directories, these were selected for use because they are the most complete and because they were published in the same year as the most complete county tax records (with racial identification) between 1876 and 1896. The Directories, however, have several faults including the omission of dozens of blacks who owned land according to tax records in 1896 and the incorrect listing of the occupations of several blacks. For example, Andrew Williams, former sheriff and largest black landowner in the county, is listed as a "laborer." R.M. Smith, former commissioner of revenue and another owner of extensive property is listed without occupation and as "boarding" at a property he owned.

19. The omission of domestic workers may result from the fact that many servants lived in the homes of their employers and therefore do not appear as heads of households in the directories.

20. See chapter 10.

21. Ibid.; Tenth U. S. Census, 1880; *HHB*, 20 November 1886; Kemp, interview.

22. Ibid., John Mallory Phillips (grandson of the first), interview, Hampton, Va., 10 August 1974; Solomon Phillips, interviews, Hampton, Va., 21, 23 July, 14, 16 August 1974; *HHB*, 23 January 1886.

23. Kemp, interview; S. Phillips, interviews.

24. James W. H. Scott interview, Hampton, Va., 13 August 1974; *HHB*, 20 November 1886.

25. *Chataigne's Directories*, ECC "Real Property Tax" Records, 1886, 1896, ECCR.

26. *Chataigne's Directories*, S. Phillips, interviews: Kemp, interview.

27. My informants have argued that *most* businesses along these two main streets were black-owned. It is impossible to determine whether they are correct. Descriptions of locations of property in tax records are vague for this period. City maps often designate "store" without designating owner. My estimate of one-half is based on my efforts to correlate information from interviews, tax records, and county maps. Ibid.; Tull, interview; ECC "Real Property Tax" Records, 1896, ECCR; "Map of Town of Hampton, May 1803," on file at the Hampton Association for the Arts and Humanities. I am indebted to Mrs. Sandidge Evans of HAAH for making this map available to me.

28. Ibid.

29. Kemp, interview; S. Phillips, interviews.

30. Ibid.; Tull, interview; *Records, Hampton Institute Students*, 1868-1880, Hampton Institute Archives.

31. George W. Fields, "Come on, Children"; Kemp, interview; McGrew, interview.

32. *HHB*, 9 March, 6 April, 11 May 1889; "Industrial Number" of the Hampton *Monitor*, August 1907; *Chataigne's Directories*. The other firm is the Phillips Seafood Company.

33. Tull, interview.

34. Edward Bonekemper, "Negro Ownership of Real Property in Elizabeth City County, 1860–1870," p. 177.

35. ECC Real Property Tax Records, ECCR. Eighteen ninety-six tax records are used because they are the first surviving complete set after the war to designate the race of the taxpayer. The 1886 figures were obtained by cross-checking for name and description of location of property in 1886 tax records in which the race of the taxpayer is not indicated. The 1886 figures are approximate because spellings of names and even description of location sometimes vary from year to year in these records.

36. Ibid.

37. Ibid.; "Land Book," 1860, ECCR. Peake's land was especially good, accessed at thirteen dollars per unimproved acre.

38. ECC Real Property Tax Records, ECCR, 1896.

39. Ibid., Will Book 5, p. 248, Will of Robert M. Smith; Will Book 9, p. 137, Will of A. W. E. Bassett, Sr., ECCR.

40. Claire Stearns, "Understanding Black History," *Casemate Chronicle* 10(1974).

41. Ibid.; *Jefferson Sinclair and Wife* vs. *Norfolk Savings Institution*, Chancery drawers 22 A and B., ECCR. (I am indebted to Mrs. Sandidge Evans of HAAH for calling these records to my attention.) Among the first to purchase Sinclair property were William Roscoe Davis, Julius Bassett, and Andrew Williams.

42. *HHB*, 27 October 1888.

43. *Sinclair* vs. *Norfolk Savings*, ECCR; *Chataigne's Directories*.

44. Kemp, interview; *HHB*, 20 November 1886.

Chapter 10

1. *HHB*, 23, May, 11, 18, 25 July 1885.

2. Ibid., 2 January 1886, Tull, interview, Mr. and Mrs. Robert Nottingham, interview, Hampton, Va., 30 July 1974.

3. Ibid., *Chataigne's Directories*; Tull, interview; McGrew, interview, Kemp, interview; "Ebenezer Baptist Church Anniversary Book, 1946."

4. Tull, interview; Kemp, interview; Naomia W. Boykin, "The History of Bethel AME Church;" *HHB*, 1 January 1887, 9 January, 13 April 1889.

5. *HHB*, 12 January, 4 February, 14 April, 16, 23 June, 20 October, 3 November 1888.

6. Ibid., 28 February, 13 June 1885, 27 February 1886; Kemp, interview, S. Phillips, interviews.

7. Kemp, interview; McGrew, interview; *HHB* 9 January 1886, 11 August 1885, 30 June, 22 September 1888.

8. Kemp, interview; S. Phillips, interviews.

9. Ibid.; *HHB*, 22 April, 28 May, 12 November 1887, 20 October, 3 November 1888.

10. Will Book 1, 1870, Will of James Bailey; Register of Marriage Book,

1899 ECCR; *HHB*, 19 January 1889; Newport News *Daily Press*, 9 February 1975.

11. *HHB*, 22, 29 September 1888, 2 December 1889, 12 April 1890.

12. Ibid., 1 August 1885, 27 March, 17, 31 July, 30 October 1886, 21 January 1887.

13. W. H. Bonaparte in *HHB*, 29 September 1888.

14. Ibid., 2 February 1889.

15. Ibid., 15 January 1887.

16. Ibid.

17. Jackson, *Negro Officeholders in Virginia*, pp. 24, 26, 30, 79. It was in the 1881-82 session, when the Readjuster coalition had a clear majority, that black representatives achieved two significant victories. They succeeded in abolishing the notorious public whipping post for crimes (usually those committed by blacks) and in creating Virginia Normal and Collegiate Institute in Petersburg. It is interesting to note that the black legislators insisted upon "and Collegiate": Virginia State was to be a true college, unlike the vision Armstrong had for Hampton.

18. Jackson, *Negro Officeholders*, p. 62; Gladys Blair, "Northerners in the Reconstruction of Hampton, Va.," pp. 92-95.

19. Jackson, *Negro Officeholders*, pp. ix, 24, 39-40, 62-63, 79. The annual tax levy was set by the county court. Smith assessed property, determined each property owner's liability and collected the tax.

20. Ibid. pp. 16-17, 36, 62; *HHB*, 10 April 1889.

21. Ibid, 20 November 1886, 7 September 1889.

22. Charles E. Wynnes, *Race Relations in Virginia 1870–1902*, (Charlottesville, VA, 1961) pp. 16–38.

23. *HHB*, 27 February, 6 March 1886, 18 June 1887.

24. Ibid.

25. Ibid., 3 April, 28 August, 4 September, 16 October 1886.

26. Ibid., 6 November 1886.

27. Hampton *Monitor*, as quoted in *HHB*, 15 June 1889.

28. T. N. Brown as quoted in ibid.

29. Ibid., 26 October 1889.

30. Ibid.

31. Ibid., 18 February, 18 September 1886, 9 June, 3 November 1888, 3, 26 January, 2 February 1889.

32. Ibid., 26 January 1889.

33. Ibid., 2 February 1889.

34. Ibid.

35. Ibid. The penalty in law for Bonaparte's crime was two to ten years at hard labor. The jury's choice of punishment was far less severe than it might have been.

36. Ibid., 4 January 1890; Phillips, interviews; Tull, interview, Mrs. Sandidge Evans to author, 5 September 1977, in author's possession.

37. *HHB*, 24, 31 August, 7 September, 7 December 1889. R. M. Smith was certainly guilty of carelessness. His records are appallingly haphazard. On the other hand, his white successor did little better. The county tax records do not acquire a semblance of good order until 1896, ECCR.

38. Ibid., 4 January 1890; Alfonso Lively, interview, Hampton, Va., 16 August 1974; Tull, interview.

39. Thomas Harmon, Luke Phillips and William R. Davis all served on City Council in the 1890s. James A Fields and John H. Robinson both served in the 1889-91 term of the state legislature. Jackson, *Negro Officeholders*, pp. 16-17, 36, 62; *HHB*, 10 April 1889.

Bibliographic Essay

Manuscript Collections

The historical reconstruction of a black community of over one hundred years ago is fraught with difficulties, but for Hampton Roads, Virginia, at least there are a number of excellent archival resources. Four sets of records stand out as particularly valuable.

The American Missionary Association Archives, now at Dillard University in New Orleans, and also available on microfilm, contain letters and reports of missionaries sent to the South during the war and Reconstruction. The Virginia file alone contains over 10,000 items; most of those for the years 1861 to 1863 are written from the Hampton Roads area. They provide a record of missionary activity there, of conflicts with the military officials, and of observations about the freedmen. Many of the letters, especially the earlier ones, also provide considerable information about the blacks and the nature of their lives in prewar Hampton.

As the missionary effort in the South expanded and the relations between missionaries and freedmen became more impersonal, the Records of the Bureau of Refugees, Freedmen, and Abandoned Lands in the National Archives, Washington, D. C., become the principal source for information about the individual blacks and their communities on the Peninsula. This study drew primarily upon the reports, letters, and endorsement books in the files of the Ninth District (later the Fifth Sub-District) of Virginia which included the Peninsula. Considerable use was also made of the "Letters Received" File for Assistant Commissioner for Virginia, Orlando Brown. This file contains reports and letters from each of the assistant subcommissioners and their subordinates to the headquarters office in Richmond. The Bureau records basically cover the period from 1863 when the Bureau of Negro Affairs was created to the end of 1869 when all Bureau activities on the Peninsula, except for supervision of freedmen's education, came to an end. These records also include correspondence between Bureau officers and freedmen, reports of freedmen's meetings, of rations issued, and records of the Freedmen's courts.

The other principal collections made use of in the National Archives were the Manuscript Census Returns of 1860, 1870, and 1880 for Elizabeth City, York, James City, and Warwick Counties, Virginia. These provide information on wealth, property, geographic distribution and occupation of blacks. They are invaluable in tracing the evolution of the area's black elites.

The third archival resource of major importance for this study is the collection of papers, manuscripts, letters, and printed reports on file at Hampton Institute. These records, unfortunately, are in considerable disarray, but are currently being catalogued. Through the help of Professor E. K. Graham, then of Hampton Institute, and his research assistant, Miss Eleanor Gilman, the author was able to see most of the records on the early years of Hampton Institute. The collection contains many letters concerning Freedman's Bureau and missionary activities not included in the papers at the National Archives nor the American Missionary Archives. The most valuable single item is Helen Ludlow, editor, "Personal Memoirs and Letters of General S. C. Armstrong: Hawaii, Williams, War, Hampton." This voluminous, unpublished manuscript contains many Armstrong letters unavailable from any other source.

In addition to these papers, the Hampton Institute Library contains numerous pamphlets, scrapbooks, and clippings on the early years of the college which are important in understanding the evolution of the school. Many "in-house" histories of the Institute were published and are in its library. Though many of them are tainted by paternalism, they offer much information about the school, its teachers, and students. Best is Francis Greenwood Peabody, *Education for Life: The Study of Hampton Institute* (New York, 1918). Others of use, particularly for their commentary on life at the Institute and records of successful graduates, are Mary F. Armstrong and Helen Ludlow, *Hampton and Its Students, by Two of Its Teachers* (New York, 1875), written with an eye toward fund raising; *Hampton Normal and Agricultural Institute* (Hampton, 1884); Mary F. Armstrong, Elaine Goodale, and Helen Ludlow, *Hampton Institute, 1868-1885: Its Work for Two Races* (Hampton, 1885); *Ten Years' Work for Indians at Hampton Institute* (Hampton, 1888); and *Twenty-Two Years' Work of the Hampton Normal and Agricultural Institute at Hampton, Virginia: Records of Negro and Indian Graduates and Ex-Students* (Hampton, 1893).

Also valuable to this study were the Records of the Elizabeth City County Court. They contain references to the ante-bellum free black community, records of taxes paid, property acquired, and the wills of many of the more prominent black residents in the post-bellum period. These records must be used with care because, for a major portion of the period covered in this study, individuals are not identified by race, and because black and white last names were often the same. As is true of so many other sets of local records, there are major gaps in the Elizabeth City set partly due to the disruption of the Civil War and partly due to haphazard record keeping in the late nineteenth century. Nevertheless, these records proved of exceptional value in reconstructing the story of black progress in the post-Reconstruction period.

Supplementing these major resources are the Armstrong Family Papers at Williams College, Williamstown, Massachusetts. These contain letters in which Armstrong expresses his most candid views of the freedmen and missionary workers. Valuable in assessing Southern white attitudes toward events during the war and Reconstruction on the Peninsula, and toward the freedmen, are the Charles A. R. Dimon Papers, the George Phifer Papers, the Edwin Ruffin, Jr., Plantation Diary, and the Mary T. Huntley Diary in the Southern Collection at the University of North Carolina, Chapel Hill; also useful are the George Neville Papers at the University of Virginia, Charlottesville and the Benjamin

Ewell Papers at the College of William and Mary, Williamsburg, Virginia. A few supplemental items on events of the war and the first year of Reconstruction are to be found in the John Augustus Wilder Papers contained in the Todd Family Papers, and, on the early years of Hampton Institute, in the Bacon Papers, both at Yale University, New Haven, Connecticut. The Virginia State Library in Richmond was also of great use for its excellent collection of Virginia newspapers and records of local election returns.

Finally, researchers for the Hampton Association for the Arts and Humanities are engaged in a major effort to reconstruct the history of Hampton. To date, their efforts have not centered on the post-bellum era, but their researchers have, nevertheless, acquired primary and secondary source materials which were helpful in this work. Most important of these were *Chataigne's Directories* for 1896 and a copy of the George Washington Fields manuscript autobiography. Also available through the Association were maps of Hampton in the late nineteenth century, photographs from that era, and capsule biographies of post-bellum Hampton's most prominent blacks and whites.

Oral Sources

Of crucial importance for the post-Reconstruction portion of this study were interviews with descendants of the first freed generation. Many nuances about the nature of post-bellum life and many leads to important written sources were acquired from these individuals. Most important among the insights gained from those I interviewed was the discovery of the extent of black property acquisition during the post-Reconstruction period. Much of that property has now reverted to white hands and few beside old time residents are aware that it ever belonged to blacks.

Concurrent with my research for this study, Hampton Institute initiated an oral history project that is still under way. As a consequence, tapes now exist of extensive interviews with many of the same subjects who contributed to this study.

Published Primary Sources

There were a number of published primary sources beside the books and pamphlets at Hampton Institute which were of value in this study. The most active missionary organization in Hampton Roads was the American Missionary Association. The problems of work with the freedmen and decisions on policy for work in the South are recorded in the Association's *Annual Reports.* The New England Freedmen's Aid Society and the Friends' Association of Philadelphia for the Relief of Colored Freedmen also sent workers to the Peninsula. Their *Annual Reports* and those of the National Freedmen's Relief Association, the American Freedmen's Union Commission, and the Presbyterian Church in the United States, Committee on Freedmen, are also useful.

The national press gave considerable attention to military and political events on the Peninsula during the war. Most helpful of the national papers was the *New York Times.* Of more value on matters directly affecting freedmen were the *National Anti-Slavery Standard* and the *Independent*, both published in New York by antislavery men. The publications of the American Freedmen's Union Commission, *American Freedmen*, and of the New England Freedman's Aid Society, *The Freedmen's Record*, were also of some use. The most valuable of the journals consulted was the American Missionary Association's *The American Missionary Magazine.* It contains reports of missionary work in Virginia and editorial discussion of the politics of the Association for most of the period covered by this study.

There were a number of Virginia newspapers published during the war and Reconstruction which were useful for this study. The Norfolk *Journal*, Norfolk *Virginian*, two Richmond papers, the *Dispatch* and the *Whig*, and the Williamsburg *Virginia Gazette* reflect the attitudes of white Southerners of the era. The short-lived Yorktown *Cavalier* (1862-64) was sympathetic to the freedmen. The most important of the local newspapers for the Reconstruction period was the *True Southerner* published in Hampton and Norfolk from November 1865 to April 1866. It published accounts of activities in the black community, advertised black businesses, and monitored the treatment of freedmen by the military, Freedmen's Bureau, and native whites. The most valuable paper for the post-Reconstruction period was the *Home Bulletin*, published by the National Soldiers (Veterans) Home located in Hampton. The paper contained news of local events, reports on black social and political activities, and advertisements for black-owned businesses.

Government documents cast some more light on events in Hampton during the war and Reconstruction. Military activities and policies on freedmen's affairs on the Peninsula are recorded in *The War of the Rebellion: A Compilation of the Official Records of the Union and Confederate Armies*, 128 vols. (Washington, D. C., 1880-1901). Also of value for the period 1865 to 1870 are John W. Alvord, *Reports on Schools and Finances of Freedmen* (Washington, 1865-1870) and Alvord's *Letters from the South* (Washington, 1870). U.S. Congress *House Reports* and *House Executive Documents* and the corresponding publications for the Senate were consulted for the period 1861 to 1877. Useful in gauging the attitude of white Virginians and the laws of postwar Virginia are the *Acts of the General Assembly of Virginia* and *Debates and Proceedings of the Constitutional Convention of 1867-1868 (Richmond, 1868)*.

Some of the chief figures in this study left memoirs and published correspondence. Among these are Edward L. Pierce, *Enfranchisement and Citizenship: Addresses and Papers* (Boston, 1896), valuable for its discussion of the first contraband; Benjamin F. Butler, *Autobiography and Personal Reminiscences of Major General Benjamin F. Butler* (Boston, 1892); and *Private and Official Correspondence of General Benjamin Butler, during the Period of the Civil War* (Norwood, Mass., 1917). Although he visited Hampton only briefly, O. O. Howard, *Autobiography of Oliver Otis Howard* (New York, 1907), is valuable for Howard's reflections about his tenure as commissioner of the Freedmen's Bureau. Of particular interest is Henry L. Swint, editor, *Dear Ones at Home* (Nashville, 1966), a compilation of letters by missionaries, primarily Lucy and Sarah Chase, AMA missionaries in Hampton Roads during the war.

Secondary Sources

Several works of a general nature were useful in providing background for this study. Kenneth M. Stampp, *The Era of Reconstruction, 1865-1867* (New York, 1965), Bell Irvin Wiley, *Southern Negroes, 1861-1865* (New Haven, 1938), Robert Cruden, *The Negro in Reconstruction* (Englewood Cliffs, N.J., 1969), offer a picture of national events affecting blacks. James M. McPherson, *The Struggle for Equality: Abolitionists and the Negro in the Civil War and Reconstruction* (Princeton, 1964), is excellent on missionary work in the South for this period. Richard Bryand Drake, "The American Missionary Association and the Southern Negro, 1861-1888," Emory University Ph.D. Dissertation, 1957, is largely uncritical and gives little attention to Hampton. Willie Lee Rose, *Rehearsal for Reconstruction: The Port Royal Experiment* (New York, 1964), treats the missionary effort on the Sea Islands of South Carolina and offers some provocative contrasts to events in Hampton Roads. The role of black soldiers during the war, many of whom were drawn from the refugee camps on the Peninsula, is documented in Dudley T. Cornish, *The Sable Arm: Negro Troops in the Union Army, 1861-1865* (New York, 1956).

Contrasting views of the Freedmen's Bureau are offered in George Bentley, *A History of the Freedmen's Bureau* (Philadelphia, 1955) which presents a positive picture of the Bureau's efforts to aid the freedmen, and in William S. McFeely, *Yankee Stepfather: General O. O. Howard and the Freedmen* (New Haven, 1968), which indicts the Bureau leadership for contributing to the organization's failures in work with the blacks. Also of interest are a biography of Howard more sympathetic than McFeely's study, John A. Carpenter, *Sword and Olive Branch, Oliver Otis Howard* (Pittsburgh, 1964), and the biographies of Ben Butler, Richard S. West, *Lincoln's Scapegoat General: A Life of Benjamin F. Butler, 1818-1893* (Boston, 1965), Howard P. Nash, Jr., *Stormy Petrel: The Life and Times of General Benjamin F. Butler, 1818-1893* (Rutherford, N. J., 1969), and Robert Holzman, *Stormy Ben Butler* (New York, 1954). Biographies of Samuel Chapman Armstrong tend to be laudatory and uncritical. Such is the case with Edith Armstrong Talbot's *Samuel Chapman Armstrong* (New York, 1904) and Francis Peabody's study with the same title (Boston, 1898). Suzanne Carson's more recent biography, "Samuel Chapman Armstrong: Missionary of the South," Johns Hopkins Ph.D. Dissertation, 1952, suffers from similar problems. It is overly sympathetic to Armstrong and superficial about the Institute's educational format.

Histories of Virginia of value for this study were Virginius Dabney's work, *Virginia: The New Dominion* (New York, 1972), Sara K. Gilliam, *Virginia's People: A Study of the Growth and Distribution of the Population of Virginia from 1607-1943* (Richmond, 1944), and Lyon G. Tyler, *The History of Hampton and Elizabeth City County, Virginia* (Hampton, 1922). The Reconstruction period in Virginia is treated in Jack P. Maddex, *The Virginia Conservatives, 1867-1879* (Chapel Hill, 1970) and Raymond Pulley, *Old Virginia Restored: An Interpretation of the Progressive Impulse* (Charlottesville, 1968).

Works specifically about blacks in Virginia which were helpful include Luther P. Jackson, *Free Negro Labor and Property Holding in Virginia, 1830-1860* (New York, 1942), a pioneering study on the life of free blacks in antebellum Virginia. Especially valuable for the post bellum period was Jackson, *Negro Officeholders in Virginia, 1865-1895* (Norfolk, 1945). Also see James H. Brewer, *The Confederate Negro: Virginia's Craftsmen and Military Laborers, 1861-1865* (Durham, 1969), an excellent study of those Virginia blacks not lucky enough to escape to Hampton. Another work on blacks in Virginia for this period is Alrutheus A. Taylor, *The Negro in Reconstruction of Virginia* (Washington, 1926) which is now somewhat dated and offers only limited insight into events on the Peninsula.

Sources about Civil War Hampton within the black community are few and difficult to locate. Oral history proved largely futile for this period because few stories of that period have been passed down among the identifiable descendants of the original freedmen. Those which exist are difficult to corroborate through other sources. Professor E. K. Graham and Miss Eleanor Gilman of Hampton Institute were helpful in providing information about the early history of the Institute and black community not otherwise available. Audrey Jackson Walker, *Centennial Celebration of First Baptist Church,* "The History of First Baptist Church" (Hampton, 1963); Arthur P. Davis, "William Roscoe Davis and his Descendants," *Negro History Bulletin* 13 (January, 1950):75-89, 95; and the *Centennial Memorial Book, Zion Baptist Church, 1863-1963* (Hampton, 1963) contain valuable material on the early black elite of the village. The *Southern Workman,* a periodical published by Hampton Institute since 1873, contains some material and reminiscences about early Hampton, but many of these are distorted by the paternalistic tone of their white authors.

An important study of the Virginia Peninsula, its freedmen, and Hampton Institute will be E. K. Graham's forthcoming *To Teach and To Lead,* the centennial history of Hampton Institute, which will contain considerable information about the black community of Hampton as well as about the Institute itself.

Index

abolitionists, perceptions of blacks, 50

accommodation. *See* Samuel Armstrong, Booker T. Washington

Addison, Dr. Thomas, 174

After Slavery (Williamson), xvi

American Missionary Association (AMA), xvii, 29, 45-65, 140-145; black workers of, 45; founded Normal Schools, 142; major focus on Virginia Peninsula, 29; mission schools, 45; new vision of freedmen and method of operation by, 140; relationship to Hampton Institute of, 139; treasury depletion of, 140

American Missionary Magazine, 51, 55, 57, 108, 141

American Palladium, The, 93

Andrew, John, 95

Armstead, Henry, 171

Armstrong, Samuel Chapman, 49, 105, 136, 139-60; accommodation advocated by, 202; as commander, 111; conditions of freedmen as his tenure begins, 113-19; credentials of, 111; crippled by stroke, 158; death of, 203; disillusionment with Bureau, 142; education for life, 136; horse, 158; independence from AMA control, 148; manual labor program, 149-50; on the courts, 124; opposition to black political organization, 131-32; population removal plan, 116-18; relations with black leaders, 147, 1 148; views on blacks, 123-26, 129-30, 143; views on Bureau's responsibilities, 128; vision for blacks, 123; vision of Hampton Institute, 143-47; winning support for Hampton Institute, 154-55

Ash William, 159

Atlantic Monthly, 28

Bacon, Leonard, 153

Bacon, Rebecca, 153

Bailey, Ann, 187-188

Bailey, James, 12-13, 132, 188

Bailey, Nancy, 12

Baker, Frank, 18

Banks, Sarah, 174

Barnes, Captain Stewart, 108

Bassette, A. W. E., 159, 175, 180

Beales, H. S., 74

Bebout, John, 61, 74

Bell, Reverend W. S., 53
Black Family in Slavery and Free-dom, 1750-1925, (Gutman), xv, 14
Black New Orleans, 1860-1880, (Blassingame), xvi
Bland, James, 159
Blassingame, John B., *Black New Orleans , 1860-1880; Slave Com-munity,* xviI
Bonaparte, W. H., 189-90; scandal of, 195-97
Brittenham, Elihu, 87
Brown, John, 16, 190
Brown, Orlando, 108, 116-17, 124; policy toward freedmen, 110; views on Bureau's responsibilities, 126
Brown, T. N., 194
Bryant, Simon, 180
Bureau of Negro Affairs (War Depart-ment), 36, 38, 40, 58
Butler, General Benjamin, 27-30, 37, 39; as Fortress commander, 18-21; return to Hampton Roads, 52
Butler Freedmen's School, 53, 87, 145, 188
Bureau of Refugees, Freedmen and Abandoned Lands. *See* Freedman's Bureau

Camp, Hamilton, 31-32
Canady, Edward, 159
Canady, Thomas, 132, 198
Carry, David, 12
Carter, Peter, 159
Cary, Major John, 20
Charles City County (Virginia), 8
Chesapeake Bay, 3, 7
Chesapeake Female Seminary, 10, 33, 47, 145
churches, 29, 45, 55, 76, 89, 133-34, 184-85, 186
Churchill, Lieutenant Rodney, 109
Circular Orders. *See* Freedman's Bureau
Civil Rights Bill of 1866, 88
Coan, Mrs. J. W., 64
Coan, William, 35
Colored troops, 111
Colton, Billy. *See* Taylor, William
Colton, Samuel, 13
Confiscation Acts of 1862, 36
contraband, 25-43; theory about, 20. *See* also Hampton blacks

Cook, Frances, 104
Cook, Stafford, 69
Cornell, Governor, 156
Corsey, William, 15
County Journal, 174
Crandall, Charles, 189
Craney Island (Virginia), 50, 52, 61, 64

Darling, J. S., 166, 170; as council-man, 193
Davis, George, 185
Davis, William Roscoe, 16, 17, 26, 31, 48, 52, 89, 91, 92, 131, 147, 185, 192, 204; in leadership role, 134, 135
Day, C. P., 32, 42, 49, 50, 54, 61, 64, 71
Dix, General John, 33-35
Dixie Hospital, 158
Dixon, Charles, 133
Douglas, Dennis, 155
Douglass, Frederick, 92
Drew, Austin, 108
Drew, Mrs. Minnie, 106
Dunlap, Alexander, 89, 91, 92

Eastern Virginia Gazette, 93
Elkins, Stanley E., xv
Elizabeth City County (Virginia), 8, 10, 81, 85; cholera in, 86; courthouse incident, 125-26; new majority, 67; political organization in, 130; refugee camps, 38; refu-gees from, 117-18; renting farms in, 75; slave-owners in, 14. *See* also Hampton
Emancipation Day, 36, 186
Emancipation Proclamation, 36-37, 52
Ewell, Colonel Benjamin, 17
eye servants. *See* missionaries

Fields, George Washington, 156, 175, 180, 203, 204; in leadership role, 134
Fields, James, 159, 185; delegate to state legislature, 192; in leadership role, 134; property-owner, 179
First Baptist Church, 10, 13, 55, 77, 89, 90, 131, 134, 184
Flagg, Captain A. S., 125
Fort Macgruder, 109
Fortress Monroe, 3, 9, 10, 22, 23, 26-28, 161, 165, 172; arrival of Lewis Lockwood, 29; arrival of General